DATE DUE

EUROPEAN POLITICS INTO THE TWENTY-FIRST CENTURY

EUROPEAN POLITICS INTO THE TWENTY-FIRST CENTURY

Integration and Division

Hans Slomp

PRAEGER

Westport, Connecticut
London

Library of Congress Cataloging-in-Publication Data

Slomp, Hans, 1945–
    European politics into the twenty-first century : integration and
division / Hans Slomp.
        p.   cm.
    Includes bibliographical references and index.
    ISBN 0–275–96800–6 (alk. paper). — ISBN 0–275–96814–6 (pbk. :
    alk. paper)
    1. Europe—Politics and government—1989–. I. Title.
JN12.S58   2000
306.2′094—dc21   99–43104

British Library Cataloguing in Publication Data is available.

Library of Congress Catalog Card Number: 99–43104
ISBN: 0–275–96800–6
        0–275–96814–6 (pbk.)

First published in 2000

Praeger Publishers, 88 Post Road West, Westport, CT 06881
An imprint of Greenwood Publishing Group, Inc.
www.praeger.com

Printed in the United States of America

The paper used in this book complies with the
Permanent Paper Standard issued by the National
Information Standards Organization (Z39.48–1984).

10   9   8   7   6   5   4   3   2

Contents

Illustrations   ix

Preface   xi

1 Introduction   **1**

One Europe or Many Europes?

Major Differences with American Politics

A Quick Historical Note

2 The Main Lines of Social Division   **13**

Language and National Culture

Religion

Region

Social Class

Coping with Division: Exclusion versus Integration

The Decline of the Traditional Sources of Division

Immigrants: A New Divide?

3 Liberals Are Not Liberals: The European Ideologies   **31**

The European Political Spectrum

Conservatism

Liberalism

Anarchism, Social Democracy, and Communism

Christian Democracy

Fascism and Nazism

New Ideologies

Regional Variations in Coping with Ideological Division

Americanization of European Politics?

4   From Elections to Governments: The Long Way   49

The European State

Where the Votes Are: Elections

Where the Power Is: Political Parties

Coalition Governments and Party Systems

Regional Variations in Elections, Parties, and Government

5   Government and Parliament   63

The Real Legislator: Government

The Final Say: Parliament

Other State Institutions

Regional Variations in Parliamentary and Government Power

Political Innovation to Cope with Division

The Short Way to a New Government: Presidential Systems

6   Between State and Society   79

New Talks Announced by the White House

Civil Society European Style

One of Europe's Favorites: Business-Labor-Government Tripartism

From Doctors to Students: Other Pressure Groups

The Commercial Revolution: The Mass Media

Regional Variations in Civil Society

Local Government and Politics

Federalism

7   Public Policy in Europe   **101**

Policy Styles in Europe

Welfare is Not Welfare

The Welfare State and Its Redefinition in Western Europe

Left and Right: Does It Make a Difference?

Redefining the Welfare State: Central and Eastern Europe

Education

Life and Death

8   Supranational Politics: The European Union   **123**

Catching the EMU-Train: EU Policies

Toward European Integration

The European Union's Structure

9   International Politics   **139**

Marking Territories in Multipolar Europe

The Bipolar World during the Cold War

Europe in the New Unipolar World

A Divided Continent in Search of Unity

Even Good Neighbors Have Their Quarrels

10   Europe by Region   **155**

Western Europe

Central Europe

Eastern Europe

Other Countries

Appendix A: Scientific Terms   173

Appendix B: The European Nations   179

Further Reading   181

Index   189

Illustrations

MAPS

1.1	Europe in 2000	5
1.2	Europe in 1988	6
2.1	The Religious Division of Europe	19
9.1	Europe in 1900	142

FIGURES

3.1	The European Political Spectrum	32
3.2	The Political Spectrum of France, Germany, and Great Britain	46

TABLES

1.1	The European Nations	4
1.2	Europe in the Twentieth Century	11
2.1	The Major Language Minorities	17
2.2	Employment in Agriculture, Industry, and Services (in percentage of the labor force)	27
2.3	Foreign Nationals (Immigrants and Fugitives) in Western Europe	30

4.1 The Impact of Electoral Systems: Share of Votes and Share 55
of Seats

4.2 Seats in Parliament and the Allocation of Cabinet Posts 60

5.1 Political Leaders in Great Britain, Germany, Italy, and France 65
Since 1980 (Italy Since 1990)

5.2 Some Examples of Referendums 73

6.1 Some Examples of Tripartite Employment Conferences 83
and Agreements

6.2 Trade Union Strength 84

6.3 Regional and Local Units 94

7.1 Left and Right Priorities in European Politics 112

7.2 Social Security in Germany 113

8.1 European Union Member States 131

8.2 Important European Council Meetings 133

9.1 Colonies that Gained Independence after World War II and
Remaining Colonies or "Overseas Territories" 147

9.2 International Organizations with Predominantly European 151
Members (except EU and CIS)

9.3 Major Regional Disputes in Europe (except Concerning 154
Minorities)

Preface

Working at a European university has the advantage of leaving time to travel through the United States and to get involved in exchange programs. The results have been two unforgettable coast-to-coast round trips, a great semester at Cornell University, and many fine meetings with Americans interested in Europe.

Working at a small European university offers the additional advantage of being able to teach both European politics and American politics, and meeting many students interested in North America.

The combination of Europe and North America has motivated me to write this short introduction to *European Politics*. It has been written for the many people in North America who are interested in European politics and society but are overwhelmed by the great (and still increasing) number of European nations. The meetings with Americans and years of lecturing on American politics have changed my teaching of European politics, from focusing on specific national features to drawing general lines. If Europe is increasingly becoming a unity, it should also be possible to discuss it as a unity, while taking into account regional variations. After two books on European labor relations, a general history and an introduction, I have now tried to discuss the wider subject of European politics, for a wider public.

I hope the book will stimulate interest in Europe and lead to even more interesting discussions of European politics and society, and comparisons of Europe and North America—on both sides of the Atlantic Ocean.

I am grateful to the many students and colleagues that commented on parts of earlier versions. A special word of thanks to my three colleagues Bert Bomert, Jan van Deth, and Huub Spoormans, who did not leave any page without comment, to Jan ter Laak for his active research assistance, to Peter Rijkhoff for drawing the maps, and to Bob Lieshout for creating the right working conditions. Jolanda, thank you most of all for Platform 7.

1

Introduction

Consider the United States. Imagine that everything West of the Mississippi is one country, whose population speaks Russian. All other states are fully independent and speak their own language, with a few exceptions. Massachusettsian is also spoken in Connecticut; two languages are spoken in both Georgia and Tennessee; and in Maryland three languages exist—Pennsylvanish, Virginian, and New Jersic.

To make things a bit more complicated, New York has three regional languages in addition to New Yorkish: Big Applish, Hudsonian, and Upstateic. Moreover, in the Russian-speaking region there are a number of smaller peoples who strive for independence. They are concentrated around the San Francisco Bay area and speak languages like Bayish, Gayish, and Siliconian.

Europe is like that. On a long trip from New York to Florida you would have to know that *aus, uit, sortie, salida,* and *saída* all stand for "exit," and only in some of the smaller states will they understand your English (or Spanish).

Although it is only slightly larger than the United States, Europe consists of more than forty nations, whose peoples speak over thirty languages. The comparison does not even express the full extent of Europe's diversity. Russians—one fifth of Europe's population—occupy half of its territory. The other forty nations and thirty languages share the other half of this crowded and divided continent.

By 2002, one of the symbols of national division will have disappeared. In that year the German mark, French franc, Italian lira, and a number of other European currencies will be replaced by a new currency, the Euro. Crossing borders will no longer imply changing money.

The trend toward more uniformity has been going on for a long period. Most Western European nations have joined the European Union and a number of Central European countries are lining up to be admitted. The European Union is the most spectacular and peaceful means ever to forge more unity in Europe. Past empires tried to reach the same goal by means of military expansion. The European Union is the first attempt to unite a large part of Europe on a voluntary base while leaving intact variations in national culture, including national languages. The Euro, which is already serving as the international currency unit of European stock markets since its introduction on January 1, 1999, is the latest effort in Europe's constant struggle to cope with division.

The international developments toward more European unity should not divert attention from the long and difficult attempts by the European nations to bring more unity within their national borders. Coping with diversity is not only an important aim of international but also national politics.

This book is a short introduction to one of Europe's favorite discussion topics: national and international politics. However, do not expect any positive observations on politics when in Europe, since Europeans do not like to admit they enjoy talking politics. Their attitude toward politics resembles the one toward the weather. It is always too hot or too cold, too rainy or too dry; but the moment you propose a radical shift in climate or migration, they start seeing some positive signs in their fate.

The book has been written to serve a wide audience, in particular in North America. Occasionally, the text refers to U.S. politics in order to clarify some points rather than attempting a full-fledged comparison. It is an effort to make Europe more understandable to American readers by stressing what European nations have in common, rather than their differences. The main body of the book is devoted to national politics, with separate chapters on the European Union and international politics.

ONE EUROPE OR MANY EUROPES?

A quick glance at a world map reveals that Europe is actually no more than a series of peninsulas on Asia's western front. Thanks to its dominant position in world history and world culture, it has claimed the status of a separate continent—and who was there to refuse it that status?

There are many Europes. People in Great Britain regard themselves as Europeans but they speak about "Great Britain and Europe" to stress their differences with continental Europe. A weather forecast in that country might even warn that "Europe is isolated due to heavy fog"; while for most Europeans this would mean that Great Britain rather than the rest of Europe is isolated. Even Swedes sometimes regard their position as one outside the European continent and then refer to Denmark as "where the continent begins." On the other hand, the Russians have always stressed their belonging to Europe. Despite the fact that Russia covers half of the continent as it is usually defined, the country is often left out from texts on Europe. Turkey wishes to be part of Europe as well, but its claim is hardly ever honored. In former times, after the Turkish Empire had conquered the Balkan Peninsula, Europe was often confined to "Christian" Europe, which was threatened by this Muslim expansion. Most treatises on Europe still only include the small "European" part of Turkey, which extends as far as Istanbul—without paying much attention to it. In accordance with the normal use of the term Europe, in this book Europe includes Great Britain and Russia, and excludes Turkey.

Europe is often divided into Western Europe and Eastern Europe. This division has its roots in the cold war period, when Europe was divided into Western Europe ("Free Europe") and Eastern Europe, which was dominated by the communist Soviet Union. The separation between the two parts of Europe ended in the late 1980s, when the Soviet Union fell apart and the communist regimes of Eastern Europe broke down. Since the end of the cold war, the term Eastern Europe has been an ambiguous one. The countries that are closest to Western Europe prefer to call themselves part of "Central Europe," a term that was previously also used by Germans (*Mitteleuropa*) for their special location between Great Britain and France to the West and Russia to the East.

The distinction made in this book between Western Europe and the rest of Europe is the usual one. Western Europe includes all countries that belonged to the "Free World" during the division of Europe. Many of them are old nations and democracies with a capitalist free market economy, which make up the European Union. In this book Central Europe includes all non-Russian nations that until recently were suppressed by communist Russia. This use of the term means that Central Europe includes more nations than in its usual demarcation, but it has the advantage of setting all small non-Russian nations apart from Russia. Central Europe constitutes the largest group by number of nations, but almost all of them are small countries. A number of them are "new nations," which have only been established after the 1989 downfall of communism and the consequent breakup of the Soviet Union, Czechoslovakia, and Yugoslavia. The Central European countries have just begun to introduce free market economies and democratic politics. The term Eastern Europe is confined to three nations: Russia, the Ukraine, and Belarus. These three nations have long shared a similar political fate. They have been part of the Russian Empire and the Soviet Union and have had the longest tradition of communist rule.

The three parts of Europe will not receive equal attention. As the leading, richer, and more traditional democratic region, Western Europe will be discussed more extensively than Central and Eastern Europe. An additional argument for this focus is that, in many respects, Western Europe serves as a model for Central and even for Eastern European nations. The three leading Western European nations will be discussed in greater detail. They are Germany (81.9 million inhabitants), Great Britain (58.8 million), and France (58.2 million).

In some chapters, Western Europe will be subdivided into three subregions. That subdivision is in line with the traditional distinction between Germanic Europe and Latin Europe, with the British Isles in a separate position. The *British Isles* comprise Great Britain and Ireland. *Germanic Europe* occupies the northern part of Western Europe. It includes Germany (Western Europe's largest country) and some ten small nations like Sweden, Holland, and Austria. *Latin Europe* consists of France and three nations in the south of Europe: Italy, Spain, and Portugal. The only

Western European nation that is geographically located in Central Europe, Greece, is added to this group. Table 1.1 lists the European nations. A comparison of Map 1.1 and Map 1.2 (Europe in 1988, before the disintegration of the Soviet Union and German Reunification) reveals the epochal changes in Central and Eastern Europe in the last ten to fifteen years. Appendix B provides more details on all nations.

This division of Europe for the greater part overlaps with language groups and religions. Most of Germanic Europe speaks Germanic (Teutonic) languages and is Protestant or Catholic (or used to be, since many Europeans no longer belong to a religious denomination). Most of Latin Europe speaks Latin (Roman) languages and has traditionally been Catholic. Most of Central Europe speaks Slavonic

Table 1.1. The European Nations

	Countries	*Group*
Western Europe		
British Isles	1 Ireland, 2 Great Britain	
Germanic Europe	3 Denmark, 4 Norway, 5 Sweden, 6 Finland	Scandinavia
	7 Holland, 8 Belgium, 9 Luxembourg	Low Countries
	10 Germany	
	11 Switzerland, 12 Austria	Alpine Countries
Latin Europe	13 France	
	14 Portugal, 15 Spain	Iberian Peninsula
	16 Italy	
	17 Greece	
Central Europe	18 Estonia, 19 Latvia, 20 Lithuania	Baltic Countries
	21 Poland	
	22 Czechia, 23 Slovakia	Former Czechoslovakia
	24 Hungary	
	25 Slovenia, 26 Croatia, 27 Bosnia, 28 Serbia, 29 Macedonia	Former Yugoslavia
	30 Albania, 31 Romania, 32 Bulgaria, 33 Moldova	Nations 26–33: Balkan Peninsula
Eastern Europe	34 Belarus, 35 Ukraine, 36 Russia	Nations 18–20, 33–36: former Soviet Union
Other	37 Iceland, 38 Malta	
	Andorra, Gibraltar, Liechtenstein, Monaco, San Marino, Vatican City	Europe's tiny Mini-states
	(39 Turkey and 40 Cyprus)	

In line with popular custom, Great Britain (2) is used instead of United Kingdom, Holland (7) instead of the Netherlands, and Serbia (27) instead of Yugoslavia.

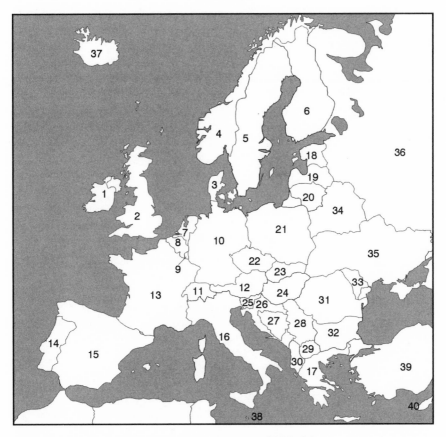

Map 1.1. Europe in 2000. For country names, see Table 1.1.

languages and used to be Catholic or Orthodox. In the three countries of Eastern Europe, which also speak Slavonic languages, the Orthodox faith prevails. Sometimes a distinction is made in different types of culture between introvert and pragmatic Germanics, extravert and passionate Latins, and patient and melancholic Slavs. These cultural variations (whatever their value) do not explain the political differences. The division made here is based on differences in political fate during the last fifty years; its only aim is to bring some order to the chaos of European states.

MAJOR DIFFERENCES WITH AMERICAN POLITICS

The fact that most European nations are democracies, or are striving to become democracies, does not mean that European politics is similar to U.S. politics. To summarize the argument of the book, four elements in particular are responsible

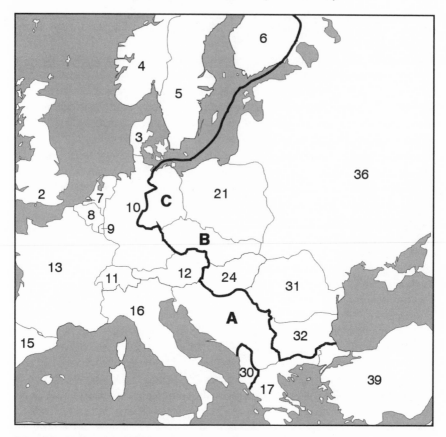

Map 1.2. Europe in 1988. For country names, see Table 1.1. Black: Iron Curtain.
A: former Yugoslavia (today's countries 25–29)
B: former Czechoslovakia (today's countries 22 and 23)
C: former East Germany (now part of 10)

for the differences between the political systems on both sides of the Atlantic: language-based nation, parliamentary democracy, religion, and social class.

Language-based nation: In Europe, national identity is often based on language, sometimes in combination with a Christian religion, either Catholic, Orthodox, or Protestant. Efforts to combine language and country, according to the principle of "each language its own nation," have been a major feature of European politics.

Parliamentary democracy: In European-style democracy, political parties compete for votes, winning them seats in the national parliament, which constitutes the highest national authority. Some of the parties build a coalition government that is responsible to the parliament. The interplay between coalition governments and the parliament, in which one or more parties support the government and others oppose it, is at the heart of European politics. Like the European kings, most European presidents are ceremonial figures with almost no political power.

Religion: Religion matters in European politics. The position of the Catholic Church, with its supreme authority in Rome has long been a source of conflict in national political and social life. Catholics have formed their own political parties, sometimes in cooperation with Protestants. One of the main religion-related issues is the influence of the Catholic Church over primary and secondary education.

Social class: Social class matters even more in European politics. In many countries it is the main dividing line. It separates working class–based political organizations like social democrats from middle and upper class organizations like conservatives and liberals. Due to the fact that social class is a major divide, social and economic policies that aim to reduce variations in living and labor conditions constitute one of the most important political issues in Europe and the core field of government policy. Like religion, the "social issue" or "social question" is now losing force. Traditional dividing lines are dwindling, which provides opportunities for new social movements and new parties.

To many Europeans these four elements are what makes European politics so fascinating—a lot more interesting than U.S. politics in their eyes—as long as the Americans come to help in case European conflicts run out of hand.

A QUICK HISTORICAL NOTE

In some chapters there are occasional references to European history. This note offers a quick reminder for those who are already familiar with European history. It has no pretension as a first introduction.

Ancient Culture (before A.D. 500)

Democracy was invented by the Greeks more than 2,500 years ago. Greek civilization had its zenith around 500 B.C. and was overtaken by the Romans who had their center in Italy, but conquered large parts of Western and Central Europe. The Romans added the notion of civil rights to democracy, but both were gradually lost after Caesar changed the Roman Republic into the more authoritarian Roman Empire before he was murdered in 44 B.C. (the most classical political assassination in European history). In combination, the Greek and Roman civilizations are known as "Ancient Culture." They heavily influenced Europe in language, philosophy (Plato, Aristotle), law, politics and public administration, arts, and general culture.

Middle Ages (500–1500)

With the breakup of the Roman Empire in A.D. 476, a period of one thousand years began in which democracy was definitely lost. Only large landowners, the landed nobility, were allowed a voice in political affairs. Under a system of feudal power they ruled over smaller landowners, with whom they controlled the dependent peasantry. During the Middle Ages, Catholicism became the major European religion, but in 1054, the Orthodox Churches broke off in Central and Eastern Europe. At the end of the Middle Ages, town dwellers wrested their autonomy from the landed nobility and developed a new urban culture, in which they rediscovered ancient culture. This "Renaissance" resulted in many new discoveries in arts and sciences, but it was confined to Western Europe and parts of Central Europe.

New Era (1500–1789)

A number of important events and discoveries ushered in the New Era.

- The Turkish conquest of what is now Istanbul (1453) marked the beginning of the Muslim domination of the Balkan Peninsula.
- Columbus' voyage to America (1492) became the start of European expansion in the rest of the world.
- The "Reformation," starting in 1517 with Martin Luther's protests against Catholic Church abuses, established Protestantism. Its spread was facilitated by the invention of book printing.

International warfare, to some extent between Catholics and Protestants, contributed to the centralization of authority in the larger European nations, where kings established absolute authority. The 1648 Peace Treaty of Westphalia, Germany, established the principle of each nation to decide on its own religion, as a form of "national sovereignty," and also recognized the independence of smaller countries like Holland and Switzerland. This recognition was the start of the European system of independent nations. In Great Britain, the nobility and the rising urban bourgeoisie were able to resist royal efforts to impose absolutism (the 1688 Glorious Revolution). They redeveloped classical and Renaissance notions about human reason as the ultimate source of all authority. In this "Enlightenment," liberalism emerged, with a focus on individual liberty and parliamentary rule.

The Nineteenth Century

The 1789 French Revolution and Napoleon's conquests spread the new idea of popular rule over the continent (in combination with the Roman-inspired codification of civil law and the metric system). Upon Napoleon's defeat in 1815, the Great Powers Great Britain, France, Prussia (Germany), Austria, and Russia established a system of mutual checks to maintain an international power balance. Smaller international revolutions in 1848 provided the liberals with opportunities to more forcefully demand or even introduce parliamentary democracy in some countries.

In the course of the nineteenth century the Industrial Revolution changed the face of Europe. Bad living conditions of the industrial proletariat gave rise to the labor movement. The labor force took part in the 1848 revolutions and gradually gained momentum as an opposition movement, either within or outside the parliament. At the end of the century, the labor movement split. The reformist wing (social democracy) abandoned the revolution in favor of participation in parliamentary politics. The communists stuck to the idea of revolution and rejected any compromise with capitalism.

During this century, Great Britain, France, and a few smaller nations established colonial rule in the African and Asian territories they dominated. Germany, which had been divided among Prussia and a number of smaller states, forged unity in 1871 after a short French-German War, but it came too late to join in colonial expansion. At the end of the century, Germany overtook Great Britain as the leading industrial power in Europe. In search of colonial expansion, it then focused on the Turkish Empire (which was in decay) as a potential prey.

The Twentieth Century

A series of international conflicts ended in World War I (1914–18), in which Germany's world power was at stake. German expansion into the Balkan Peninsula and the Middle East posed a threat to the established colonial powers Great Britain and France, and to the main Russian shipping routes. These three countries fought against Germany and the Austro-Hungarian Empire, which had actually started the war by an action against Serbia. Wartime hardship allowed the communists under Lenin to seize power in Russia in the 1917 Revolution and to establish the communist Soviet Union. After the war, the Austro-Hungarian Empire was split into a number of autonomous states in Central Europe. Amidst a wave of international turmoil and social unrest, the German Empire made way for the "Weimar Republic," named after the town where the new constitution was framed.

The economic crisis of the 1930s brought widespread unemployment and a very authoritarian political reaction in the form of fascism and Nazism, after the example of Italy. In that country, Benito Mussolini had established a fascist dictatorship in 1922, in response to postwar social upheaval. In Spain, the fascist rise to power occasioned the Spanish Civil War (1936–39).

The German Nazis, under Adolf Hitler who came to power in 1933, blamed the Jews for the crisis and Germany's defeat in World War I, and they started the Holocaust and World War II (1939–45). The Germans occupied large parts of Europe, including the Soviet Union, but the Russians, under the iron fist of communist dictator Josef Stalin, forced them back after the 1942 Battle of Stalingrad. At the Western Front, the allied invasion in France on D-Day (June 6, 1944) forced the Germans to retreat until they finally surrendered on May 8, 1945. Even more than World War I, World War II has left deep scars throughout Europe.

Following World War II, the Soviet Union imposed its communist rule in Central Europe, where its Red Army had beaten the Germans. This Russian domination resulted in the cold war and the division of Europe through an "Iron

Curtain" between Free Western Europe, helped by the U.S. Marshall aid, and communist Central and Eastern Europe. The Iron Curtain also split Germany into a western and an eastern part.

In Western Europe, France and Germany took the initiative in a new form of international cooperation, in order to prevent a new war between these two nations (they had fought three wars in less than eighty years). The outcome was the European Union, which started in 1952 as a coordinating body for the steel industry, and then developed as a "Common Market" for agricultural produce. Almost all the Western European nations have now joined the European Union.

During the booming 1960s (the Golden Sixties), Western Europe greatly expanded its social policies, to become full-fledged "Welfare States." The 1968 student revolt in Paris unleashed a youth protest movement, directed against traditional authority. The movement resulted in the emergence of "new social movements," and contributed to the decline of religion and the expansion of the welfare state in Western Europe. The spell of permanent economic growth and social development was broken by two consecutive oil crises, in 1973–74 and 1979–80, when the oil-producing countries multiplied the prices of crude oil and for the first time changed the balance-of-payments in favor of nonindustrialized countries outside Europe. The challenge posed by the Japanese economy added to the dismay of the European economy.

In Central and Eastern Europe, the reform campaign by Mikhail Gorbachev in the second half of the 1980s undermined the ossified communist structures. In 1989, communism broke down and the Soviet Union fell to pieces. Yugoslavia and Czechoslovakia also fell apart and Germany was reunified. Most Central European nations started a new course toward democracy and free enterprise, and a number of them applied for admission to the European Union.

The main events of the twentieth century are summarized in Table 1.2. Among the pressing political issues Europe faces in the first decade of the twenty-first century are the development of the European Union, including the introduction of a common currency (Euro), the integration of the waves of overseas immigrants and fugitives in Western Europe, the political and economic transformation of Central Europe, and its relations with the European Union. However, the position of Russia in Europe might well become the most urgent problem.

Table 1.2. Europe in the Twentieth Century

1900s	Spread of the labor movement. At the turn of the century labor leaders are voted into the national parliaments in Western Europe. Growing German interest in the Balkan Peninsula and the Middle East as a way to compensate for its lack of colonies leads to international tension.
1914–18	World War I. Great Britain, France, and Russia (later assisted by the United States) fight Austria and Germany.
1917	The Russian Revolution establishes the Soviet Union with communist dictatorship under Lenin.
1918–19	Revolutionary movements in Central Europe and Germany result in the disintegration of the Austro-Hungarian, the German, and later also the Turkish Empires. New nations emerge in Central Europe. Under labor pressure, universal (male) suffrage is implemented in most of Western Europe.
1922	Benito Mussolini establishes fascism in Italy.
1927	Josef Stalin starts the forced industrialization of the Soviet Union, followed by the suppression of millions of opponents and "class enemies" in several "purge campaigns."
1933	The Nazis under Adolf Hitler rise to power in Germany, followed by other fascist dictatorships.
1936–39	Civil War in Spain between the Republic under a labor government and the fascists, who take over.
1938	In Munich, Great Britain and France consent in the German claim of parts of Czechoslovakia.
1939–45	World War II, after the German invasion of Poland. Germany occupies large parts of Europe until it is driven back by the Russians in the East and the "Western Allies," including the United States, in the West. Millions of Jews killed in the Holocaust.
1948	Marshall aid to help European reconstruction. Beginning of the cold war, in which Europe (and Germany) are divided by the Iron Curtain, and of the arms race between East and West. The first Asian colonies become independent, the beginning of the process of decolonization.
1952	Foundation of the European Coal and Steel Community, precursor to the European Union.
1956	Soviet invasion of Hungary, followed by "Peaceful Coexistence" between West and East Europe.
1957	Treaty of Rome, start of the European Economic Community, the later European Union.
1958	President Charles De Gaulle founds the French Fifth Republic, with a presidential political system.

continued on next page

continued from previous page

1960s	Booming economic conditions. Western Europe develops the welfare state.
1961	Berlin Wall erected to stop the flow of fugitives from communist East Germany to West Germany.
1968	Soviet invasion of Czechoslovakia; a student revolt in Paris unleashes a wave of spontaneous actions in favor of a democratization of society.
1973–74	The first oil crisis puts an end to the booming sixties.
1979–80	Following the second oil crisis, unemployment and budget deficits become major state concerns.
1985	Mikhail Gorbachev initiates his *Perestroika* reform program, resulting in the breakdown of the communism in the Soviet Union and of the communist regimes in Central Europe.
1989–90	Disintegration of the Soviet Union and Reunification of Germany. Yugoslavia also falls apart.
1993	Introduction of the internal "Open Market" in the European Union.
2000s	Negotiations on admission of a number of Central European nations to the European Union.
2002	Introduction of the Euro, the common European Union currency.

2

The Main Lines of
Social Division

War between Serbia and Croatia, civil war in Bosnia, NATO intervention, and Serbian atrocities in Kosovo. . . . Will Macedonia be the next victim?

When former Yugoslavia fell apart in 1992, five new states were created, of which only one, Slovenia, was ethnically homogeneous. The other four new states comprise sizable ethnic minorities. Croatia contains Hungarian and Serbian minorities; the Bosnian population consists of Muslims, Croats, and Serbs; in Serbia and Macedonia there is a large Albanian minority. The Albanians in Serbia were concentrated in the Kosovo region, where they constituted an overwhelming majority of the population, at least until their forced exodus in 1999.

As the Bosnian and Kosovo conflicts show, the ethnic fragmentation of former Yugoslavia and the Balkan Peninsula in general is not merely an internal problem of these nations. It is also an international problem, first of all because most of the ethnic minorities speak the language of a neighboring country and feel akin to that country. In response, these neighbors often claim some responsibility for their "brothers and sisters" at the other side of the border. Increasingly, suppression of minorities has also become a source of international concern, and has prompted United States and European Union pressure—even military intervention.

What does "ethnicity" stand for? Mostly it points to a different language, sometimes in combination with a different religion. Since language and religion are major forces in shaping a culture, ethnic minorities often have a different culture from the majority, even if they have lived in the same country for a long time. "Ethnic Albanians" speak Albanian and are Muslims; both characteristics set them apart from Serbians and Macedonians, who share the Orthodox faith. Muslim Bosnians are also considered a separate ethnic group, despite the fact that they speak more or less the same language as the Catholic Croats and the Orthodox Serbians that live in Bosnia. In their case, religion has shaped their distinct culture. Exceptionally, two peoples with the same language and religion may still consider themselves as different, especially when they have lived in separate countries for a long time. In that case, divergent national histories have led to different nationalities. Examples are Austria and the eastern part of Switzerland. Both speak German and share the Catholic religion of the bordering regions of Germany, but they have grown apart from the Germans in the course of time. Mostly, however, language or religion has been at the root of "ethnicity." In this chapter, language, religion, and other sources of division in European politics are discussed.

LANGUAGE AND NATIONAL CULTURE

Thirty languages and three different alphabets (Latin, Cyrillic, and Greek) in a territory half the size of the United States—doesn't that cause a lot of problems? Indeed, as the main means of communication, language is the most important of all lines of division. Holding one's hand at moonlight is preferable at times, but after a while speech comes in, and many international holiday love stories soon stop after the exchange of "I love you" and "Te quiero" because of the lack of other words.

Europe speaks over thirty languages, yet most Europeans just speak their mother tongue, with a mouthful of French (old and rich people), German (the other elderly), or English (young people). Russian no longer serves as an international language, since the Central Europeans, who had to learn it at school, now refuse to understand it. With a few exceptions like Finnish and Hungarian, European languages belong to three groups: Germanic, Latin, and Slavonic. Even within each group, however, people normally do not understand each other's language. As the table in Appendix B shows, even the smallest nations have their own language.

Why is language so important in European politics? Language is an expression of culture and at the same time it shapes cultural identity. Language and language-based national identity have been sources of conflict throughout European history. They have also given rise to that most important of all political organizations, the nation. The national issue has consisted of two distinct efforts, both of them geared toward creating single-language nation-states and "ethnic nationality," mostly based on a common language. The first activity is to get all those who speak the national language within the national boundaries ("one language, hence one nation"), the second is to impose the national language upon all national citizens ("one nation, hence one language").

The first principle, "one language, hence one nation," has caused the largest problems. Important steps in that direction were the German Unification in 1871 (after centuries of German longing for unification of the many independent German states), and the break up of the multiethnic Austro-Hungarian Empire immediately after World War I. The latest developments have been the disintegration of the Soviet Union and Yugoslavia into a number of language-based nations and the Reunification of West and East Germany in 1989. National poets and novelists have often played a role in the growth of national consciousness.

They have contributed to the emergence of a real "language," out of what might have been no more than a regional dialect. Of course, poets that hailed the glorious past of the group involved were celebrated most of all. It is this national literature that often decides whether a language is more than a regional dialect.

Although the first principle "one language, hence one nation" has served as a powerful ideal in Europe, it has not been fully realized. In particular German, Hungarian, and Russian minorities have caused international tension and conflict. The outcome of World War I, the 1918 Versailles Treaty, dissolved the Austro-Hungarian Empire, which had been the most prominent example of a multiethnic state. A number of single-ethnic nations emerged. However, the Treaty consciously imposed restrictions on the principle of "one language, hence one nation" to Germany, (German-speaking) Austria, and Hungary. These countries were held responsible for the war and they were deprived of territories in which their language was the majority. Eventually, this deviation from the principle was to become one of the causes of World War II. It fueled German resentment against the peace treaty and provided the Nazis a pretext to justify the start of World War II in 1939 in order to get these Germans back into the nation. After World War II, the issue of German-speaking minorities was solved by the forced expatriation of millions of Germans from Central and Eastern Europe.

The Hungarian borders that were established in 1918 have resulted in the presence of Hungarian-speaking minorities in all surrounding countries, a source of friction between Hungary and its neighbors. Since the disintegration of the Soviet Union, Russian minorities pose a threat to national unity in the three Baltic States, Estonia, Latvia, and Lithuania, which made up part of the Soviet Union. In these new nations, Russians comprise up to one third of the total population.

The second form of language policies has been to integrate all inhabitants into a national culture by having them speak the national language, according to the principle of "one nation, hence one language." The Russification of Eastern Europe before and under communism has been the greatest effort in this respect. Nowadays we think mainly of ethnic minorities that are forced to speak the national language, yet even in countries without such minorities it has taken a long time to implant the "official" language in the whole nation. Primary education, conscription in the army, and more recently the mass media have been the means to bring about national integration.

In Central and Eastern Europe, not only the fact that many minorities speak the language of a neighboring country, but also that most of the countries involved are new nations, aggravates the problem of minority tongues and minority cultures. Their present borders date from the end of World War II, or from only ten years ago, when Russia, Yugoslavia, and Czechoslovakia disintegrated. These new nations now vehemently attempt to construct national unity by way of imposing the majority language in education, the army, and the mass media. Moreover, the effort of national integration coincides with their liberation from communist domination during which Central Europe forcibly imitated Soviet Russian political culture. National traditions—expressions of the majority culture that were suppressed under communism—were rediscovered, including the restoration of churches and the revival of old customs. Minorities are forcibly integrated, for instance, by a ban on the use of the minority tongue in schools. How important a distinct language is for national integration is shown by the rediscovery or re-invention of the Byelorussian language in Belarus and the Ukrainian tongue in Ukraine, and their promotion to the status of national languages. Even the presidents of both countries, who only spoke Russian, had to learn their new national languages.

Although these examples are mainly drawn from Central and Eastern Europe, minority languages and culture as sources of political division are not confined to that part of the continent. Western Europe also has a long history of minority suppression. Until the 1970s, Catalan—spoken by over six million people—and Basque were banned from the schools in Spain. Moreover, the most successful effort in Europe to impose the national language has not been accomplished by the Russians, but by the English. English has become the dominant language in Ireland, while Gaelic, the old Celtic language that was spoken there traditionally, has almost disappeared. Ireland is now attempting to revive Gaelic by making it a compulsory subject in education, but hardly any people are able or willing to speak it.

In Western Europe, most nations have had more time than in Central Europe to impose one national language and to seek solutions for minority groups. Common solutions have included regional autonomy for ethnic minorities, and full-fledged federalism. The best known examples are Switzerland and Belgium, where three languages are spoken. While Switzerland is the oldest federal system of the world, Belgian federalism dates from the 1970s. It was introduced when the Dutch-speaking part overtook the French-speaking part, which had dominated the economy and national culture until then. Belgian federalism has not solved all problems. The bilingual national capital Brussels, located in the Dutch-speaking part, is gradually expanding and forcing surrounding towns to become partially bilingual as well.

Table 2.1 shows the major language minorities in Europe in terms of their share in total national population. The table neither includes Russian minorities in Ukraine and Belarus (where even many nationals speak only Russian) nor the minorities in Bosnia because of the current division of that nation into two states. As the table makes clear, language minorities are the largest challenge to national integration in Central Europe. In Belgium and Switzerland, the French speakers do not regard themselves as French, but as Belgians or Swiss. In spite of their different language, they do not consider themselves to be ethnically distinct. In contrast to the efforts of federalism in Western Europe, "no special rights" in Central Europe may actually imply subtle or overt forms of suppression.

The European Union is sometimes regarded as the ultimate effort to introduce a federal political system, while leaving all national and regional cultures intact. It would guarantee not only lasting peace, but also close cooperation among the fifteen member states (and the Central European countries that stand in line to be

Table 2.1. The Major Language Minorities

Country	Population (millions)	Minority	Share (in %)	Minority Position
Belgium	10.2	French-speaking	42	Federal nation since the 1970s
Latvia	2.5	Russian	33	New nation; no special rights
Estonia	1.5	Russian	29	New nation; special rights
Macedonia	2.0	Albanian	23	New nation; no special rights. The share is that before the 1999 invasion of fugitives from Kosovo.
Switzerland	7.1	French-speaking	19	The oldest federal nation in the world.
Serbia	10.6	Albanian	17	Concentrated in Kosovo. The share is that prior to the forced 1999 exodus.
Spain	40.5	Catalan	16	Special rights; country is being federalized
Moldova	4.5	Ukrainian	14	New nation; no special rights
Moldova	4.5	Russian	13	New nation; no special rights, separatist movement
Slovakia	5.4	Hungarian	11	New nation; no special rights

admitted). It is a unique experiment in world history, since it might lead to a political system with at least ten different languages without any form of formal domination by one single language. Even if the outcome stops short of the ideal, the amount of cooperation achieved so far is already a great accomplishment. Imagine what would have become of the United States if the thirteen founding U.S. states had to bargain in ten languages.

The nature of most European countries as nation-states anchored on one language and a national culture implies that national identity is mainly based on language. Consequently, education in the national tongue within the family makes a child a member of the nation. Most Europeans do not consider themselves national citizens because they live in a particular country, but because they speak that particular language. Any conversation between two persons of the same tongue, even abroad, reinforces their national allegiance. Although large Mediterranean camping sites may appear very international meeting points, Danes speak with Danes, Dutchmen with Dutchmen, and Italians with other Italians. As a consequence of this process of national integration based on a common language, European nations generally make less intensive use of national symbols like the national flag or the national anthem than the United States. A national holiday and a regular soccer match, preferably against Germany, help to confirm national identity.

This national identity based on language is one of the basic differences with the United States, where ideas (or dreams) of democracy and free enterprise serve as foundations of the nation. Many Europeans have lived through too many nightmares (fascism, war, and communism) to believe in dreams.

RELIGION

The 1998 Nobel Peace Prize was awarded to two politicians from Northern Ireland, the Protestant prime minister and a leading Catholic politician. Both men were praised for their strenuous efforts to forge peace between the Protestant majority and the Catholic minority in their country. (Although it is subject to British rule, Northern Ireland is not a part of Great Britain; together with Great Britain it constitutes the United Kingdom.) The religious division had been a long-lasting source of violence, with bomb attacks in the regional capital Belfast and even in London. While Catholics demanded joining Ireland, which is a Catholic nation, Protestants rejected any compromise in that direction as the beginning of "Papal" rule. After long negotiations, which involved the two communities in the region, as well as the Irish and British governments, the long overdue 1998 "Good Friday Agreement" introduced a kind of autonomy under common British-Irish rule.

As the conflict in Northern Ireland shows, culture and ethnicity are not shaped by language alone. Religion is a second force at work. Although the last major wars mainly fueled by religious motives were fought centuries ago, religion continues to be a cause of division between nations and within nations, not only in Bosnia and Kosovo. The British and the Irish now share one language, but their cultures are far apart, due also to different religions. While most British are Protestant, the Irish are Catholic, and the clash between these religions is the major cause of conflict in Northern Ireland, though not the only one.

As Map 2.1 shows, the three main religions in Europe are Catholicism, Protestantism, and the Orthodox faith. European history has been full of political tension between these religions, but now one religion predominates in most countries. Catholicism is most widespread, but a few nations in the north, like Scandinavia, are totally Protestant, and Eastern Europe is Orthodox. In the three countries that are divided between Protestants and Catholics (Germany, Holland, and Switzerland), conflict has traditionally been reduced by the regional concentration of the two religions. Dominant Protestantism prevails in the North and the Catholic minority is concentrated in the South. The two denominations now cooperate in one political movement: Christian democracy. This leaves Northern Ireland as the only lasting example of Catholic-Protestant conflict.

The main type of friction caused by religion is not one between religions, however. It is the dividing line between Catholics (clericals) and anticlericals, who oppose the influence of the Catholic Church in social life. This line of conflict is most pronounced in Catholic countries. While Protestantism and the Orthodox religion have founded national or regional Churches, which accept the authority of the national government in political affairs, the Catholic Church has always tried to keep a prominent say in political and social affairs. During the nineteenth century, the liberals became the core of an anti-Church movement in the Catholic countries. They hailed individual freedom and opposed the dominant role of the Church in politics and society. In the course of the twentieth century, social

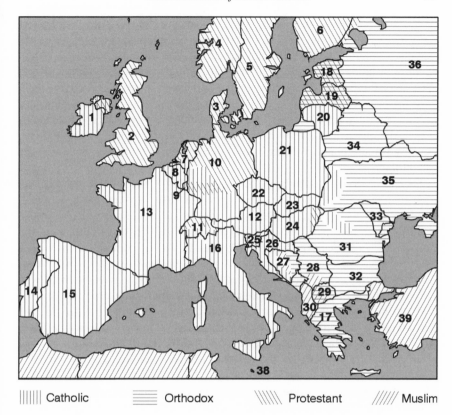

Catholic ‖‖‖‖‖ Orthodox ≡≡≡ Protestant \\\\\ Muslim /////

Map 2.1. The Religious Division of Europe. For country names, see Table 1.1.

democrats, and even more communists, have taken over as the leading anti-Church force in Catholic countries. In France, the 1789 French Revolution fixed the front line between clericals (Catholics) and anticlericals. French Catholics still speak in different and more negative terms about the French Revolution than the anticlericals—in striking contrast with the unanimous American praise of the American Revolution.

The strong clerical/anticlerical strife in countries in which almost all people are Catholic may come as a surprise. As a matter of fact, fierce anticlericals fighting Church influence in politics and society may be Catholics, at least in name. However, many Catholics in the Catholic countries have very weak links with the Church. They only come to church for their weddings, the baptisms of their children, Christmas celebrations, and their own funerals.

What is the political relevance of religion in Europe? First, although most European nations adhere to the separation between state and religion, that separation is far from complete. The British queen is the head of the national Anglican Church, and in Sweden all citizens were officially registered as members of the

Protestant Lutheran Church until 1996. In some of the Central and Eastern European countries, the fall of communism has prompted a revival of the Catholic Church, notably in Poland, and of national Orthodox Churches as part of the rediscovery of national heritage. In several European countries, either Protestantism, Catholicism, or the national Orthodox Church enjoys special facilities, for instance in tax exemptions, state support of church construction, and facilities for religious education. Often, however, these privileges are matched by support of nonreligious institutions as well, to provide for equality-under-the-law. Equality is more important than a total American-style separation between state and religion.

Second, national governments, and the Catholic Church have clashed over education, most of all. For the governments, this "School Issue" has been a matter of national integration; for the Church, an attack upon religion. All Catholic countries have had their "school conflict" about the rights of Catholics to run their own schools, state funding of such schools, and the right of others to send their children to nonreligious schools. A recent incident took place in Bavaria, Germany in 1996, when people protested against the Catholic crucifix on the wall of public schools. The German Supreme Court decided that the crucifix had to be removed if pupils or their parents demanded so. Catholic politicians then denounced the Supreme Court as biased—a capital sin in Germany, just as it is in the United States. Incidentally, the issue of specific Catholic school is revived when governments reorganize the school system or announce cuts in the education budget. Catholic education is no longer the major religious issue, however. Christian religion now mainly plays a role in moral issues like abortion, sexual morals, and the rights of homosexuals.

Third, religion serves as the base of Christian democracy, one of the leading European ideologies, and political movements. Christian democracy has dominated politics in the German Federal Republic since World War II and has been powerful in several other countries as well.

Islam is the latest religious issue. In Central Europe, Muslims have lived in Albania, Bosnia, and in Serbia (Kosovo) for several centuries. In Kosovo, the Muslim Albanian minority had to face Serbian suppression, which reached its tragic finale in 1999 at the time of the NATO military intervention. Hundreds of thousands of Muslims then were forced to leave the country overnight. In Western Europe, Islam is a new issue and will be discussed at the end of this chapter.

REGION

In 1996, the mock republic of Padania was proclaimed in northern Italy. The new "state" was a propaganda act of one of Italy's new political movements, *Lega Nord* (Northern League), which claims independence for northern Italy. Lega Nord sprang up after the collapse of the traditional political parties. The Christian democratic and social democratic parties broke down under heavy accusations of links with the Mafia, the communist party because of the international demise of communism. The media-tycoon Silvio Berlusconi, who aspired to a political career, and Lega Nord filled the gap. The Lega argues that southern Italy has only exported to the North "backward" migrant workers, the Mafia, and corrupt politics. Both this movement and its claim are new elements in European politics, because, by way of exception, in this secessionist movement language and religion are not the main issues, and it is located in the most prosperous part of the country.

Although most claims for regional autonomy in European nations are based on differences in language or religion, region may serve as a political issue in yet another form. The divergence between the political "center" and the "periphery" may give rise to protest or even separatist movements in the periphery. The center often consists of the national capital, as the political center, or more generally of the most prosperous regions in the country, as the economic center. They attract most investment, and often most government attention. The periphery comprises less developed rural areas far from the political and economic center and with a marginal role in the national economy.

Resentment between center and periphery may be mutual. The center complains about the backwardness of the periphery and the cost of public assistance to the less developed areas. The periphery points to the fact that it is either dominated or forgotten by a far-off government. Even when language and religion are not involved, the division often includes a cultural component. The rural periphery defends its "authentic" culture against "progress" (and taxes) imposed by the "big city." The most conspicuous example of the divergence between the national capital—as the economic, political, and cultural center of the nation—and the rest of the country, is France. The Parisians consider the rest of France as *la Province*, (backward since it lacks all vices for which Paris is so famous). The rest of France complains about Parisian government spending and control. Italy is a prominent example of divergence between the economic center in the North and the economic periphery in the South. The mock republic of Padania was an expression of that division, in which the national capital Rome hardly plays a role.

A new kind of center-periphery division arose in the 1980s, and it made clear that traditional "centers" may become new "peripheries." The change was due to the rise of unemployment and the shift from traditional industries to service-oriented economies. Old industrial areas like the German Ruhr area (Essen, Duisburg, and Dortmund), and northern England (Manchester, Liverpool, and Leeds) were plagued by the closing down of many factories and by high unemployment. From being economic centers of the nation, they to some extent became a new kind of periphery. Investors preferred the high-tech enterprises in other parts of these countries, like the south of Germany and the southeast of England. These regions then seemed to become the new centers of gravity of the national economy and motors of economic progress. In Western Europe, most old industrial areas have been able to attract new investments, however, and they have gradually retaken a prominent place in the economy. In Central Europe, the economic reforms have hit the old industrial centers harder. The opening of the economic borders has made them easy victims of international competition. Industrial regions that used to be the pride of the nation as showpieces of industrial progress under communism are now changing into slum areas.

The latest type of center-periphery division developed in Germany following 1989 German Reunification, when former communist East Germany was integrated in the West German Federal Republic. The East German economy has not survived the competition with West German enterprises and has crumbled down, resulting in high unemployment. East Germans ("Ossies") are discontent with the domination of their economy and politics by the "Wessies." The Wessies complain about the lack of gratitude among the Ossies in spite of the billions of German marks that flow from West to East as reconstruction funds.

The political relevancy of the center-periphery issue is not only shown by separation movements like the one in Italy, but also by differences in voting behavior or even by the rise of political parties that defend the periphery. In some countries, farmers' parties act in that way.

SOCIAL CLASS

Language, religion, and center-periphery have been age-old sources of conflict and motivated internal and international warfare. With a few exceptions, they no longer dominate politics within the European nations. Since the turn of the century a fourth divide—social class—has established itself as a prominent political issue. It has marked twentieth century European politics and has been the predominant dividing line since the end of World War II.

During most of European history, peasants used to be the "poor" class. They were often exploited by the nobility and other landowners. In the course of the Industrial Revolution, which spread across Europe in the nineteenth century, a new class of poor people arose, the industrial working class. It was concentrated in industrial towns and cities and in large mining communities. Prominent examples were the mining and steel regions in the north of England and the German Ruhr area, which have now lost their position as the national economic "center."

Although millions of town and village laborers migrated to the New World during the second half of the nineteenth century, Europe did not develop a notion like the U.S. "Open Frontier." Within the national borders there were hardly any opportunities to evade harsh labor discipline or to escape political oppression. These conditions encouraged industrial labor to raise its voice in industrial protest, social revolt, and even in national revolution.

Toward the end of the nineteenth century, manual workers in industry established the labor movement, which drew attention to the appalling living and labor conditions of the industrial "proletariat" and demanded more social and political equality. Labor succeeded in making social class the core political issue in many

European nations, separating the industrial working class from the middle and the upper class. The term working class refers especially to manual workers in industry (blue-collar workers) but also to office workers (white-collar workers). What sets this class apart is that they are employed by others and are dependent on wages for a living. The middle class comprises all people that are self-employed and have some capital from which they derive income, in the form of a shop or an enterprise. The upper class forms the wealthy top of this middle class.

The labor movement attacked "bourgeois" politics by the small groups of middle- and upper-class industrialists, landowners, and professionals that enjoyed voting rights, but denied that right to the working class. The national labor movements then set up their own political organizations and trade unions in order to improve working class living and labor conditions. The two leading labor movement ideologies have been reformist social democracy and revolutionary communism. A third trend, revolutionary anarchism, has occupied a more marginal position.

In many European countries, the struggle between social democrats and communists on the one hand and liberals and conservatives on the other has constituted the basic divide in national politics since World War II. Of course, the border line has been blurred, in particular by the rise of a "new middle class" of office workers who are wage-earners but identify more with the middle class. However, partly due to the existence of the large and politically oriented European labor movement, the split between the working class and the middle class is still stronger in Europe than in the United States. European labor has emphasized the common interests of the working class and created a sense of community among industrial workers. In most of Europe, skilled workers in large and heavy industry, like steelworks, machine works, and automobile factories have formed the backbone of the labor movement. They also appealed to unskilled workers to join the movement in order to give it more weight in politics and in contacts with employers. This appeal has resulted in a higher degree of "class identification" of manual workers with their social class than in the United States.

The strong divide in Europe based on social class is one of the main differences with U.S. politics. In American politics, the trade unions traditionally support the Democratic Party, but that party is not an exclusive working class party—just think of the Democrats in the Old South.

COPING WITH DIVISION: EXCLUSION VERSUS INTEGRATION

Language, religious affiliation, regional disparities, and the social structure of society have been disruptive forces in European politics. They have caused international conflicts, civil strife, and political division within nations. Several means have been tried to cope with this kind of division. They range from violent exclusion of minorities to peaceful efforts to integrate them in national society, while granting them specific rights to continue their culture.

Regretfully, efforts of violent exclusion or even extermination have been most common in European politics, up to modern times. The "ethnic cleansing" campaign by Serbs and Croats in Bosnia, and by the Serbs in Kosovo, have only been the most recent examples. By far the largest extermination campaigns during the twentieth century have been the Nazi Holocaust and the Soviet purges of "enemies of the working class" in the course of the 1930s. The Holocaust was one of the few times in which race played a dominant role in European politics. Before that time many European towns housed Jewish communities. Throughout European history they were chased at times, tolerated at times, and discriminated against most of the time. Following the Holocaust, many survivors migrated to Israel. The extermination of "class enemies" in the Soviet Union under Josef Stalin affected not only middle-class people and farmers but also all opponents to the communist regime. Most of the victims died in the concentration camps in the far north of Russia and Siberia. One of the survivors wrote about the large number of concentration camps as an "archipelago" in the Arctic areas of Russia.

Although no one would call it that way, the largest "ethnic cleansing" campaign after World War II actually took place immediately after the war. Millions of Germans were removed from Central and Eastern European countries, where they sometimes had been settled for over centuries, to Germany. This removal was not only a reaction to the war but was also meant to prevent any new German claims on foreign territory.

Political exclusion may also assume less violent forms, like denying access to national politics or refusing participation in the national government. This strategy affected Italian communists since World War II. Although they regularly received a quarter of all votes in national elections, they were systematically left out of government between 1948 and 1998, partly under U.S. pressure. The Americans feared for the strength of NATO if communists would hold power positions in any of the larger member states.

Integration in the national political system might look like the opposite of exclusion but it may actually amount to the same. This is especially the case when integration takes undemocratic and violent forms and the majority does not take into account the minorities' different culture. Once again, the most repressive forms of integration were Nazi Germany and the Soviet Union. The Nazis banned all organizations of the labor movement and chased communists and social democrats. New and state-controlled organizations, with compulsory membership, were set up to integrate workers in Nazi society. The Soviet Union used the power monopoly of the communist party and the ban on all rival organizations to guarantee the integration of the working class in Soviet politics and to exclude minority interests.

Except for multilingual Switzerland, the combination of special rights and of peaceful national integration doesn't have a long history in Europe. In Western Europe, most developments in that direction date from the postwar period, and in most of the new nations of Central Europe special rights are still a hot issue.

A special way to prevent conflicts between various language or religious groups, in particular when they are not regionally concentrated, is the segmentation of social life. Society is then subdivided into a number of religious or ideological segments or "pillars" which do not have frequent mutual contact. Each of the segments has its own network of schools, hospitals, recreational facilities, and other provisions, within which people live their lives "from womb to tomb." That segmentation or "pillarization" of society links people within the same group together and limits contacts and reduces conflicts with members of other groups. In particular, social democrats and Catholics have built solid and separate blocks, for instance in Austria and Belgium. In Scandinavia, farmers and social democrats had their own networks of organizations. Holland had a Catholic, a Protestant, and a social democratic bloc or "pillar" and used to be the most prominent example of pillarization. Catholics were called upon by their political and religious leaders to join Catholic clubs and organizations, buy in shops owned by Catholics, read Catholic newspapers, look at Catholic television channels, and send their children to Catholic schools. In short, they should prevent any contact with Protestants and social democrats. The latter two acted in similar ways for their own groups. In order to prevent conflict between the leaders of the pillars, some rules of the game have to be observed, like proportional representation of all pillars in official committees and a proportional distribution of state funds. Although this kind of reducing mutual contacts has worked well for a long period as a device to reduce contacts and conflicts, it may also feed hostile feelings toward each other. Members of the different groups do not get any opportunities to come into contact with the other groups and develop a positive posture toward these fellow human beings. By way of contrast, frequent and close contacts between members of different groups might reduce feelings of hatred or envy. On the other hand, such frequent contacts are no panacea for peaceful living together, either. The civil war in Bosnia between Muslims, Croats, and Serbs shows that even where people have a lot of contacts, a spark of hostile feeling may easily arouse hatred and lead to open conflict.

The various social and cultural divides sometimes overlap. In case the same groups of people are not only divided on one line of division but on two or three, overt conflict is more likely and once broken out, it is harder to solve. In Northern Ireland, social class and religion coincide to some extent as lines of division, with poor Catholics opposing middle class (and less poor working class) Protestants. On the other hand, lines of division may also crosscut. (Political scientists then speak of crosscutting social cleavages.) In that case, conflict arises less easily because the opposing groups share some common loyalties. Where part of the working class is Catholic (and not just in name), it is more difficult for social democrats to mobilize these workers for their parties. The Catholic workers not only feel class-based loyalties toward their fellow workers, but also "inter-class" loyalties to middle-class and even upper-class Catholics. The social democrats regret these class-overstepping loyalties, of course, but they cannot fight the

Catholic Church too ardently. That would drive the Catholic workers even more into the arms of the Church and tighten the Catholic pillar or block even more.

THE DECLINE OF THE TRADITIONAL SOURCES OF DIVISION

While some of the traditional sources of division are weakening, new divides challenge European politics. In most of Western Europe, language and ethnicity are no longer hot issues. Only scattered and isolated terrorist groups are now fighting for independence in Basque Country (Spain) and for autonomy on the French isle of Corse. Partly under pressure of the European Union, several Central European countries are introducing modest variants of minority rights as a precondition for admission to the European Union. Only in a few Central European countries such issues remain as yet unsettled and may lead to armed conflict in the future.

Religion, in the sense of Catholic-Protestant or clerical/anticlerical conflict, has also lost much of its political force. Many people do not go to church and neither do their children attend Catholic or Protestant schools any longer. The religion-based schools and universities that continue to exist have become far more tolerant and open-minded than twenty years ago. The combination of decline of religious affiliation and weakening of the impact of religion on politics is called "secularization." Secularization has contributed to the gradual decline of the segmentation or pillarization of society. People no longer accept strict rules on their behavior by religious or political leaders. In Central and Eastern Europe, the long period of communist rule (during which religious expression was banned) "secularized" society in a less democratic way. In Europe, going to church is no social obligation, as it is in large parts of the United States, and in particular in towns and cities only old people go to church regularly and fulfill other religious duties.

Center-periphery contrasts have also lost much of their force. The labor force in agriculture is now only a fraction of the total population in most European countries and there are no "rural states" as in the United States (see Table 2.2). Rural areas that are close to towns have been turned into "suburbia" and are populated by urban dwellers looking for a house with a garden and more rest than in the old quarters of large towns. Farmers' parties still exist but they are small and have to look for support outside agriculture.

Even more important than any of these changes is the transformation of the social structure, which has reduced the prominence of social class in national politics. Many European nations are no longer industrial economies but "post-industrial" and service-oriented economies, in which most people are employed in the services sector, rather than in the industrial sector. Traditional industries with large numbers of manual workers have given way to commercial and non-profit services whose employees form the "new middle class" of office workers and do not feel strong bonds with the traditional working class. Most employees

**Table 2.2. Employment in Agriculture, Industry, and Services
(in percentage of the labor force)**

Country	Agriculture		Industry		Services		Comments
	1973	1996	1973	1996	1973	1996	
Western Europe							
Denmark	10	4	34	27	57	69	A major agricultural exporter!
France	11	5	40	26	49	70	Also a major agricultural exporter.
Germany	7	3	47	38	45	59	Industry continues to be more important than in the surrounding countries.
Greece	37	20	28	23	36	56	The lowest income EU member state.
Holland	6	4	37	22	58	74	Europe's most service-oriented economy.
Portugal	27	12	34	31	39	56	The second lowest income EU member.
Central Europe	1989	1993	1989	1993	1989	1993	
Czechia	11	7	50	45	40	49	Central Europe's leading industrial nation.
Hungary	16	9	38	34	47	57	Central Europe's largest services sector.
Romania	28	36	45	36	27	28	Many people returned to the agricultural sector after the collapse of industry.
Eastern Europe	1989	1993	1989	1993	1989	1993	
Russia	14	15	43	40	44	45	Also a movement back to jobs in agriculture.

Data for the USA: agriculture 4–3; industry 33–24; services 63–73.
Source: *OECD Employment Outlook 1996*; UN, ECE, Economic Survey of Europe in 1994–1995.

think of themselves as middle class, live in middle-class suburbs, and display a great variety of lifestyles, to which they are more attached than to their "class status." This change of social structure has reduced the "class identification" of the working class and affected the attractiveness of the labor movement. In particular the social democratic parties have changed from exclusive labor parties to more general parties, appealing not only to manual workers but also to office employees and professionals. As Table 2.2 shows, even Central European nations have become service-oriented economies.

New divisions have not (yet) replaced the old ones. An important new line of division is gender. The women's movement has come to enjoy political influence. It emerged during the 1960s and 1970s, partly due to the weakening of religion and social class as sources of identity and division. Nowadays, women's role in society is a general issue in European politics. Political parties run by women are still a rarity in Europe, however, and so are female party leaders.

Age might well become another source of division, due to the growing number of old-age pensioners. Since many of them are dependent upon state pensions, they are increasingly organizing as pressure groups or even as political parties, in order to fight cuts in state pensions. Their organization is hampered by the fact that leaders do not last long in organizations of the elderly.

Increasingly, however, Western European society is characterized by what could become the strongest source of political conflict, the waves of immigrant workers and political fugitives.

IMMIGRANTS: A NEW DIVIDE?

In 1993, girls wearing the traditional Muslim headscarf were refused admittance to a school in France. Such religious symbols were considered a violation of the separation between the state and religion. Others objected to what they saw as an encroachment of civil and religious rights. Later, similar incidents were reported, without a final solution. While some ten years ago Europeans used to look amusingly at efforts by the American religious right to introduce a Biblical version of the creation of the world in American schools, they now quarrel about religious headscarves themselves. As the incidents show, even national governments have not yet become accustomed to the spread of Islam in a predominantly Christian continent. The issue of Islam arose in Western Europe in the course of the 1960s and 1970s, when millions of Muslim workers from Turkey and North Africa migrated to the industrial cities in the more prosperous countries of Western Europe. Since they have larger families than the Western Europeans, their share in the population has risen continuously. In Western Europe, Muslims have erected their own mosques (often partly paid by Saudi Arabia) and have also humbly asked the same rights that Christians have enjoyed for centuries—but in which many are no longer interested. Why should Christian church bells wake up Muslims, and Muslim muezzins not be permitted to call for prayer?

According to some, the growing importance of Islam, "imported" by millions of immigrant workers and political fugitives, is threatening Europe's language-based and "secularized" national societies. The argument is that the influence of the Islam, and in particular of very conservative religious leaders who reject any form of integration in Western European society, undermine democracy and civil liberties, as well as "national virtues." Nationalist and even outright racist parties focus on this loss of classical national virtues, while forgetting their nation's "glorious past" as colonial or imperial oppressors. Their opponents point to the fact that many children of Muslim migrants (the second-generation migrants) are raised in democratic traditions and are willing to adapt to national social life. The social and political integration of this second generation is jeopardized, however, by their marginal position in economic life. Generally, they have a lower level of training than the children of the indigenous population, and they are more plagued by unemployment. The "ghettos" of poor African-Americans and other ethnic minorities in the United States serve as a powerful incentive for European governments to step up the efforts of integration, including social measures to get these people to work. "Are we going the American way?" is a popular headline story in Europe after each outburst of racial discontent in the United States. In Europe, the minority issue has explicit racial overtones in Great Britain, where the larger cities house concentrations of blacks from the former colonies. Many of them share the fate of unemployment and other social problems with the Muslim migrants in the rest of Western Europe.

Although debate focuses on Muslim immigrants, recent migration waves have also included many nationals from "Christian" European nations, especially in the South (southern Italy, Portugal, and Spain) to the more prosperous countries of Western Europe. The largest flow of migrants enter from outside Europe, however, and most of them are Muslims: Two-and-a-half-million people from Turkey and almost two million from North Africa (Algeria and Morocco). The two million fugitives from former Yugoslavia, who left their countries because of Croatian-Serbian warfare, the Bosnian Civil War, and the Kosovo conflict have been the largest group of migrants during the 1990s. In the year 1992, over 400,000 of them fled to Germany. Foreigners now make up nine percent of the German population, the highest share in Europe. Table 2.3 shows the spread of foreign migrants over the main immigration countries of Western Europe. In these countries foreigners comprise between five and nine percent of total population. Table 2.3 does not include large numbers of people from former colonies that have the nationality of the country they have immigrated to (see also Table 9.1 for the former colonies).

Although the share of foreigners in the total population is not very high, migrants are often concentrated in large cities. In some quarters of the larger Western European cities and in industrial towns they form a sizable minority. In Paris, Algerians constitute the largest foreign community with over 300,000 people; in Berlin, Turks are the largest minority with over 140,000.

The integration of foreign migrants and fugitives is mainly a Western European problem, in particular of the more prosperous Western European countries. In that part of Europe, it is now by far the most pressing political issue and also a topic of lively debate in public and private discussion. In Germany, debate now focuses on easier immigrant access to German nationality. In particular, those born in Germany in immigrant families should be allowed to become German nationals without much bureaucratic delay. This concession to foreigners implies a partial shift from the principle of nationality based on family descent, which is the common form in Europe, to the American principle of nationality based on place of birth. The American principle, which also applies in France, often allows for a "double nationality," in case the parents do not give up

Table 2.3. Foreign Nationals (Immigrants and Fugitives) in Western Europe

Country	Population (millions)	Main countries of origin	Comments
Germany	81.9	Turkey (two million), Serbia, Italy, Greece, Poland, Bosnia	Country with largest population of foreigners (nine percent of total population). During the 1990s, large numbers of political fugitives were admitted.
Great Britain	58.8	Ireland, Pakistan, India	Additionally, there are many people from former colonies, who are British nationals.
France	58.2	North Africa (Algeria, Morocco)	The oldest immigration country, with many Latin European immigrant workers. Additionally, many immigrants have arrived from former colonies, who are French nationals.
Holland	15.5	Turkey, North Africa (Morocco)	Additionally, there are many immigrants from Dutch Guyana (Surinam), who are Dutch nationals.
Belgium	10.2	Italy, North Africa (Morocco)	An old immigration country with miners from Italy and Poland.
Austria	8.1	Former Yugoslavia	Many fugitives have traveled to Germany, others have stayed in Austria.
Switzerland	7.1	Italy	Italians are employed in manual work. Due to a small number of Italian-speaking Swiss, Italian is one of Switzerland's official languages.

Countries ranked in order of population size.

their (and their children's) original nationality (even when they officially have to). German opponents of double nationality fear that it will lead to split national allegiance and to increasing numbers of foreigners that only use their German passports for social security benefits or even for criminal purposes, without considering themselves as Germans.

In Central Europe, the problem of fugitives has been mainly confined to former Yugoslavia and Albania. Serbs fled from Croatia, and Bosnian Muslims fled from the parts occupied by the Bosnian Serbs. The largest flow of fugitives consisted of Albanian Muslims who were deported from Kosovo and fled to Albania and Macedonia. In both countries the large flow of fugitives almost endangered sheer national survival, and in Macedonia it also threatened the fragile ethnic balance between the Macedonians and the large Albanian minority.

All of these outbursts of ethnic conflict in former Yugoslavia implied "ethnic cleansing," a new term for the deportation of ethnic minorities. Although the Serbs were most active in pursuing this kind of atrocities, they fell also victim to it themselves when hundreds of thousands of Serbs fled the eastern part of Croatia in 1995.

3

Liberals Are Not Liberals: The European Ideologies

Anarchists, Bolsheviks, Christian democrats, environmentalists, feminists, Gaullists . . . As if forty nations and thirty languages are not enough, Europe is also heavily divided among a great variety of ideologies, at least one for every letter in the Latin alphabet. To many Europeans, the wide range of the political spectrum enhances the fascination of European politics. To most Americans, it is a source of frustration, since some terms may cause confusion. European liberals are quite different from American liberals and Christian democrats are not Europe's "religious right." Better still, most European liberals are more conservative than the Christian democrats.

THE EUROPEAN POLITICAL SPECTRUM

The usual way to bring order in the apparent chaos of ideologies is to rank them from left to right on a horizontal line. This ranking is based on their position with respect to the issue of state intervention in the free-market economy in order to protect the working class and bring about more social equality. Labor movement ideologies that totally reject the free-market economy, like communism, are placed on the left end, while ideologies that oppose any state intervention in the form of social policies are located on the right end. However, there is one complication to start with. The political right not only consists of free-market apologists but also of people that support state intervention in the economy or even state control of the national economy for other reasons than promoting social equality. It might serve a strong state or foreign expansion, for instance. In between the two extremes of "social intervention" versus "no intervention" or "no social intervention," are parties that advocate or accept some form of social state intervention, like social democrats and Christian democrats. This line of division is at the heart of European politics. Most Europeans define their political position in left-right terms, and social equality and social policies constitute the core issue in European politics.

European politics is not that simple, however. An older line of division continues to play a role, as well. It relates to freedom and authority in moral values and family life, including sexual morals and abortion. Here the contrast is one between conservatives who stress authority by the state, a Church or one's parents, and liberals who espouse individual liberty. This second source of division, between authoritarianism and libertarianism, may be represented by a vertical line, which crosscuts the horizontal line.

As a consequence, the European political spectrum is a combination of two lines of division, a horizontal line for the left-right division, and a vertical one for the authoritarian-libertarian contrast. Political discussion is impeded by the fact that for both dividing lines, the qualifications "progressive-conservative" are used. Progressive stands for a position to the left on the horizontal line but also for a libertarian position on the vertical line; conservative denotes a place to the right and to the authoritarian side. Moreover, ideologies that are progressive in the issue of social state intervention in the economy may hold conservative views with respect to moral issues.

Figure 3.1 shows the location of the most important European ideologies on the horizontal and the vertical lines. Communists, who are the most radical with

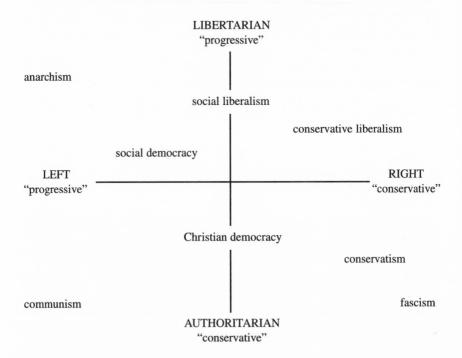

Figure 3.1. The European Political Spectrum.

respect to the social issue and at the same time extremely authoritarian in moral issues, are placed below in the left corner. Conservative liberals, who are conservative with respect to the social issue but at the same time libertarian in moral issues, are in the upper right corner. Social democracy is located to the left and more upward than Christian democracy.

Is the greater number of ideologies the only difference between the European and the American political spectrum? No, they also differ in other respects. First, in the United States the two lines (left-right and libertarian-authoritarian) more or less overlap. This is to some extent due to the American two-party system. Republicans are more to the right (more conservative in social issues) as well as more authoritarian (more conservative in moral issues) than Democrats. The fact that the two lines of division do not overlap in Europe makes European politics more difficult to understand than American politics.

Second, the left-right division does not dominate American politics to the extent it does in Europe. The American labor movement has not been successful in promoting social equality as the core issue of politics, and moral issues count just as much, or even more, than social issues. Third, the American political spectrum as a whole is more "conservative" on both lines than the European one. The European labor movement has widened the left part of the horizontal line, and in so doing, it has pulled the whole political spectrum to the left. In combination with liberals, it has also pulled the whole spectrum upward, toward the progressive side in moral issues. As a consequence, several large European parties occupy positions that are more "progressive" on both lines (more social equality oriented as well as more libertarian) than that of the Democratic Party, and only a few European parties share the Republicans' attitudes in social and moral questions. Probably to Jesse Helms's pleasure, it would be difficult to find someone in Europe matching his ideas. European politics, then, lean more to the Democratic than to the Republican side.

Yet another difference is that the terms Democrats and Republicans do not have any meaning in Europe. Several ideologies call themselves democrats, so one has to add a typical European adjective (liberal, Christian, or social). Republicans only exist in France, and less so in Italy. They are the defenders of the Republic against opponents to the right (very conservative Catholics and old-fashioned royalists in favor of a strong king). In the existing European kingdoms, abolishing monarchy is not an issue and there are hardly any republicans in those countries. The main difference in terms between Europe and the United States, however, is in the meaning of "liberal," to be discussed next. The ideologies appear here in the chronological order of their emergence.

CONSERVATISM

"Once upon a time there was a king . . ." After some problems in finding a suitable prince for the princess, such fairy tales always end up with a happy royal family and consequently also happy subjects.

Conservatism is the oldest ideological trend in Europe. Its core ideas are hierarchy and authority. The conservative vision of society is based upon the traditional view of the family as a "natural" unity, in which the father exercises authority over his wife and children and takes care of them. Other forms of authority, like that of employers over their employees, and of kings over their subjects, are patterned after this family relationship. This relationship of inequality benefits both sides. The subordinates are under the obligation to obey, but in return they are well looked after by the men of authority. That fatherly care enables the subjects to live in peace, free from concern.

In addition to traditional fairy tales about a "Golden Past" with well-beloved kings and lovely princesses, conservatism has found its expression in the "organic" analogy of social life, which compares society with the human body. In this vision, all parts of the body (and of society) constitute a harmonious and organic unity and perform necessary functions for a person's (and society's) well-being but a clear distinction is made between "lower" and "higher" organs. "Lower" parts like the feet and internal organs have to obey a higher organ like the head, otherwise the body will dysfunction. Conservatives abhor rebellious lower parts.

On defending authority, conservatism is located at the bottom of the political spectrum. In its attitude toward the free-market economy, conservatism is less unambiguous. Originally the free market was rejected as a threat to social life, since it disrupted family life and undermined traditional authority. Nowadays, most conservatives strongly speak out in favor of the free-market economy. There are also conservatives that advocate state intervention in the economy, but as a means to reinforce state power rather than to pursue social goals.

Of course, conservatism has traditionally been supported by those in power, including absolute kings and the aristocracy. However, people without any power have also embraced conservative ideas on society as a "natural order." This attitude is more pronounced on the countryside than in the towns, and it is cherished especially in peripheral rural areas. Conservative political parties do not exist in all European nations. In some countries, conservative liberals dominate the right end of the political spectrum. In Eastern Europe, communists are now the main conservative parties in support of strong authority and a strong state. The two major conservative parties in Western Europe are the British conservatives and the French Gaullists, who are named after former French president Charles de Gaulle. They differ in their attitude toward the free market. In that respect, the British conservatives, like conservative liberal parties, favor state abstention. The Gaullists have long advocated state intervention in the economy to serve French *grandeur* in the international economy and international politics. Charles de Gaulle, who was French president during the 1960s, was probably the most prominent conservative statesman in Europe since the war. The reigning French president, Gaullist Jacques Chirac, is more of a conservative liberal in favor of state retreat in the economy.

LIBERALISM

"Men living together according to reason, without a common superior on earth with authority to judge between them, is properly the state of nature," according to the seventeenth century British philosopher John Locke in his "Two Treatises on Government." These individuals' only aim in creating a commonwealth (state) was to punish crime "for the preservation of the property of all the members of that society."

According to liberalism, individual freedom is the core element in society: freedom from pressing bonds of authority and from total responsibility for subordinates. Society does not consist of rulers and subjects but is based on a voluntary "social contract," in which free individual citizens confirm their intention to form a civic community and create "civic nationality," based on citizens' rights. In this self-chosen community, all citizens should be able to develop their faculties. The only limit to individual freedom is that one should not harm others, or better yet, should not reduce the freedom of other citizens. Two elements are important for individual self-development: education and private property. Education is the base of human freedom, since it enlarges one's capacities and capabilities and widens the range of opportunities available. Private property is the stake one has in society and provides the material base of engaging in nonproductive activities, like culture and political debate.

Liberals were the early defenders of both free-market competition and parliamentary democracy (which is also a kind of competition). In early liberal thought, people without education and private property were not full citizens and could not participate in political decision making, since they had no stake in society. Their degrading position was regarded as the result of free choice, or a lack of initial capacities. State social policies designed to improve that situation would only interfere with free choice. The only state tasks were national defense and preventing and fighting crime.

After the rise of social democracy, the liberals split into two trends: conservative liberals and social liberals. Traditional or conservative liberals continue to defend state abstinence, while social liberals have come closer to the social democrats in accepting social legislation. Both trends are at home in the upper half of the political spectrum. Conservative liberals occupy a place at the right end, social liberals in the middle.

Liberalism finds its defenders in the towns and cities, and most of all among the urban (higher) middle class. While businessmen are more inclined to conservative liberalism, professionals and intellectuals ("Massachusetts or California style") constitute the backbone of social liberalism. Conservative liberal parties exist in most European countries, but apart from the British Conservative Party, which might also be called conservative liberal, they do not dominate national politics. Former British Prime Minister Margaret Thatcher was the most prominent conservative liberal hawk in Europe. Social liberal parties are less common and much smaller.

As Figure 3.1 shows, European liberals are not the same as American liberals. American conservatives need not be afraid of European liberals, they might even be their friends. Most European liberals are conservative liberals, located at the right end of the left-right line, exactly the opposite of the American liberals' position. When transplanted to the United States, they would occupy the left wing and the center of the Republican Party. Only the less numerous social liberals resemble American liberals. In contrast to the United States, they are not located at the left end of the political spectrum, since that place is occupied by the ideologies of the labor movement.

ANARCHISM, SOCIAL DEMOCRACY, AND COMMUNISM

"Society as a whole is more and more splitting up into two great hostile camps, into two great classes directly facing each other: Bourgeoisie and Proletariat," stated Karl Marx and his friend Frederick Engels in *The Communist Manifesto* in 1848. At the end of what is probably Europe's most influential political manifesto ever, they appealed to the proletariats to unite and forcibly overthrow all existing social conditions, since the workers had "nothing to lose but their chains."

The three major labor ideologies are anarchism, social democracy, and communism. Anarchism embraces individual and spontaneous worker actions against their exploiters. The anarchist ideal is a wave of such actions that leads to large general strikes and ultimately results in international revolution. In the course of the revolution the old small-scale artisanal workshop, a remnant of preindustrial society, is to be re-established as the dominant form of production without any central authority. Preferably, private property should be abolished in favor of communal or "socialist" property. The rejection of the free market economy and of any authority whatsoever places anarchism in the upper left corner of the spectrum.

At the end of the nineteenth century, a new labor movement ideology emerged: Marxism, inspired by Karl Marx. Marx rejected anarchism as a backward movement because it denied industrial progress. Instead, industrial development would constitute the base of "socialism." In Marxist theory, capitalism would develop until it would eventually collapse under its own disruptive forces and under the revolution of the organized working class. The working class would then take over industry and establish a new socialist order of common (social) property. In contrast to anarchism, Marxists established large organizations, which overtook anarchism as the leading ideology of the labor movement. At the turn of the century, the Marxist movement split into social democrats and communists.

Social democrats are often called socialists, and some of them prefer that name. Their first aim was general voting rights and they soon started to organize political parties in order to participate in national politics. They expected that the workers' vote would provide them with a majority in the national parliament and enable them to take over national government. With its demand of universal suffrage, social democracy was not only a social class movement but also a democratization movement, addressing both the issues of social policy and of parliamentary democracy. Instead of a mere ethnic nationality based on a common language—or some other form of ethnic community that was pursued by national governments—and the form of civic nationality that liberals promoted for the middle and upper class, social democrats demanded civic nationality for the population at large, and voting rights to start with.

The social democratic participation in national parliaments made them stress reform rather than revolution. This transition from a revolutionary to a "revisionist" or reformist movement took place in the early twentieth century. Since then, social democracy has become the largest labor movement ideology, and after World War II also the most widespread ideology in Europe. It has been the major protagonist of social policies that protect not merely the working class but the population at large. Its position is on the left side of the political spectrum. Because of its tolerance in moral and family values, in combination with its support of extensive educational and cultural policies, its position on the vertical line is about halfway between libertarianism and authoritarianism.

Communists opposed the revision of Marx and stuck to revolution as the major goal of working-class organization. The 1917 Russian Revolution and the establishment of the Soviet Union sealed the breach between the two Marxist trends. Democracy and the free-market economy have been the major issues in this split. Social democracy has become one of the staunchest defenders of parliamentary democracy. Communism has rejected "bourgeois" democracy because it helps the ruling class to exploit and oppress the working class. Instead, the working class (proletariat) should exercise dictatorial power over the other classes in order to fight working-class enemies and to terminate class differences. In the Soviet Union and other countries under communist control, this "dictatorship of the proletariat" amounted to a form of totalitarian state authority. It was actually exercised by the Communist Party, the "vanguard of the proletariat," and implied severe sanctions against any deviation from the official doctrine. Within the Communist Party power was concentrated in the hands of the party leader, who suppressed all opposition within the party and was officially hailed as a "Hero of the Working Class."

Social democrats have not only abandoned revolution, but also the idea that a free-market economy could be fully replaced by a socialist economy under one central authority. Instead, the functioning of the market economy is to be mitigated by extensive social policies. After the Russian Revolution, by way of contrast, the communists under Lenin implemented a strict disciplining of all workers by the state. Lenin argued that technological and economic progress could only be reached in a centrally planned economy and under conditions of uncompromising state control of all economic and social activities. In the communist "command economy" almost all enterprises were state property. Investment and production were subject to a very rigid system of central planning under the ultimate control of the Communist Party.

The communist position in the political spectrum might seem to be clear: to the far left and on the authoritarian side. However, its position to the left is not undisputed. Communism may also be called a form of conservatism, since the communist power monopoly over the economy in communist countries has served a strong state rather than the social interests of workers. Communism would then belong to the trend within conservatism that appreciates a strong state, and the Russian communists that now oppose economic reforms in the direction of the free market might be dubbed conservatives—in both meanings of that term.

In the course of the century, social democracy and communism have become even more hostile toward each other. Communists have denounced social democrats as "traitors of the working class" and in Soviet Russia and other countries where communists gained power, they suppressed social democracy and anarchism. Communism and social democracy have retained some common symbols and rituals, however, like their red banners and their common song *The International* ("Arise ye Pris'ners of Starvation . . ."), sung at party meetings, demonstrations, and strikes. These rituals may easily mislead non-Europeans to think that the two trends share a common ideology, which is not the case. Like two brothers who have grown apart, they have come to nurture hostile feelings toward each other, and have only joined hands under the pressure of very serious conditions.

Social democracy is supported by the working class. Manual workers are its traditional backbone but it has also succeeded in attracting office workers and sections of the middle class. In contrast to the United States, there is nothing politically wrong with social democracy in Europe. It has made a great contribution to the development of democracy and occupies an important place in the European political spectrum. All European countries have large social democratic parties and at present a great majority of government leaders in Western Europe are social democrats. Notable social democratic leaders were German Chancellor Willy Brandt, French President François Mitterand, and Spanish Prime Minister Felipe Gonzalez. Rising stars are Great Britain's Tony Blair and Germany's Gerhard Schröder. The Kennedy Brothers would have been prominent social democratic leaders if they had been born in the right continent for such a career.

Social democracy has survived both anarchism and communism. Following World War II, communist regimes were installed by Soviet Russia throughout Central and Eastern Europe. They imitated the Soviet power monopoly of the Communist Party and the Soviet "command economy." In Western Europe the communist appeal has been confined to the manual working class in a few countries, notably France and Italy. Since the collapse of the Soviet Union, communism has dwindled. In most of Central Europe, communist parties have either fallen to pieces or transformed themselves into democratic and reformist parties. Both in Western and in Central Europe, many former communists now embrace democracy and call themselves social democrats or socialists. Where they are still engaged in a process of ideological reorientation, communists are often simply called "post-communists." Only in Eastern Europe are old-style communists still a strong force in national politics.

What about socialism? Doesn't that exist in Europe? In France and other Latin countries, social democrats prefer to call themselves socialists instead of social democrats in order to stress the importance of rank-and-file initiative and their nature as a movement rather than an organization (a remnant of anarchist influence), as well as their less-compromising politics. However, communists have also used the term socialism to denote the nature of society under communist rule. In their view, "real" communism would be the final stage of societal development to be reached much later. In order to prevent confusion between these two meanings, the term socialism is not used in this book.

CHRISTIAN DEMOCRACY

Condemning the Marxists' class struggle, Pope Leo XIII in his 1891 encyclical "Rerum Novarum" called for "harmony between the divergent interests and the various classes that compose the state" and for "concerted action" by "men of eminence" among employers and working class' leaders.

Christian democrats reject the liberals' individualism and the social democrats' preference of social state action. They emphasize the social role of the family and of voluntary organizations, like business associations and trade unions. Instead of fighting each other, employers and workers' organizations should join hands to take care of social measures. Their "corporatism" (activities by the organizations or "corporations" at both sides) is regarded as a form of "subsidiarity": keeping the state in check by leaving activities to voluntary sector and branch organizations of business, workers, and others.

Christian democracy was developed mainly by Catholics as a reaction to the rise of Marxism. Its ideology combines a preference of authority with social measures, a kind of "conservatism with a social face." The Catholic Church has not only underlined its own authority, but also a hierarchical structure within the Catholic organizations. In a few countries, Protestants also established separate organizations with roughly similar ideas about social measures. This common outlook has allowed Catholics and Protestants to cooperate in one Christian democratic movement, in which the Catholics, due to their more centralized system of authority, often predominate in the leading positions.

Christian democrats are not the European "religious right." They are neither to the right on the left-right line, nor extremely authoritarian on the other line, but they occupy a position halfway across the left-right line, and a bit to the authoritarian side. Christian democracy is supported most of all by the Catholic middle class and farmers, who are attracted by its devotion to authority (and religion) but it has also attracted sizable parts of the working class. Its appeal to Protestants has been weaker. More than Catholics, Protestants have been inclined to support social democratic and other nonreligious political movements.

Christian democrats occupy central positions in the political spectrum of several countries, notably in nations with a mixed Protestant-Catholic population and in some Catholic nations. Their central position is due to competition with the social democrats for working-class support. Compromise has become the Christian democratic trademark. Its latest heavyweight was German Chancellor Helmut Kohl.

If the Christian democrats are not the European "religious right," who are? Actually, the "religious right" is very small in Europe. It consists of small ultra-right Catholics within conservative parties, and a few "biblical" Protestant parties in Protestant countries. Neither of the two reject evolutionist theory on the origins of man.

The rise of Christian democracy in the beginning of the century more or less completed the patchwork of major ideological trends that still play a role in European politics. A more violent response to the rise of the working-class movement was yet to appear, however.

FASCISM AND NAZISM

"Outside the State there can be neither individuals nor groups . . .," wrote Benito Mussolini during his fascist dictatorship in Italy between the wars. The "nation is created by the State, which gives to the people, conscious of its own moral unity, a will and therefore an effective existence."

Fascism represented the most extreme reaction against the 1917 Russian Revolution and the growth of social democracy. It denounced the social democratic and communist division of national society into two classes and proclaimed national unity and a "national cause." In some cases the national cause required foreign expansion, for which the nation as a whole should be mobilized. Hence its banner was the national one; its favorite music military marches; its favorite dress military capes and boots. Its conservatism was expressed in the appraisal of hierarchy and order. Mussolini introduced fascism in Italy in 1922. Germany followed his example in 1933, when the Nazis under Adolf Hitler took power. Both movements proclaimed their national leaders to be the personification of national unity and the people's will, and endowed them with almost absolute power.

Fascism became a widespread phenomenon during the economic recession of the 1930s. Mass unemployment and growing international tension provided national leaders with an easy motive to install a fascist order. Hitler's Nazism, the most fanatical movement, reinforced national hierarchy and order to absolute dimensions, with total repression of all opposition and the extermination of millions of Jews in the Holocaust. Fascism and Nazism succumbed at the end of World War II. Only in Portugal and Spain did much weaker versions dating from the 1930s survive until the 1970s.

As a very authoritarian movement, fascism is located at the bottom of the political spectrum. Although fascist leaders implemented a number of labor reforms, fascism is not located to the left, but to the right. Fascism owes its place on the spectrum to the fact that the main aim of state involvement in the economy was not social equality, but a strong state and foreign expansion. The stress on hierarchy and the suppression of the labor movement made fascism an attractive ideology for conservative people in rural areas. Nazism was more of an industrial ideology and enjoyed a wider appeal, especially among small entrepreneurs and other sections of the urban middle classes. However, manual workers and large industrialists also supported it. Nowadays, there are hardly any parties that explicitly call themselves fascist, but new racist parties bear some similarities to them.

Fascism was the last of the epoch-making European ideologies. Since its decline, the other ideologies discussed before represent the "traditional" European ideologies. Since the 1960s and 1970s, new ideologies have gained prominence.

NEW IDEOLOGIES

Feminism

Feminism's primary target is the sexual or gender division of labor in society between two social spheres, a public sphere and a subservient private one. The public and dominant sphere consists of paid work in economic, social, and political activities, all of them dominated by men. In the private sphere—the family—the main aim of unpaid female labor is to raise children and provide an ambiance of emotional intimacy for men, which enables men to be active in the public sphere.

The first women's movement emerged at the turn of the century, focusing on the introduction of universal suffrage instead of only universal male suffrage, as demanded by the social democrats. It also wanted easier access to higher education for girls. The second feminist movement arose during the late 1960s as a part of the youth revolt against traditional authority. It demanded equal treatment on the labor market, including wage equality, and equal access to social provisions, including social security benefits, not only for single women but also for married women, independent of their husbands' position. The second feminist movement has also raised the new issue of female autonomy. That idea was also stimulated by the introduction of the contraceptive pill, which gave women more autonomy in sexual relations. Rights of women in sexual matters, and the right of abortion became the unifying issues of the new women's movement. Feminism has also pointed to the difference in power between men and women, and its reflection in all kinds of expressions of culture, including daily speech.

The feminist movement has hardly given rise to separate political parties. Even female leaders in social democratic, Christian democratic, or liberal parties are still exceptional. Although the feminist movement has made its voice heard especially in social democracy, which is more open to demands of equality, the other ideologies have been influenced, too. Equality on the labor market and a ban on sexual harassment have become popular political issues.

Environmentalism

The oil crises of the 1970s stimulated public discussion on energy consumption and intensified environmental concerns. During the late 1970s and 1980s green action groups, like Greenpeace, arose, as well as green political parties, some of which had started as anti-nuclear power protest groups. A serious 1986 accident in the nuclear power plant at Chernobyl, Ukraine, widened the appeal of the green cause. Nowadays, hardly any change in infrastructure is introduced in Western Europe without green protests and without investigation of the ecological effects.

As a political movement, environmentalism has become a left-wing alternative to social democratic parties (a transition from red to green). Its main supporters are young people in the towns and students. Its place is to the left, to the libertarian side, because of its tolerance (or lack of interest) in family values. Green political parties now exist in many Western European countries, but they are very small. In Central and Eastern Europe, politics is still dominated too much by economic reforms and economic problems to create much latitude for environmentalist parties.

New Nationalism and Racism

The emergence of nation-states in Europe was accompanied by nationalism. It focused on the building of a nation that was based on language or other forms of ethnicity. The change in economic conditions in the 1970s gave rise to a new form of nationalism and to racist outcries. While the new nationalism fights the alleged depreciation of national culture by the influx of foreigners, racism even proclaims the superiority of the indigenous population over foreigners, in particular over those from overseas. Racism has deep roots in European history, exemplified by international slave trade until the nineteenth century and the treatment of Jews throughout European history. Its current victims are foreign workers and political fugitives, most of them Muslims. The immigrant workers were called in during the Golden Sixties. Due to the disappearance of traditional industry many of them are unemployed, and they are accused of being idle and refusing to accept work. Recent waves of political fugitives from Africa and the Middle East (many of them Muslims as well) reinforce nationalism and racism.

At first, new nationalism and racism embarrassed the other ideological trends and political parties who feared a revival of fascism. To their relief, racism has remained a single-issue movement, without leadership, cult, or public manifestations of mass hysteria, in contrast to fascism. Its main theme, stricter immigration rules, is now generally adopted in order to reduce its appeal. However, the introduction of stricter rules on political asylum continues to be a tricky topic in Western Europe. Since there are not many immigrant workers and political fugitives in Central and Eastern Europe, racism that focuses on recent immigrants is mainly a Western European affair. In many countries there are small racist parties, like Jean-Marie Le Pen's *Front National* in France. Racist parties mainly draw their support from people in towns and cities where migrants have settled in great numbers.

Neo-conservatism

The oil crises of the 1970s also prompted a new kind of economic policy and economic thinking: neo-conservatism. It attributes rising inflation and unemployment and large state deficits to the expansion of state policies. Governments should no longer regulate the economy but take their hands off and let the free market do its work again. Increasingly, neo-conservatism has extended from a new economic "paradigm" to a full-fledged ideology, demanding more opportunities for private initiative and individual responsibility, which is actually more in line with classical liberalism than with conservatism. Neo-conservatism has heavily influenced European politics. State intervention in the economy and state regulation have sharply decreased (deregulation), and large public sectors have been privatized and commercialized (privatization). The state budget and the national debt have become primary political concerns. The European Union has contributed to these developments by imposing strict limits on state subvention of enterprises and by opening up public sectors for international competition from the other member states. The reappraisal of the free market has affected all traditional ideologies. Even social democrats have mitigated their traditional claim of more state social policies. Under the pressure of state deficits and high unemployment, they have partially shifted their attention to private initiative and speak less and less about state action. That shift has yielded a general turn to the right on the horizontal line, with more interest in the free market and less concern for social equality.

REGIONAL VARIATIONS IN COPING WITH IDEOLOGICAL DIVISION

The great variety in sources of division and political ideologies makes European politics a highly complex affair. Europeans have found a way to deal with this political and ideological divergence, however, in the form of coalition governments that are composed of various parties. The formation of coalition governments is facilitated by the fact that not all ideologies exist in all countries. In most nations the political spectrum is confined to three or four major parties, including social democrats, Christian democrats, liberals, and conservatives. These major political parties still reflect and express lines of division that already existed in the beginning of the twentieth century. For this reason, political scientists speak of a "frozen" party system in Western Europe, with only small green parties and racist groups as newcomers. There are some regionally distinctive patterns, however. The division of Europe in a few groups of nations reveals the regional variations in the composition of the political spectrum.

Great Britain occupies an exceptional position in many respects and also in this one. Its political spectrum is smaller than that on the continent. The two main parties (Labour and Conservative) are primarily based on social class. To some extent they also express regional interests: Scotland votes Labour. The two distinct regions, Scotland and Wales, already had their own soccer and rugby teams, but they are now being endowed with more powers in a process of "devolution" toward more autonomy. (Northern Ireland is a different story, as we have seen.) Notwithstanding the multinational character of the British state, the intensity of regional identity is limited and English is generally accepted as the only language. Religion does not act as a dividing force either. Many people are members of the national Anglican Church but it occupies a marginal position in social life. Although social class is by far the main line of division, it is not very disruptive, since the Labour Party has never had a revolutionary ideology and there is no extreme left. Consequently, Great Britain is one of the least divided societies in Europe.

In Scandinavia (Denmark, Norway, Sweden, and Finland), the political spectrum is relatively small, too, and the degree of conflict between left and right is limited. There are hardly any language minorities, and in these Protestant countries religion is not politically relevant either. Recently some small Christian democratic parties have come up, in which Protestants predominate. This type of Christian democracy in which Protestantism prevails is a new feature in European politics. As is the case in Great Britain, social class has become the main line of division, and large social democratic parties dominate national politics. The political right is divided among conservatives and conservative liberals. The line of division between the national capitals (the only big city in these nations) and the countryside has given rise to farmers' parties, which make up part of the divided right, but are positioned left of the conservatives.

In Germany and other Germanic nations (Holland, Belgium, Luxembourg, Austria, and Switzerland), the political spectrum is also small but more lines of division are operative. Belgium and Switzerland are Western Europe's most prominent multi-language nations, but both countries possess federal structures. In contrast to Great Britain and Scandinavia, religion plays a prominent role in politics in all five nations and the political spectrum is dominated by the Christian democrats (mostly Catholics), who also represent the interests of farmers. In Germany, this role of religion implies a division between the protestant North, where social democracy gets most of its support, and the Catholic South, dominated by Christian democrats. In the smaller Germanic nations, the Christian democrats occupy a position in the middle of the spectrum and they are flanked by social democrats to the left and by conservative liberals to the right. Both are forced to keep the distance toward Christian democracy small, in order to be acceptable as coalition partners for the Christian democrats. Moreover, in addition to the social democratic labor movement there also exists a Catholic labor movement, or at least a "labor wing" within the Christian democratic parties. That makes the Christian democratic parties sensitive to the issue of social equality. In combination with the Christian democrats' center position, this sensitivity reduces the saliency of social class as a dividing line.

In Latin Europe, including France, Portugal, Spain, and Italy, the political spectrum completely changed during the 1980s and 1990s. France and Italy used to have large communist parties that were often excluded from participation in the government by the parties to the right. More in general, the political spectrum was far wider than in Germanic Europe or Great Britain, with communists and even anarchists to the left and conservative parties to the right. The division between social classes was reinforced by the fact that the left was anticlerical, while the conservative parties were supported by Catholics. That composition of the spectrum—in which social class and religion to some extent coincided as sources of division—caused lots of conflict between left and right. As political scientists say, there was a high degree of "polarization," because the left and the right parties were located to the extreme "poles" of the left-right line with a large distance in between. (Mind that polarization is quite distinct from "pillarization," discussed in Chapter 2, which tended to reduce conflicts between the "pillars" or segments of society.) The strength of the social class issue has left fewer opportunities for the rise of green parties. The greens are much weaker in Latin Europe than in the Germanic nations.

Communism has now almost disappeared as a force in national politics and social democracy has taken over as the leading party to the left in Latin Europe. At the same time, conservatives and conservative liberals, who were strongly represented in the countryside, have also tried to widen their base of support and have become less radical. These moves have reduced the degree of "polarization" and the likelihood of conflict between left and right. One source of division that still stands is the pressure for more regional autonomy, in particular by language minorities in Spain and in Italy. Figure 3.2 shows the political spectrum of the three largest European nations, apart from Russia.

In Central Europe new political movements have sprung up in recent years. Although some of them resemble Western European trends, like social democracy, Christian democracy, and farmers' parties, the political spectrum is not comparable to that in Western Europe. The main dividing line is not social class but it is based on the still formidable issues of national integration (nation building) and the pace of economic reforms (the transition toward a free-market economy). The first issue is highly contentious because of the language minorities that are (or may become) politically active. Economic reforms are underway in all of Central Europe in the form of the transfer of public enterprises into public hands. Once most of the economy is privatized, which is the main thrust, the basic dividing line will probably change.

Consequently, the political spectrum in Central Europe has probably not yet reached its "final" extension. It is a few leading personalities, rather than more stable groups or organizations that dominate national politics, and they may change policies during their term of office. In the least, the degree of polarization is pronounced, with post-communists on the one hand, and Christian democrats,

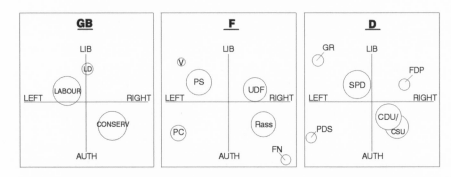

Figure 3.2. The Political Spectrum of France, Germany, and Great Britain.

Great Britain: LD: liberal democrats.

France: FN: racists; PC: communists; PS: social democrats; Rass(emblement): Gaullists; UDF: conservative liberals; V(erdes): Greens.

Germany: CDU: Christian democrats; CSU: Bavarian Christian democrats (in permanent alliance with the CDU); FDP: conservative liberals; Grünen: Greens; PDS: (post)communists; SPD: social democrats.

social democrats, and liberal parties on the other. In spite of its great number of its political movements, Poland has probably the most clear cut political division, between former communists who are now embracing economic reform and liberal virtues and conservative Catholics. The Catholics are an offspring of Solidarność, which was the first opposition movement under a communist regime in the early 1980s and now espouses traditional Catholic values. The Romanian division, by contrast, seems to become one of authoritarian post-communists versus more democratically minded (and even libertarian) Christian democrats.

Eastern European politics is even more dominated by personalities, in the form of strong presidents, and it is difficult to speak of ideological movements. In particular the presidents of Belarus and Russia are autocratic rulers, who already occupied high government posts under communism. Language, or ethnicity in general, is an issue in Russia and the Ukraine. Some minorities claim regional autonomy or total independence, as in Chechenia and in the Crimea (a peninsula in the Ukraine that would like to join Russia). Religion is less of an issue, since all three presidents seek the support of the national Orthodox Churches for their regimes. Old-fashioned communism continues to exercise a wide appeal in Eastern Europe due to the economic uncertainties during the current stage of economic reform—even if the direction of that reform is not always clear. Communists pay lip service to the principle of democracy but do not like political competition or a reduction of state control of the economy. Other political movements have yet to arise.

The difficulty of comparing the Eastern European political spectrum with that in Western or even Central Europe is clearly revealed by the position of the (former) Russian president Boris Yeltsin. Where would he have to be located in the political spectrum? His positive attitude toward economic reform does not make him progressive, since that outlook implies a mere shift from one form of conservatism (in favor of a strong state) to another (introducing elements of the free-market economy). Because of his reform policies, he is often regarded as progressive, however, in contrast to his conservative communist opponents who cling to a strong state. President Yeltsin's autocratic leadership would put him at the authoritarian side of the vertical line, but his communist opponents are still more authoritarian. So, Eastern European politics seems to be far more conservative (in both meanings of the term) than Western or Central European politics. This is not surprising after centuries of autocratic Tsarist rule and seventy years of communist dictatorship.

AMERICANIZATION OF EUROPEAN POLITICS?

The decline of the traditional sources of division and the weakening appeal of the major ideologies is currently changing European politics. Farmers' parties can no longer rely on farmers' votes only, Christian democrats have to reckon with the weakening of religious affiliation, and social democrats have to take into account the dwindling of their traditional backbone, the manual working class in industry.

One of the traditional means to cope with division, the segmentation or "pillarization" of society, with networks of social organizations for each religious group or social class, has also come to an end. Many young people no longer identify with such catholic or social democratic blocks and establish friendship bonds independent of such blocks.

These changes are also reshaping the composition of the political spectrum in Europe. The left-right division continues to prevail as the major determinant of political attitudes and voting behavior but it has lost some of its importance. The authority-liberty line is now regaining attention. Many young people are no longer very interested in material values, but take more interest in the fulfillment of nonmaterial needs, like individual self-expression in rock music, new religious movements, and the environment. This turn away from material values (and social equality) is called post-materialism. It favors libertarian values at the expense of social ideas. Post-materialism is especially pronounced in the generations that have been raised in peace and relative affluence after World War II. For part of Europe's youth the left-right line is an outdated one. They consider the social democrats and conservatives as being obsessed with material values and not paying attention to differences in lifestyle and to the preservation of natural resources. Some even predict the emergence of a completely new line of division, of post-materialists versus materialists. This new distinction does not (yet) make much sense, however, since almost all Europeans would still have to be counted as materialists.

The result of ideological decline and the rise of post-materialism may be a gradual transition from politics based on social class or religious affiliation to a new kind of politics. It is centered on political issues that do not necessarily have to do with class, religion, or region, and may be even more focused on persons. In their election campaigns, politicians try to appeal to large sections of the population rather than to their own religious group or one social class only. This wider appeal may entail a growing prominence of persons instead of ideologies in election campaigns, and a greater focus on the personal qualities of the contestants rather than the policies they propose. Pessimists(!) call this the "Americanization" of European election. The term refers to the shift in attention away from party platforms and the parties' past performance to personal characteristics ("An experienced leader," "Just read his lips") and in particular to the more superficial ones (how to look when on television, dress, style your hair). Americanization implies growing attention for personal appearance, family life, and even the sex life of the political leaders rather than for what they stand for. United States presidential elections are always more personal than parliamentary elections, of course. In Europe the trend toward more personal campaigning has to do with the decline of traditional ideologies. Politicians reinforce this decline by only making short one-liners like "more change" rather than discussing their political views. England's Tony Blair is considered as a prominent example of this kind of person-oriented and "superficial" political campaigning. Blair's record is then compared to that of Margaret Thatcher, prime minister during the 1980s, who was very pronounced in her political priorities. As one the most drastic European leaders in her efforts to reduce the amount of state involvement in the economy, she was called the "Iron Lady." Since the trend toward more personal politics is to some extent the outcome of weakening traditional sources of division, it may also involve less political conflict. In that sense Americanization might seem to be an asset rather than a source of evil.

4

From Elections to Governments: The Long Way

Europe's longest serving democratic prime minister since World War II was not German Chancellor Helmut Kohl with his sixteen years in office, but Sweden's Tage Erlander, a social democrat who held office from 1946 to 1969 (almost six U.S. presidential terms!). However, the person who served as prime minister most times during the last twenty years is the Belgian Christian democrat Wilfried Martens. Let us look at Martens' governments.

- April 1979: After four months of coalition building, the cabinet Martens 1 is formed, consisting of Christian democrats, social democrats, and a regional party.
- January 1980: The regional party quits. Cabinet Martens 2 is formed, consisting of Christian democrats and social democrats.
- May 1980: Liberals are invited to join. Cabinet Martens 3 is formed, consisting of Christian democrats, social democrats, and liberals.
- October 1980: Liberals leave again. Cabinet Martens 4 is formed, consisting of Christian democrats and social democrats.
- April 1981: A Christian democratic colleague takes over.
- December 1981: Advanced elections are held. Cabinet Martens 5 is formed, consisting of Christian democrats and liberals, which lasts for almost four years.
- October 1985: Advanced elections are held. Cabinet Martens 6 is formed, consisting of Christian democrats and liberals.
- 1987: Social democrats are included as well. Cabinet Martens 7 is formed.
- December 1987: Elections. After five months of coalition building, cabinet Martens 8 is formed, consisting of Christian democrats and social democrats, which holds out until 1991.

Belgian politics is not always like this. Frequent cabinet turnover in the early 1980s was due to the oil crisis and even more to the federalization of the country, separating the Flemish from the Walloons. To those who wonder about this seeming instability of Belgian politics: Look at it from the other side. The country, one of the most divided in Western Europe, had the same political leader for over ten years, and his party dominated all cabinets. In many other countries national politics is even more stable, with one or two prime ministers during each decade but with less cabinets, and with a more decisive role of elections than in Belgium.

THE EUROPEAN STATE

The term "state" has a double meaning in Europe. It is used to denote both independent countries and the countries' political authorities. Independent states, as they exist nowadays, developed some three to four centuries ago when the Catholic Church to some extent abandoned its right to interfere directly in national politics, and when the larger European powers recognized the independence of smaller nations like Holland and Switzerland.

In the second meaning, the state is not merely government, it is the "State," the highest authority in the nation. Until the nineteenth century (in parts of Europe until the twentieth century), kings and emperors exercised the highest authority. Ordinary people spoke with great respect about this 'State,' if only to escape imprisonment. Since absolute kings and emperors had increasingly centralized their hold over the country and fixed national borders, dissenters could not easily escape the State police. Migration to the colonies and later to the United States offered an outlet but generally European nations did not have an "Open Frontier" for those who wanted to shape their own future, without any state involvement. Even under the Russian Tsars, the vast territory of Siberia already served more as a location for prisons than as a voluntary refuge (except for escaped prisoners).

Consequently, protest and opposition were more addressed to the State, and politics became more of a general concern than in the United States. The 1789 French Revolution and later efforts to dethrone absolute kings and emperors changed the nature of State authority, but not the central place of the State in European society. Almost all political ideologies have focused on the State rather than on the individual person. With its political demands, the continental labor movement also addressed the State and added to its strength. The notion of the State as highest authority within the nation still permeates European political discussion. The term "State" is only a bleak translation of the French *l'Etat*, the German *der Staat*, the Spanish *el estado*, let alone the Russian *gosudarstvo*. The word "government" is an even bleaker alternative for these European terms. This chapter and the next one discuss the nature of European state authorities, or in more down-to-earth terms, the nature of European "government." In other words, how the political movements described in the previous chapters come to power and exercise government.

Similar to U.S. politics, European government in a broad sense consists of three branches: The legislative power, vested in the national parliament; the executive power, vested in the national executive, often called the government; and the judicial power, executed by courts of justice.

The combination of three powers is called *Trias Politica*, a Latin term. The distinction between the three powers was developed before the 1789 French Revolution by the French philosopher Charles de Montesquieu. It was an expression of the idea that the king (the executive power) should be subordinate to the general rules set by the representation of the citizens, the parliament (the legislative power). The third power was added because citizens should have the opportunity to defend their own rights against the kings. In most of Europe the struggle for supremacy between parliament and the king was decided in the nineteenth or early twentieth century. The change was effectuated in national constitutions, and is therefore called the transition from absolute monarchy to constitutional monarchy.

In contrast to the United States, the three branches are unequal in power and there exists hardly any "separation of powers" between the legislative power (parliament) and the executive power (government). Since the parliament is by far the highest ranking of the three, the European political systems are called parliamentary democracies. Parliament enjoys the right to nominate and dismiss the government and to appoint the national court judges. In practice, European politics is dominated by the interplay between the parliament and the national government; the judiciary plays a marginal role only. In several countries the right of judicial review is curtailed, or does not exist at all. The reason behind this is that it is the parliament, as the representation of the people, that has framed the constitution and it is also the parliament that serves as its watchdog. No institution is allowed to tell parliament what parliament had in mind when framing the constitution and subsequent legislation based on the constitution.

European politics is parliamentary politics. In addition to the difference in the base of national identity, this is yet another basic difference with the United States. Europeans are not primarily represented by a President but by members of parliament and that representation serves to promote their cause: their language, their religion, their regional interests, their social class, and the various ideologies related to these lines of division. There are only a few exceptions to the preponderant role of the parliament. In a few nations the president is elected in separate elections and is not responsible to the parliament. Until some years ago, France and Finland were the only examples of this system, but some countries in Central and Eastern Europe are now also experimenting with an independent president. Presidential politics will be discussed in the next chapter.

With the parliament as the core of the political system in most of Europe, the election of the parliament and the role of political parties making up the parliament are of primordial interest. This is a clear contrast to American politics, where presidential elections dominate the political scene.

WHERE THE VOTES ARE: ELECTIONS

Once every four or five years, European citizens are supposed to go to the polls in order to decide about the composition of the national parliament. In practice they go more often, up to every other year, following a government breakdown. (The government may also dissolve parliament and call for advanced elections, but that action is usually confined to periods of crisis in the coalition.) Except for the few nations with an elected president, the day of parliamentary elections is the most important event in national politics. It is preceded by the parties' campaigns and followed by the parliamentary decision about government composition. National, regional, and local elections are often held at different times; national elections are the most popular ones, with a turnout of over seventy percent in most countries (higher than in the United States). In most of Europe you do not need to register as a voter. The state takes care of that and it has no interest in non-registration, since the tax bill (or the welfare payment) is sent to the same address.

There are two electoral systems operative in Europe. In both of them, the country is subdivided into a number of constituencies (voting districts). The most common system, proportional representation, is used in almost all smaller countries. Under this system each of the voting districts (constituencies) may elect a fixed number of representatives. The parliamentary seats available for each voting district are allocated according to the total number of votes that parties win. A party that obtains ten percent of the votes in a district also gets ten percent of the district seats in parliament. This system is called proportional representation because the number of seats for each party is roughly in proportion with the number of votes for each party within the voting districts. Since parties will lose varying numbers of remaining votes in each district after the allocation of seats, however, the number of seats that parties win is never totally in proportion to the national number of votes nationwide. For that reason, some countries with proportional representation use a special device to increase that proportionality of seats with the number of votes nationwide. They allocate a number of seats on a nationwide basis to those parties whose total share of the nationwide votes outnumbers their share of parliamentary seats, once all constituencies are taken together. This "second tier" allocation corrects for disproportionalities that might arise from the constituency elections. Holland has an even simpler form of reaching almost complete proportionality between number of seats and share of votes. It treats the whole country as one constituency. In most other small nations the number of constituencies varies from four to fifty.

Under the second system, called the majority or plurality system, the number of constituencies equals the number of seats in parliament and each constituency may only return one representative to the parliament. The candidate who gets a relative majority (more votes than any competitor) or an absolute majority (more than fifty percent) of the district votes is elected, hence, the name majority system. It is also called "first past the post," or "winner takes all," because each district has only one winner and the votes for the other candidates are lost.

Traditionally, Great Britain was the only country that applied the majority system. France has switched back and forth between the two systems and now has a majority system with two consecutive rounds of voting, except in those constituencies in which one candidate obtains an absolute majority in the first round. The "second ballot," as the system is called, allows parties to forge coalitions for the second round and withdraw their own candidates in favor of those of the coalition parties, if necessary. In this second ballot the largest number of votes decides; an absolute majority is not required. In Germany, proportional representation is the dominant system, but it is complemented by an additional vote in which regional party candidates may carry a district, as is the case in the majority system. This refined and intricate system of "dual votes" is exceptional in that it offers voters the opportunity of a split ticket in a single election. They may vote for a regional candidate of one party (this is called their first vote) and use their second vote for the party list of that same party or a different one. In accordance with proportional representation, it is that second vote, for the party list, that decides on the total number of seats for that party. Similar systems of dual votes have been introduced in Eastern Europe, both in Russia and Ukraine.

The difference between the two systems accounts for quite a range of other variations in national politics. The majority system tends to reduce the number of parties. This serves the country's governability, since it facilitates the decisions in parliament about the parties that will participate in the government. Under proportional representation the parliament better reflects the various interests in society. Small political parties have a much better chance to enter parliament, especially when their supporters live scattered over the country. However, a number of countries try to prevent a proliferation of small parties by means of a threshold. This is a German invention and in that country the threshold stands at five percent of the votes. Other countries have followed the example, with thresholds that range from two to five percent of the votes. Its introduction in Poland in 1992 reduced the number of parties in parliament from twenty-nine to six. Under the majority system there is less need of a threshold. Small parties survive only if they are highly concentrated locally and able to carry a number of constituencies.

Ideally, under proportional representation the total number of seats for a constituency should be in proportion with the number of voters. The larger the constituency, the more representatives it should return to parliament. In a similar way, under the majority system all districts or constituencies should contain the same number of voters, since all of them only elect one representative. The implication could be a constant rearranging of district borders in case of the growth of new suburbs and new towns, or migration from one region to another. Especially under the majority system, such redrawing of district borders leaves a lot of room for arbitrary decisions ("gerrymandering," as it is called in the United States). Parties may try to redraw the district borders in such a way as to ensure them with a number of narrow victories, rather than a few overwhelming landslides: Better to carry two districts with fifty-five percent than one with eighty and lose the second with thirty percent. This leads to a lot of quarreling and cheating, which is unknown under proportional representation. French governments in particular often started their term of office with efforts to redraw district borders, in order to ensure yet another electoral victory. On the other hand, the majority system can point to a stronger relationship between voter and representative and a better

representation of local interests. Local minority votes are lost but that puts the representative under the moral obligation to represent the local people who did not vote for her or him, too, and to take care of local interests more generally. Under proportional representation, differences in local and regional interests are often played down in favor of a reflection of the national electorate.

Why does Great Britain occupy an exceptional position once again with its tradition of majority voting? During the nineteenth century the majority system was common in other countries as well. On the continent, social democrats, Christian democrats, and others pressed for proportional representation, especially if their followers were locally concentrated, like the laboring class in a few industrial towns, or Catholics in rural areas. Under the majority system they only carried a few districts, under proportional representation they would win a larger number of seats. The relative weakness of the various lines of division in Great Britain reduced the pressure to change its electoral system and helped to keep the number of parties small. In its two-party system, only Conservative and Labour play a role in government building. Smaller parties do exist, but they are unable to keep either of the two large parties from winning the elections and building a (one-party) government. All continental countries, by contrast, are multiparty systems. More than two (dominant) parties compete for seats, and government building normally requires coalitions between two or more parties. The number of parties represented in parliament may vary from four or five (Germany) to twenty-nine (Poland in 1991). Table 4.1 shows the impact of electoral systems. A comparison of the continental nations makes it clear that the more parties that fail to pass a threshold, the more extra seats for the larger parties. Most small and traditional democracies of Western Europe, like Denmark, have relatively large numbers of political parties, due to a low threshold.

The difference between a two-party and a multiparty system has a great impact on the role of elections in politics. Great Britain is the only country in which the election results directly decide which party will govern the country and who will be the government leader. In "winner takes all," the winner gets all government posts, without any concessions to other parties or coalitions. On the continent, elections are less decisive, as the introduction to this chapter has shown. The losers may even prevent a clear winner from participating in government (except in the case of a highly exceptional fifty-one percent victory, of course).

Due to the gradual waning of traditional lines of division, voices are raised in favor of introducing more elements of a majority system on the continent. Stronger competition among the local candidates would reinforce their local involvement. That would reduce the alleged distance between voters and representatives and between citizens and politics generally. In Italy, the majority system was introduced in 1993 in order to clean up the party system and reduce the number of political parties. One of its effects, however, was to reinforce the political gap between North and South—and the birth of the mock republic of Padania.

Table 4.1. The Impact of Electoral Systems: Share of Votes and Share of Seats

Country	Election	Parties	Votes	Seats	Comments
Czechia	1996	ODS (conservative)*	29.6%	34.0%	New nation since
		CSSD (social democrats)	26.4%	30.5%	the split up of
		KSCM (communists)	10.3%	11.0%	Czechoslovakia in
		Christian democrats*	8.1%	9.0%	1992, with propor-
		SPR-RSC (nationalists)	8.0%	9.0%	tional representa-
		ODA (conservative liberals)*	6.4%	6.5%	tion and an
		Others	11.2%	0%	effective five
					percent threshold.
Denmark	1998	SiD (social democrats)*	36.0%	36.0%	Proportional repre-
		Venstre (liberals)	24.0%	24.0%	sentation with a
		KF (conservatives)	8.9%	9.1%	low two percent
		SF (green social democrats)	7.5%	7.4%	threshold that
		DF (moderate nationalists)	7.4%	7.4%	hardly affects
		C-D (social democrats)	4.3%	4.6%	smaller parties.
		RV (social liberals)*	3.9%	4.0%	Ten parties are rep-
		Rød-Grønne (greens)	2.7%	2.9%	resented in the
		KF (Christian democrats)	2.5%	2.3%	parliament. Many
		FP (moderate nationalists)	2.4%	2.3%	governments are
		Others	.4%	0%	minority cabinets.
Germany	1998	SPD (social democrats)*	40.9%	44.5%	Proportional repre-
		CDU/CSU (Christian democrats)	35.2%	36.6%	sentation with
		Grünen (Greens)*	6.7%	7.0%	elements of a
		FDP (conservative liberals)	6.2%	6.6%	majority system
		PDS (post-communists)	5.1%	5.2%	and a five percent
					threshold, but
					hardly any small
					parties.
Great Britain	1997	Labour*	44.4%	63.4%	Majority system
		Conservative	31.4%	25.0%	favors large parties
		Liberal-Democrats	17.2%	6.9%	and in particular
		Others	7.0%	4.7%	the winning party.

*Parties that are represented in government after these elections

WHERE THE POWER IS: POLITICAL PARTIES

In 1997, Tony Blair introduced a new style of election campaign in Great Britain, stressing his youth and personal dynamics rather than the Labour program he stood for. In contrast to the European tradition of leaving wife and children at home, in relative anonymity, he showed up on television with his wife and children in an American-style campaign. Some party members accused him of forgetting about the traditional values of the party, but they soon fell silent after his victory, the first Labour success after several failed attempts by others to take over. He even managed to get the highly partisan anti-Labour popular press on his side, which hailed his landslide with headlines like: "YES! Tony rips 'em apart with 160 majority." In 1998, Gerhard Schröder imitated Blair's success after a similar personality show, together with his fourth wife. Disregarding objections from within his party about his lack of policy plans, he turned the tide for the German social democrats after several failed attempts by others to oust Christian democratic Chancellor Helmut Kohl.

Both campaigns raised complaints about the decline of the role of ideologies in politics and the "Americanization" of political campaigns, mentioned in the previous chapter. A first and conscious move toward ideological decline was made by the social democrats. After World War II, they increasingly gave up part of their Marxist ideology, as well as symbols and rituals, in order to appeal to the new middle class of office employees and to win middle class votes. It was a response to the fact that conservatives, liberals, and Christian democrats appealed also to a portion of the working class. The trend toward such "catch-all parties," which pay more attention to popular appeal than to ideology, has been followed by a decline in party allegiance (political "de-alignment" as political scientists say). The number of "floating voters," who switch from one party to another, is on the rise, which in turn increases the influence of the mass media.

In spite of de-alignment, most Europeans still vote for a party, not for a person. European politics is party politics, and even in Great Britain's majority system there is no direct relation between voters and their members of parliament. That relation is an indirect one with the political party in between. It is not the representative personally who matters but the party he "represents." Why this party dominance? The answer is simple. Catholics want to be represented by Catholics and operate as a unity, and the same applies to social democrats, farmers, liberal industrialists, and others. In Europe, it is the party platform rather than the party ticket that counts. Political parties express ideologies and represent segments of the population. They make up the lists of candidates for seats in the parliament. Representatives do not air their own opinion, but speak on behalf of their party and their speeches are weighed accordingly. Many voters only know one or two names on the party list they vote for. Often the first name on such a list gets all the votes, the others just the votes of their families, friends, and colleagues. Exceptionally, candidates may be so popular that they receive a lot of personal votes. In general, parties do not appreciate such a kind of personal vote, as it reduces the party hold over the representative.

It is the party that selects the candidates and that finances and carries on the election campaign. In return, the candidate promises to express party views and to vote in accordance with the party line, at least on major items. If the candidate deviates too often, that person may be refused a next term of office. Interestingly, this vision of the representative as a party mandatory violates the oath that new members of parliament have to swear to in most countries. That oath states that they will decide independently. To most Europeans, this discrepancy between norm and practice is no problem, since the new member of Parliament participates in the party decisions that she or he has to comply with. Individuals that seek a seat in parliament as independent candidates without party support are exceptional.

Most Europeans still vote for a party, not for a person. What then, are these parties? European political parties are standing organizations. Their head office is located in the national capital. The members pay party dues and are organized in networks of party locals, which are also active in local politics. The locals organize regular meetings for their members, at which political issues are discussed or a member of Parliament speaks. The party members elect regional representatives who attend the party congress, which is held once a year or less. There, the long-term policy lines are discussed, and especially in the social democratic parties the party locals table a lot of motions. In all parties, the discussion is well prepared by the party committee or party council, a small group of people elected by the congress. It constitutes the factual party top, meets every (other) week and takes all organizational decisions. In between the congress meetings, a smaller "national council" decides about major points.

This rather bureaucratic structure reduces the amount of influence ordinary party members may have. Their influence is curtailed even more by the fact that the party leader is a member of Parliament, or even a minister in the government, and in the latter case he is bound by his loyalty to the government. In practice, party leaders only need to defend themselves before party meetings after a heavy defeat in elections, which is often a reason for retreat (and their acceptance of better paid posts in private enterprise). The other party representatives in parliament only lose credit in case they cast too many deviant votes or are too passive in fraction meetings or party meetings.

How to get on the party list? U.S.-style primaries are unknown in Europe, since they focus on candidates rather than issues. Preferably, two conditions should be met: connections with relevant pressure groups and expertise in a specific policy field. Most parties maintain formal and informal relations with a number of pressure groups and may even offer them the guarantee of one or more parliament seats. Christian democratic parties reserve a number of seats for small business owners and farmers, social democrats for trade union leaders, and liberal and conservative parties persuade prominent businessmen to join their list. This allocation of a number of seats does not mean that parties are mere combinations of interest groups. Rather, they aggregate interests that are expressed by pressure groups. At the same time, both parties and pressure groups try to prevent too strong a mutual dependency. As for expertise, the larger parties have their specialists in all policy fields. These experts speak on behalf of the party when issues in those fields are being discussed. Often, they are the same people that have connections with pressure groups in a specific field.

A long experience with distributing election flyers during rainy evening hours does not bring one much further toward a seat in parliament and neither does money. Election campaigns are financed by the parties, not by candidates. The parties get financial support from a variety of sources, including membership dues and voluntary contributions from individuals and companies. Company money has increasingly become suspicious, however, since it may easily cross the borderline between a normal donation and bribery. In several countries there have been scandals about financing election campaigns with the help of "secret" gifts from companies looking for state contracts. In 1997, accusations of that kind were among the first challenge that Tony Blair's Labour government had to face, and they also caused the breakdown of a Czech cabinet. In 1998, NATO Secretary General Willy Claes had to resign since he was under suspicion, and later condemned, for accepting such secret campaigning funds at the time he was still a leading politician in Belgium. In a number of countries political donations must be made public, but liberals and conservatives, leaning more on this kind of support than social democrats or communists, have preferred to keep them secret "for privacy reasons." This secrecy about finance is in line with the more general reluctance of Europeans to tell how much money they make and what their sources of income are. The state also provides the parties with funds. Parties represented in parliament often get state money, for instance for research and other activities, and also to cover the costs of election campaigns. In addition, they also get time on public broadcasting channels, at fixed hours. Buying additional time at commercial rates is unpopular or even forbidden.

Who decides the ranking of the candidates? That is the prerogative of the party top or the party members. The party leaders submit a provisional list to the members, who discuss it in their branch meetings, followed by the final decision in the party committee or the party council. Recently, the share of women and ethnic minorities has become a popular issue. Women attempt to secure a minimum number or even a fixed quota of seats and have organized "women vote for women" campaigns in their parties. In the European Union member states, women now occupy twenty-two percent of the seats in the national parliaments and twenty-six percent of the cabinet posts.

COALITION GOVERNMENTS AND PARTY SYSTEMS

In Great Britain, the name of the new head of government is known the very moment the last election results from remote areas come in. On the continent, with more than two parties playing a role in national politics, a clear majority for a single party is often absent, and yet another question has to be solved: Which parties will participate in the government? Sometimes that decision has been made before the elections, when the parties in government announce their determination to continue their cooperation. However, even then an election debacle may encourage one of the parties to quit, in the hope to win back its voters by means of a more pronounced opposition role.

The person who will start the negotiating talks and form a new cabinet is elected by the parliament. Usually he is the leader of the largest party. In a few countries, he is appointed by the formal Head of State, which is a remnant of the time that the cabinet ministers were no more than advisors to the king ("His

Majesty's Government"). In many nations, the parties prefer a solid government program or government declaration as the basis of a coalition. As a result, the coalition negotiations may cover the core policy fields in detail and last for a while, up to several weeks or even months. The 1998 red-green coalition negotiations in Germany took three weeks, the Belgian periods of four and five months mentioned in the introduction to this chapter are exceptionally long. Outsiders sometimes see this period as one of political crisis, which it is not. It is a period of laying the foundation of a new cabinet, and laying a foundation always gives the impression that nothing happens—in politics as in construction and in putting on makeup. The periods of coalition building would point to crisis only if they would last longer than the resulting cabinet, which incidentally happens in Italy. If the parties in government have won a majority, the coalition talks may be confined to changes within the cabinet, to have its composition better reflect the new numerical force of the participating parties.

In the government program, the coalition parties lay down the main policies that they have agreed upon and will defend in parliament. This shows an important function of party discipline. Without such discipline, all representatives of these parties would be free to withdraw their support at any moment, thus making stable governments impossible. After the parties involved have pledged their support, the person that built the coalition officially invites prominent members of the coalition parties to join the new cabinet as ministers. Sometimes this process may involve new bargaining on the allocation of cabinet posts among the participant parties and about the people to be selected. Once this "cabinet building" is completed, the cabinet leader becomes prime minister, the nation's chief executive. He and his ministers are sworn in by the Head of State, a ceremonial activity and often the only occasion at which the Head of State meets the full government.

Usually a distinction is made between narrow coalitions (comprising just enough parties to form a majority government) and broad coalitions. Narrow coalitions have the obvious advantage of less construction costs and less coordination trouble, but they often provide disproportionate power to the second or third party that is needed to secure majority support in parliament. This is especially the case in Germany, where the two largest parties, social democrats and Christian democrats, always need the support of a much smaller second party, either the conservative liberals or the green party. In broad coalitions and especially in coalitions that comprise more parties than is strictly necessary for a majority, the power of each party in the cabinet tends to be more in proportion to its number of seats (see Table 4.2). Parties that are too arrogant may count with a reaction from the other parties or may even be thrown out of the cabinet. Broad coalitions often serve to reduce opposition and to widen popular support for unpopular measures.

In addition to coalition governments, one-party or multiparty minority governments also belong to the regular stock of variations in European government composition. Such governments do not dispose of a majority in parliament, but they either get the tacit support of other parties or count on support from various

Table 4.2. Seats in Parliament and the Allocation of Cabinet Posts

Country	Year	Parties in Government	Seats (%)	Cabinet Posts (%)	Comment
Germany	1998	SPD (social democrats)	44.5	73.3	Two-party coalition favors smaller coalition partner.
		Grünen (greens)	7.0	20.0	
Great Britain	1997	Labour	63.0	100	One-party government.
Latvia	1995	Saimnieks	18	26.7	Very broad coalition, in which cabinet posts are allocated taking into account not only the number of parliament seats but also the importance of the cabinet posts.
		LC	17	20.0	
		TUBS	14	26.7	
		LNNK	8	13.3	
		LVP	8	6.7	
		LZS	8	6.7	
Slovenia	1995	LDS (liberals)	28.4	44.4	SLS broke apart from an alliance in order to participate in this cabinet, in which the prime minister came from LDS ranks.
		SLSi (conservatives)	21.6	50.0	
		DeSUS (social liberals)	5.7	5.6	

sides, depending on the issues at hand. Minority governments especially prevail when the parties involved occupy a strong position in parliament and face a divided opposition, that consists of parties that are unable to combine and bring down the government.

REGIONAL VARIATIONS IN ELECTIONS, PARTIES AND GOVERNMENT

In accordance with the degree of party discipline and the nature of divisions, there is a great deal of regional variation in type of government.

In Great Britain, the elections decide about the government. They are the clearest left-right contest in Europe. Great Britain is the country of one-party government by the party that wins the elections.

In Scandinavia, elections are a contest of the social democrats versus all others. In that sense, they are also a clear left-right contest but they do not necessarily decide about the government. A social democratic minority government is the most common type, and it is relatively independent of the number of votes for the social democrats. It faces opposition from the left (communists) and the (highly divided) right, but often the two opposition forces are unable and unwilling to join forces against the social democrats. During the late 1970s and 1980s, conservative and liberal coalitions were in power for some time, but in the 1990s, the social democrats have taken over again.

In most other Germanic countries, Germany included, Christian democrats are the dominant party and elections are less of a left-right contest. In Belgium and Holland, the Christian democrats—as the political "center"—either build "center-left" coalitions with social democrats or "center-right" combinations with liberals. Elections mainly decide whether both options dispose of a majority or not and are available to the Christian democrats. Social democratic/liberal coalitions are exceptional. In Holland, such a "purple" (red-blue) coalition has come to power in 1994, which put an end to almost a century of Christian democratic government domination. In Germany, the small conservative liberal party used to be the coalition partner of both major parties. That favorable position has secured its participation in government for a longer period than both large parties. In 1998, Gerhard Schröder put an end to that situation by opting for a "red-green" coalition, one of the first times a green party participates in a national government.

In Latin Europe either the left or the right governs, preferably in a one-party social democratic or conservative government. As a consequence, elections are a real contest between left and right, similar to the British elections. Coalitions are not very popular and where they are necessary they are confined to either left or right parties. In accordance with the greater degree of polarization between left and right, broad coalitions that comprise parties from the left and the right are virtually absent.

Italy is an exception. In that country, a tradition survives that also existed in France before the introduction of the presidential system. In this Latin tradition, parliament has, to some extent, remained an open marketplace for debate between individual representatives. Classical oratory in the French *Assemblée Nationale* used to be an appeal to individual reason, either in line with party views or not. With the exception of the communist party, the parties involved are neither willing, nor able to impose party discipline. Even the term "party" is suspect in France for that reason. French parties prefer to call themselves *Rassemblement*, *Front*, or *Mouvement*. The absence of party discipline means they cannot count on the support of their own representatives and the government is not ensured of the permanent support of the participating parties. For those reasons, broad coalitions are preferred, which strengthen the government's base. Such governments continue to predominate in Italy but the outcome has not been more government stability. During the postwar period, both Italy and France have enjoyed the privilege of being governed by more than fifty governments, on the average one new government each year. In Italy, a week without a new government is still considered a lost week.

An interesting difference between Germanic and Latin nations is in the share of women in national parliaments. In most Germanic nations, women occupy more than a quarter of all seats. Belgium tails the group with less than fifteen percent, but that is still a higher share than in the Latin nations, with the exception of Spain. The difference shows that, like the environmentalists, feminists are more successful in Germanic than in Latin Europe.

In Central Europe almost all nations are ruled by coalition governments, which often include a number of parties, or alliances, of political parties. Such alliances, either ad-hoc or more stable, are typical of Central Europe. They consist of groups of political parties that promise to work together either in government or in opposition, but they fall apart as easily as they are built. Most Central European governments include social democrats. However, the terms social democrat and socialist are used by a variety of political parties, including not-very-democratic former communist parties (Bulgaria), former communist parties that now resemble Western European social democrats (Poland), and parties that have been newly created (Czechia). The first ten years or so of democratic politics has revealed remarkable variations in government stability. While Czechia had only one prime minister, leading two consecutive cabinets during the first five years of its national existence, Poland has had a new prime minister almost every year since 1989. However, stability need not always be an asset, since it may also point to the domination of politics by a strong man, as is the case in Croatia and Serbia. In these former Yugoslav republics, the presidents are "war heroes" from the time Yugoslavia fell apart and new nations sprang up that soon engaged in war.

A fine example of Central European complexity is Macedonia, the southern part of former Yugoslavia, and now one of the smaller states of Europe. In that country, the former communist party split into three parts, and in addition to several other parties, three parties exist that specifically represent the Albanian minority. The 1997 government consisted of three parties. They included two of the three offsprings of the former communist party, which called themselves socialist and liberal. The third party in government was an alliance of two of the three parties representing the Albanian minority. The government faced an opposition that comprised the third party that had grown out of the former communist party, the third Albanian party, together with a number of other parties.

5

Government and Parliament

MP, *standing*:	Does the minister know that his policy. . . .?
Minister, *seated*:	*Nods an affirmative.*
MP:	Does the minister know that many people are now worse off?
Minister, *standing*:	The Right Honourable Gentleman and his political friends know very well that I know that this policy improves the conditions of. . . .
Backbenchers, *loud*:	Hear, hear.
Speaker, *louder*:	Order! Order!

The question hour in the British Parliament, the oldest parliament in the world, is one of the finest (and most amusing) democratic rituals. Members of Parliament (M.P.s) pose questions and the prime minister answers. Their political friends support them by functioning as the background vocals with sounds that resemble something in between muttering and shouting, which allows the chairperson (Speaker) to drown them all out, and call for order and new questions. Newcomers in parliament are seated in the last rows (backbenchers). The ritual may look a bit out of date. However, the whole world recognizes the Houses of Parliament on a postcard from London, while hardly anyone knows in what building the French *Assemblée Nationale* meets or even in which city the German *Bundestag* met before its removal to Berlin. Do you?

THE REAL LEGISLATOR: GOVERNMENT

European governments consist of at least two layers. The government as such represents the first layer. It comprises all ministers and vice ministers, often over thirty people in total. Full meetings of this group only take place incidentally. More frequent are the meetings of the second layer, the cabinet, in which only the "full" ministers participate. These fifteen or so people meet every week and they form the "real" national government. In everyday usage, the words government and cabinet are used indiscriminately for this Council of Ministers, as it is also called. Cabinet ministers have two functions to fulfill: To run their department and develop policy in their field, and to take part in the process of collective decision making by the cabinet as a whole during the weekly meetings. The cabinet decides on the most important issues, the ministers individually take the other decisions.

Prime ministers and ministers are mostly recruited from the ranks of the members of parliament. The implication is that the party's main speaker in a policy field is more or less certain of nomination as a minister in case the party participates in government. The persons involved will follow the coalition negotiations with distrust, to see to it that their field of expertise is not claimed by one of the other coalition partners. A small minority of cabinet ministers in Europe consists of former civil servants or businessmen, selected because of their expert knowledge and administrative skills in addition to their political persuasion.

Within the cabinet two important subgroups exist that may overlap: First, the group consisting of the leaders of the parties that are represented in the cabinet. Their task is to keep the coalition together. Second, the small circle consisting of the ministers of finance, economic affairs, and social affairs. It meets in between regular cabinet sessions, in order to provide a quick response to changes in economic and social conditions like inflation and employment, and to maintain contacts with the two major pressure groups in European politics: trade unions and business associations.

The prime minister, called chancellor (*Bundeskanzler*) in Austria and Germany, chairs the council of ministers and sometimes heads a small ministry of "General Affairs." This does not mean they are mere "first among equals." They are the political leaders of their countries, the "face" of the nation and they often exercise considerable power over the cabinet and their own political party. This may imply the competency to carry through any changes in the composition of the cabinet without prior notice. Increased television coverage of politics and regular international summits have reinforced the preponderance of the prime ministers. Due to the growing concern with budget deficits since the early 1980s and the development of the European Monetary Union, ministers of finance have also become key figures in national politics.

Prime ministers resign right after elections (to prepare for a new term of office if they win the elections), or as soon as one or more of the coalition partners withdraws its support. The prime minister may then attempt to build a new cabinet without elections, which allows him to stay in power during a number of cabinets. As the introduction to the previous chapter has shown, it is even possible to change the prime minister and forge a new coalition in between elections.

In case of collision between a minister and the parliament, or with the rest of the cabinet (or in case of a scandal of some kind) the minister involved may resign, without jeopardizing the cabinet. Formal votes of distrust are popular only in a few countries. Table 5.1 lists the British, German, and Italian prime ministers, as well as the French presidents over the last twenty years.

Table 5.1. Political Leaders in Great Britain, Germany, Italy, and France Since 1980 (Italy Since 1990)

Great Britain	Germany	Italy	France
Prime Minister	*Bundeskanzler*	*Presidente del Consiglio* Since 1990	*Président de la République*
Margaret Thatcher (conservative) 1979–1990	Helmut Schmidt (social democrat) 1974–1982	Giulio Andreotti (Christian democrat) 1989–1992	Valérie Giscard d'Estaing (conservative liberal) 1974–1981
		Giuliano Amato (social democrat) 1992–1993	
John Major (conservative) 1990–1997	Helmut Kohl (Christian democrat) 1982–1998	Carlo Ciampi (independent) 1993–1994	François Mitterand (social democrat) 1981–1995
		Silvio Berlusconi (conservative) 1994–1995	
Tony Blair (Labour) 1997–	Gerhard Schröder (social democrat) 1999–	Lamberto Dini (independent) 1995–1996	Jacques Chirac (Gaullist) 1995–
		Romano Prodi (Christian democrat) 1996–1998	
		Massimo D'Alema (post-communist) 1998–	

THE FINAL SAY: PARLIAMENT

The national parliaments in Europe often look like university conference halls during the last minutes of a written examination, with only a few students left, who pretend they still have something to say. Aren't the members of parliament interested in making laws, then?

No, they are not. Although law making counts as the primary function of the parliament, its main activity is not to make rules but to check the cabinet. Ireland has even had a period of forty years without a single law that was initiated by a member of Parliament. In Europe, governments make the rules and parliaments have to approve them. The governing parties are bound by their support of the government, however, and are no longer free to reject major government bills, at the risk of a cabinet crisis.

Once a government has been formed, the parliamentary function of checking the government may be divided into three distinct activities. First, the parliament decides on all laws by adding "amendments" and casting the final vote. In this process the cabinet or individual ministers defend the bill before the Parliament. The major bills are discussed first with the minister in parliamentary committees. The committees consist of party specialists in a particular field, the meetings take place in a rather informal way, and the focus is on the details as much as on the main thrust of the bill. For these reasons, the committee meetings (whether behind closed doors or in public) allow more room for influence by the opposition parties than full parliamentary sessions. The committees' agenda is determined more by the minister involved, however, than by the committee chairman or its members. The discussion will be continued in the main hall, between party specialists and the minister. Television broadcasting of the plenary sessions often shows an empty hall, since most representatives will come in for a final vote only.

The second parliamentary task is to scrutinize and approve the government budget. The budget talks constitute the main confrontation between government and parliament. They decide on the business of government and the continuity of state services and subsidized organizations. Due to the wide scope of the talks and the possible implications for government continuity, these meetings are at the heart of the parliament's work. They get wide coverage in the national mass media and most representatives are present.

The budget debate mostly starts right after the annual reading of the government's program (the national "State of the Union") and the presentation of its budget. In some countries, the government program is read by the Head of State in a ceremonial meeting, with due pomp (in particular in the kingdoms). The general debate is followed by discussion and a final vote on each minister's budget. All parties propose a number of changes. Even the parties supporting the government do so, but they will check that the minister does not consider them as an attack on the coalition. If the parliament rejects the total budget, the government will change the budget or resign. If parliament rejects a specific ministry's budget, either the government or the minister involved resigns and in the latter case the government recruits a new minister, and adapts the plans. When a cabinet falls, it often stays on until new elections are held or a new cabinet has been formed. In case of such conflicts the current budget will be continued until the coming of a new cabinet or a new minister, in order to guarantee the payment of salaries and subventions. Almost all schools and universities would have to shut down if such a provision did not exist.

The third parliamentary activity is the regular "question hour" in which the prime minister and other ministers are questioned about the implications of their plans for specific groups, unforeseen effects of their policies, and current developments in general—in short—about everything. Rather than written questions, these oral questions are a fine opportunity for the opposition to show its oratorical skills in attempt to tackle a minister. The members of the parties supporting the government defend the minister or reduce his loss of face by proposing small adjustments in policy. Although the question hour is often the liveliest part of the parliament's activities, especially when an experienced opposition debater has the floor, it is also the least important one because of its limited effect on national policies.

In between the parliamentary meetings, the representatives keep in contact with organizations and individuals that are active in their field of specialization. Going back to the constituency is mainly important in Great Britain, with its majority electoral system. Parliamentarians only have a small staff but they can also rely on party assistants and the party's research or documentation departments, which are often subsidized by state funds for the parties represented in parliament.

National parliaments leave almost all initiative to the government. They mainly respond to government activities and bills in direct contact with cabinet ministers. That relationship does not create much latitude of logrolling or pork barrels American-style. Members of Parliament do not mutually negotiate without government participation (logrolling) and neither does the government negotiate package deals with individual members of Parliament (pork barrels), except when these M.P.s act as the official speakers of their parties. In accordance, the factual relation between government and parliament in most countries is not so much one of hierarchy with the parliament on top, but a power balance between the two: a situation of "dual power." Governments must be responsive to constructive changes in the original coalition plans by the parties represented in government. Parliament may send home a minister or vote down the cabinet, but more exceptionally the government may also dissolve the parliament and force new elections. It will do so especially if it is unable to build a new cabinet after a party has withdrawn its support, in the case of strong disagreement between the coalition partners, or under heavy pressure of political protests outside the parliament.

The strong links between parliament and government—with regular visits over and across and with the ministers often occupying seats in the parliament—are reflected in the interior of most houses of Parliament. Like the American Congress, all continental parliaments are seated in a half circle. They look toward the speaker in front of them, who (unlike in the American Congress) is often a cabinet minister. In the British Parliament, by contrast, the Parliament does not face the speaker who has the floor but the two main parties face each other and the ministers occupy the more prominent seats on one side. Here it is not the Parliament facing the government but two parties, one of them constituting the government, that face each other.

This survey of parliamentary activities has focused on the main chamber of Parliament. Most European parliaments consist of two chambers: a lower house or "Chamber" and an upper house or Senate, but the names vary across nations. The Chamber is the real representation of the nation, it has more weight and gets far wider attention in the media. The Senate is often smaller and has less power than the Chamber (for instance a Senate veto may be overrun by the Chamber). Often the Senate is not elected by popular vote, but by local or regional government or by governments of the federal states, as a representation of regional interests. Nevertheless, it is party affiliation that counts and decides about nominations for the Senate and voting patterns in it. In contrast to the U.S. Senate, most European Senates that are based on regional or federal state representation take into account the relative size of the constituent units. Switzerland is an exception with two seats for each of the cantons in the upper house. In the German *Bundesrat*, the best known example of a federal Senate, federal *Länder* dispose of three to six votes, depending on population size.

Most senates are directly elected by the people of the constituent units, and in that respect the *Bundesrat* is an exception. It is not elected but consists of the representatives of the sixteen federal state governments, often cabinet ministers. The delegation of each *Land* has to vote as a bloc. This composition makes the *Bundesrat* an even stronger federal representation than the U.S. Senate, but one could argue also a less democratic one. When the opposition parties dispose of a majority in the German *Bundesrat*, they are able to veto any national government plans. Facing a hostile *Bundesrat*, the German government sometimes attempts to prevent a deadlock through negotiations with the opposition. In 1997 the Kohl government concluded a pact with the social democratic party to carry through tax and old age pension reforms. However, mostly the German Senate remains in the shadow of the real Chamber, the *Bundestag* (Federal Meeting).

A number of smaller countries (as well as Ukraine) do without a Senate. A strange relic from the past is the British "House of Lords," in which a large number of seats were reserved for nobility and for elderly statesmen that have been promoted into the nobility ranks. They use the House to take their nap while tourists swarm the bedrooms in their castles. In 1999 their quiet nap turned into a nightmare when the Blair government introduced a reform of this institution in the direction of more democratic composition.

(To answer the question in the introduction to this chapter: The French *Assemblée Nationale* meets in the Palais Bourbon, on the Seine bank, facing the Place de la Concorde. The German Parliament met in the city of Bonn, on the Rhine, South of Cologne, until it moved to the *Reichstag* building opposite the Brandenburger Tor in downtown Berlin in 1999.)

OTHER STATE INSTITUTIONS

Head of State: King, Queen, or President

Except in France and Eastern Europe, the Head of State is not the head of state, but its symbol. Until the mid-nineteenth century or even early twentieth century, most Heads of State were hereditary kings. National constitutions reduced their power or removed them from office, and by doing so transformed absolute monarchies into constitutional monarchies or into republics. The European presidents are often elderly statesmen elected by the Parliament. Like the constitutional monarchs they mainly exercise ceremonial tasks, such as eating *folies bergères à la belle-mère* with other Heads of State and drinking a fine *Château Discord 1976* to wash down the taste. Great Britain, Scandinavia, and the Low Countries continue to appreciate their royalty as a fine relic from the past. It brings in an element of stability in national allegiance. It offers a century-old object of identification (Who dreams of being a president as an infant?) and some juicy sex scandals of idle crown princes and the husbands of reigning queens. (As busy elder statesmen, presidents are less interesting in that respect.)

The main function of the Heads of State in politics is to sign laws. This may provide them some informal influence in the contents of laws, facilitated by regular working visits by the prime minister to the presidential or royal palace. The Heads of State are no longer in a position to refuse to sign, however, as is shown by a fine incident. In 1990, the Belgian king refused to sign a law relaxing the rules on abortion. The Belgians then found a creative solution by having him declared unable to reign (which he was at that moment!). The combined houses of Parliament then took over his powers and signed the law. The next day they restored their king into power.

The Constitution

All European nations possess a constitution. In Western Europe its main function has been to limit royal power, and to protect civil liberties, like free speech, freedom of religion, freedom of gathering, and a free press. In Central and to some extent in Eastern Europe, new constitutions have been framed in the early 1990s to introduce democracy and to protect these same civil liberties.

In general, the older the democracy is, the less the constitution is referred to in everyday politics and the less opportunities of judicial review. Great Britain, as the first country to limit royal power in a series of documents, some of them dating back to Medieval times, does not even have a written constitution in the strict sense. The idea behind this absence of a formal constitution is that a longstanding democracy hardly needs a constitution, and in the hypothetical case in which a dictator takes over, a written constitution won't stop him.

France is the only long-standing democracy that has lived through a number of constitutions (a bad sign in British and American eyes), to serve the consecutive French republics. Like France, all countries that have become democracies since World War II (Germany, the Iberian Peninsula, and Central and Eastern Europe) not only appreciate their constitution, but have also introduced judicial review of laws. Often, a special Constitutional Court has been established for this activity. The best known example is Germany, where the constitution is regarded as a sacred document, not to be spoken about in a belittling way, since it is considered as an effective guarantee against the rise to power of terror movements. Judicial review in Germany has been patterned after the U.S. Supreme Court and plays a prominent role in German politics, in particular in ethical questions like abortion.

Although the idea of *Trias Politica* might suggest otherwise, ordinary courts and judges are not supposed to play a role in politics. In most countries, the courts only function to interpret laws and apply them to specific cases. Even in their interpretation they have no free hand but must look at what the government had in mind when framing the law, in other words, they must take into account the intentions of the law, rather than its actual contents. In continental countries this application of law is facilitated by the fact that law, based on Roman Empire law, has been codified in a civil code, a penal code, and a few other codes. It goes without saying that Great Britain is the only country that does not enjoy civil law. Its system of "common law" (which prevails also in the United States, but in combination with a well-enforced constitution) leaves British judges a greater range of freedom in their jurisdiction than their colleagues on the continent. They do not have to look at the legislator's intentions but only at the text of the law. In interpreting laws, British judges mainly follow precedent (earlier verdicts in similar cases). In the absence of precedent, judges—to a limited extent—may shape new law, rather than merely interpreting existing legislation.

The European Union has introduced a new form of judicial review. The European Court of Justice may decide on the conformity of national legislation with the European treaties. Some of the treaties include civil rights and have come to function as a kind of European constitution, with the possibility of judicial review of national legislation.

The Bureaucracy

An institution that occupies a prominent position in politics throughout Europe is the standing bureaucracy in the ministries or government departments. They are headed by a minister or vice minister but managed by a senior civil servant. With their specialized knowledge, higher civil servants may sometimes dominate a minister who is new in the field. The basic distinction in the nature of the civil service is the one between Great Britain and the continent. In Great Britain, senior civil servants are "generalists," selected not because of their expertise in their policy field but because of their general administrative skills and their adherence to group norms (and the use of upper class English). All of these skills are learned at the universities of Oxford and Cambridge. Most of the continent prefers civil servants with technical knowledge in the policy field involved, for which any university or technical college will do. This preference for specialization probably goes back to the standing military bureaucracies on the continent. Great Britain, as an island, lacked a standing army. For a long time its major state service was the Royal Navy, which did not play a role in domestic politics but ruled the waves. On the continent, France is a bit exceptional with its special educational institutes for top civil servants, the *Grandes Ecoles*. They create a closed elite, which shares the same educational background.

In all of Europe the civil service is considered to be apolitical but in some countries new ministers may appoint a small group of personal assistants or consultants, who will leave again when their minister resigns. (This is not unlike the American "spoils" system, but on a more limited scale and not as a reward for campaign activities or funds.) Additionally, in several countries, the rule is observed that the top of the civil service should reflect the political divisions in the country at least to some extent. This kind of "political investiture" may be an informal affair, or even a public secret. Of course, the department will stress that technical knowledge was crucial in appointing someone, but the rest of the country knows that the appointee had also (or only) the right political affiliation.

State bureaucracies and public services are often very hierarchical organizations, with strictly defined competencies and tasks. These static institutions are currently being changed into more dynamic and business-like organizations. This transition from "public administration" to "public management" originated in the United States and in Great Britain under Margaret Thatcher. Although most governments rejected Thatcher's crusade against big government as too radical, the British example of public management is now imitated in a number of countries, in order to increase efficiency.

REGIONAL VARIATIONS IN PARLIAMENTARY AND GOVERNMENT POWER

The regional differences in the relation between government and parliament are just as pronounced as those in social and ideological division.

Great Britain's combination of majoritarian electoral system, predominance of two parties, and prevalence of one-party government is called the "Westminster" model, after the location of the Parliament in London. In the Westminster model, the existence of stable one-party governments increases the government's power vis-à-vis the parliament. Many backbenchers of the ruling party mainly support their government, while the opposition party has hardly any influence at all.

The Westminster model of strong one-party cabinets, which rely on stable majority support and do not compromise with the opposition, contrasts with the "consensus" model. That system of government-parliament relationship is especially found in the smaller Germanic nations. Governments are either minority one-party cabinets (in Scandinavia) or multiparty coalitions that have to take care not to lose majority support in parliament. The cabinet listens carefully to what the opposition has to say and preferably tries to integrate some of the opposition's ideas in its policies, if only because the major parties in opposition might well be the next partners-in-government. In Scandinavia, parliaments consist of one chamber only. Influence of the opposition is secured by means of the parliamentary committees. The committees play a more active role than their counterparts elsewhere and they allow for intense exchange of views on state policies. In other Germanic nations, committees are less influential but national government still seeks to find some kind of compromise with the opposition, hence the term "consensus system." The most far-reaching example of consensus seeking is Switzerland, where the major parties in parliament are always represented in the government as a permanent broad coalition. In Germany, the parties are less consensus-oriented but a hostile *Bundesrat* (Senate) and the federal system by itself encourage regular negotiations between government and opposition.

While Great Britain has the best supporters and Germanic Europe the best listeners, Latin Europe, where emotions may run a bit higher, enjoys the privilege of having the best speakers, and as a result also the liveliest meetings. With the exception of Italy, however, the Latin European parliaments are now under strict "party surveillance." Party discipline no longer provides ample opportunities for sending the government home every now and then or even for practicing oratory skills. Only occasionally there is some old-fashioned cursing or even a small fight, with CNN right on the spot as the most qualified reporter. Although most governments are coalitions, the stronger left-right division does not encourage consensus-oriented talks with the opposition. In Great Britain, the opposition's role is to criticize the government, in Germanic nations its role is to influence the government, and in Latin Europe its role is to undermine the government until it breaks. The Senates in these countries mainly serve to express local and regional interests. Particularly in France, mayors occupy a number of seats in the *Senat*, where they promote the local cause.

In Central Europe, democratic parliaments have only a short history. The first democratic elections did not take place until the early 1990s. A number of the smaller nations (like the Baltic states and Slovakia) have established a one-chamber parliament and often the parliamentary right to send home the government has been curtailed, in order to guarantee government stability. The very process of coalition building is already a difficult and tiresome effort to forge some form of understanding and agreements among parties and alliances of parties. That does not leave much time or energy for consensus-seeking talks with the opposition. The fierce opposition between former communists and ardent anti-communists, with often one side in government and the other in opposition, does not facilitate consensus, either. Moreover, in several of these nations, strong prime ministers or presidents occupy the forefront of national politics. In the less democratic states they dominate the political scene, like Milosevič in Serbia, and are able to silence most of the opposition, sometimes by mobilizing their supporters to threaten and beat up opponents. That applies even more to Eastern Europe, with their presidential systems.

POLITICAL INNOVATION TO COPE WITH DIVISION

The principle of parliamentary representation is currently being criticized because of the "gulf" it creates between citizens and politics. The partial replacement of proportional representation by a majority system is one of the solutions forwarded to bridge the gap. It supposedly intensifies political competition, because there is only one seat to win in each district. A second solution is to introduce elements of "direct democracy" in the form of a referendum (a popular vote on an issue, instead of the regular vote for seats in parliament). Only in Italy, and even more in Switzerland has the referendum been a traditional and longstanding part of politics. In Switzerland any change in the federal constitution requires a nationwide referendum, and in both countries all kinds of other issues may also be the subject of a referendum, after 50,000 citizens (Switzerland) or 500,000 citizens (Italy) have signed a petition to that order. Ireland has also been quite active in calling for a referendum, especially on ethical questions like abortion and divorce. Most other nations have only organized such expressions of "direct democracy" on specific occasions, in particular on joining the European Union, or other changes in the international position of the country (see Table 5.2). The referendums dealing with European Union membership have gotten widest publicity. Protagonists of direct democracy praise the advantage of citizen involvement, while opponents point to the power of those who formulate the

Table 5.2. Some Examples of Referendums

Country	Year	Subject	Comment
Austria/Finland/ Norway/Sweden	1994	Joining the European Union (EU)	Only Norway rejected membership, as it had done in a previous referendum in 1972.
Switzerland	1995	Setting up a Swiss United Nations Peace Corps	Rejected, in line with the traditional Swiss dislike of international obligations.
Italy	1995	Twelve simultaneous referendums on commercial TV stations, trade union rights and shop opening hours and other subjects	The referendums on commercial TV were a victory for media-tycoon and politician Silvio Berlusconi, who was allowed to own more than one TV station. Longer shop opening hours were rejected.
Poland	1996	Privatization program of state enterprises	No decision, since only thirty percent of all voters showed up.
Belarus	1996	Granting the president dictatorial powers	The nation's Supreme Court and parliament had declared the referendum illegal, but the dictatorial president got his majority.
Great Britain	1997	Introducing regional parliaments in Scotland and Wales	Regional referendums. Both regions were in favor, the Welsh with a very small majority.
Serbia	1998	Outside mediation in the Kosovo conflict	A majority voted against international mediation. Western democracies condemned the referendum as dictatorial.
Denmark/ Ireland	1998	Ratification of the EU Treaty of Amsterdam	In the other EU member states the national parliaments decided on this issue.
Switzerland	1998	1. Ban on arms export 2. Cuts in unemployment pay 3. Anti-drug policies, including free heroin for drug addicts	1. Rejected by a large majority. 2. Rejected by a small majority. 3. Approved by a large majority.

questions. This objection has materialized in Central and Eastern European countries, where referendums have been used by presidents to put parliament aside.

The referendum may reduce division over an issue by expressing a clear majority opinion. However, it may also intensify division between the majority and the minority, without opportunities for compromise. In contrast to the referendum, most previous changes in the system of parliamentary representation have served to improve government stability by means of reducing the impact of division on the formation and the functioning of government. One general device of doing so is the "de-politicization" of hot issues, by first asking outside expert advice. Royal Commissions (in Great Britain) or Joint Committees (on the continent), consisting of university professors, elder statesmen, or prominent businessmen, are normal features of European politics. Sometimes they serve de-politicization very well, and the issue will be forgotten by the time that the committee publishes its final report.

In addition to judicial review, its federal system and the system of two votes in national elections, Germany, with its problematic past, has introduced a number of other new novelties in the past decades in order to guarantee democratic stability. A German innovation has been the widely imitated vote threshold (*Sperrklausel*). Parties need to win at least five percent of the votes (or carry three districts) to be represented in Parliament. This device reduces the number of small parties. The small German liberal party has regularly fallen victim to this threshold in the German states, which has endangered its position as a standing minor partner in government.

A second German innovation has been the "constructive vote of no-confidence." Parties may only vote down the Chancellor by means of a vote of no-confidence on the condition that they are able to vote in office a new Chancellor (hence the term constructive). This new departure in the no-confidence vote is to prevent large parties that are unwilling to cooperate in a coalition from forcing a government to retreat. In the 1930s the Nazis and the communists did so and contributed to the breakdown of democracy and Hitler's rise to power. The constructive vote of no-confidence has been used once, in 1982, when the small liberal party changed sides from the social democrats to the Christian democrats and voted Helmut Kohl in power. The constructive vote of no-confidence has been adopted in a couple of other nations, including Spain and Poland.

Interestingly, Russia has adopted some of the German innovations, in particular in the election and composition of both Chambers of Parliament, though not the constructive vote of no-confidence. As is the case in Germany, all voters may bring out two votes for the Russian Lower House (*Duma*). One half of the *Duma* is elected by means of proportional representation, with a five percent threshold, the other half through the majority system. Like the German *Bundesrat*, the Russian Senate—called the Council of the Federation—is not elected. All eighty-one regional and local governments in the country are represented in it, with two votes each.

One would also expect innovations in that apparently most unstable of Western European nations, Italy. Like the leaning Tower of Pisa it seems to crumble almost permanently but it still stands. How does it cope with its political instability?

First, until recently the major party in government, which also provided most prime ministers, always was the same, the Christian democrats. They dominated Italian politics, leaving small margins for other parties. Second, more than any other country, Italian politics has been characterized by family based "clientelism." This phenomenon consists of offering favors like a job, social security benefits, approval of company plans, or other forms of preferential treatment, in return for electoral support. In the rest of Europe, clientelism is condemned as an almost certain source of corruption, but it has the advantage of providing stability in party allegiances. A third element that contributes to stability is the limited impact of politics on Italian society. Both in the prosperous North and the poorer South, politics in Rome is far off, not very relevant, and hardly to be complied with. While governments come and go, business tycoons in the North, like the Agnelli family (which rules the Fiat empire), as well as party (and Mafia) bosses in the South, have a rather free hand to manage their business.

The introduction of the majority system in 1993 has not been of much help in creating a more stable party system, as many Italians had hoped. Voices are now raised to shift to a presidential system. That system has been the greatest political innovation in European politics.

THE SHORT WAY TO A NEW GOVERNMENT: PRESIDENTIAL SYSTEMS

In 1993, after a long blockade of his reforms by the Parliament, Russian president Yeltsin announced constitutional reforms by presidential decree. He suspended all functions of the *Duma*—the communist-dominated Russian Parliament—until new elections would be held. In response, Parliament started a kind of impeachment procedure and elected the communist vice president to be president. When that person tried to impose his rule, Yeltsin sent troops to the White House (the *Duma* seat, not the other one). After some fighting, the troops set fire to the White House and arrested Yeltsin's rival. In yet another new constitution, Yeltsin increased his own powers. Interestingly, during this period several democratic leaders, including the U.S. president, supported him as the democratically elected defender of democratic reforms in Russia.

In contrast to the United States, Europe has hardly had any experience with democratic presidential systems, in which both the president, as the head of government, and the Parliament are elected by popular vote and are independent of each other. The three presidential systems in Eastern Europe (Belarus, Russia, and Ukraine) can hardly be called democratic, and the French system is not a fully presidential one.

Although Finland was first, one might say that France has introduced the presidential type of political system in Europe. Under the interwar Third Republic (1918–1940) and the postwar Fourth Republic (1944–1958), government instability was a serious problem, and in some years the French were governed by a sequence of various governments. This lack of continuity was compensated to some extent by the strong network of top civil servants recruited from the *Grandes Ecoles*. Their power reduced the impact of parties and government on state policies—which is yet another form of de-politicization.

In 1958, Charles de Gaulle, leader of the French liberation army during World War II, put a drastic end to frequent party deadlocks. He introduced the Fifth Republic, in which the parliament and the president are both elected by the French people. Yet, it is not a full presidential system, because the national government is responsible to both the *Assemblée Nationale* and the president. In a full presidential system like the United States, the ministers are responsible to the president only. For that reason, political scientists use the term semi-presidential to describe this hybrid system. The 1958 Constitution and the French Fifth Republic, which was introduced through that Constitution, have made the French president the most powerful Head of State in Western Europe. In combination with the seven-year presidential term, which is exceptionally long for European standards, the change finally has provided France a stable face in Europe. The president has to take into account the composition of parliament when he appoints a government and he lacks explicit powers in domestic affairs, but he enjoys extensive powers in foreign policy.

Due to this presidential power, the French prime minister is no longer to be compared with the other prime ministers in Europe, who are the political leaders of their countries. Although some French presidents, including de Gaulle himself, preferably used to treat the prime minister in public as their senior assistant, he is much more than that, yet less than his "colleagues" outside France. The unclear division of competencies between president and prime minister creates tension in case a president faces a hostile parliament and has to accept a prime minister with opposite views. In that case, the French speak of *cohabitation*, which resembles a kind of uneasy living together of two people without shaking hands in the morning (which requires unusual restraint in France). *Cohabitation* is even more of a predicament for the president than the hilarious situation in which an American presidential candidate would have to accept a hostile person as running mate, because unlike U.S. Vice Presidents, French prime ministers are real policy makers in domestic politics. Actually, the situation looks a bit like a U.S. President who has to deal with a hostile Senate majority leader.

The French president may attempt to stop *cohabitation* through dissolving Parliament and calling for new elections. In 1997, President Chirac, a (conservative liberal) Gaullist, called new elections in which he hoped to enlarge his majority in the *Assemblée Nationale*. Surprisingly the social democrats won and Chirac had to appoint their leader Lionel Jospin as prime minister—the beginning of a period of *cohabitation.* (Chirac had experience with *cohabitation.* He had served as prime minister under President François Mitterand, a social democrat.) Actually, both a hostile and a friendly prime minister may serve as a "fuse," getting all the blame for economic and social problems, while the president gets all the credit for France's international position.

The presidential elections have also changed the political landscape in France by reducing the number of parties: Socialists and communists on the left, conservative Gaullists and conservative liberals to the right, with the racist Front National as a newcomer. In parliament, the traditional factionalism is continued, but in the presidential elections the parties show a stronger commitment.

A number of Central European countries have been transformed into parliamentary democracies but at the same time they have endowed their presidents with more power than those in Western Europe, except France. In several democratic countries like Poland and Romania, the president is elected by popular vote and has a voice in the building of a cabinet. In less democratic countries like Albania and Serbia, the presidents have been able to absorb great powers irrespective of the constitution.

The presidential or semi-presidential systems of Eastern Europe provide the presidents most power. The president may veto parliamentary decisions and, as in France, may dissolve parliament and call for new elections. An easier means to bypass parliament is to issue presidential decrees rather than formal legislation, or to organize a referendum on hot issues. In Belarus the authoritarian president and the majority in parliament are all (former) communists, which has reduced the rate of conflicts between president and parliament. Already before impeachment became a general topic of discussion due to the Clinton case in the United States, a couple of small Ukrainian parties tried to start an impeachment procedure of their president—motivated by his wrong policies—but they failed. The relatively smooth relationship between the reformist president and the communist-dominated parliament in Ukraine is quite a difference with the almost permanent deadlock between Russia's President Yeltsin and the communist-dominated *Duma*, as shown by the introduction to this section. During the second half of the 1990s, the communist majority in the *Duma* almost permanently announced their intention to start an impeachment procedure. On various occasions they also rejected the prime ministers' budgets. The stalemates were not solved until the president threatened with reduction of the *Duma*'s power, or fired the prime minister. Actually, removing prime ministers was one of Yeltsin's favorite measures. He did so if they were unable to foster economic growth, when they became too popular and could be a threat to his own popularity, or, so it seemed, merely for the fun of it.

The Russian combination of a German style parliament and French style presidential power has yet to prove its viability. Russia is trying to combine the best of Western European political innovation, but in a country with no democratic tradition at all.

6

Between State and Society

NEW TALKS ANNOUNCED BY THE WHITE HOUSE

Washington: The White House has announced a new meeting with business representatives and trade union leaders after today's successful talks about wage restraint and employee training facilities. The White House speaker said that trade unions were convinced of the need to reduce wage claims below productivity growth levels in order not to endanger the government's employment policies. Business representatives promised a boost in training provisions for their employees to catch up with Germany and Japan. The concessions will be laid down in an official business/trade union/government pact later this month. On leaving the White House, AFL-CIO secretary Boy Dime declared that his organization was very positive about the president's initiative and inspiring leadership during the talks. Business leader Boss Dinero said the talks had been hard but fair. He would blame AFL-CIO for any wage claims in violation of the pact.

While Americans may be appalled, to many Europeans this kind of "tripartite" (government/business/trade union) contacts are part of normal political life. Why are they so popular in Europe?

CIVIL SOCIETY EUROPEAN STYLE

Most Europeans are members of one or more organizations, which may be politically active at times and act as "pressure groups," trying to receive state funds or pressing for specific policies.

The organization of social life by means of voluntary groups, with or without government support, is an important ingredient of democracy. It constitutes the basis of "Civil Society," a society in which citizens share social responsibilities by means of voluntary groups and organizations. The term has become popular under the influence of various developments. In Western Europe, Christian democrats have reappraised "subsidiarity," one of the classical ideas of Catholic social doctrine, which recommended common activities by voluntary organizations as an alternative to state social policies. Social democrats have come to embrace this same idea, in line with their shift from state to private activities, intended to bring about more equality. Some neo-conservatives have also pointed to the need for voluntary organizations in their crusade against state overspending. In Central Europe, the term civil society is basic to the transition toward democracy and a (partially) free-market economy. Civil society contrasts with an overactive democratic state that leaves hardly any room for private initiative, but even more with a communist-controlled society in which the communist party controls all other societal organizations.

Organizational life and pressure politics in Europe are different from those in the United States. First of all, membership of voluntary groups is much less widespread in Europe. This difference is partly due to more extensive state policies in Europe. Ad hoc groups and local community groups sponsoring local culture or removing highway litter are not very common. Europeans expect local or national government to take care of these concerns. Under pressure of budget deficits and the reduction of state activities, however, business sponsoring and private promotion of cultural and recreational activities are on the rise. The smaller membership rate has also to do with a second difference between American and European pressure groups. Most European pressure groups are well organized, display nationwide activities, and are coordinated by national peak organizations. Many of them maintain links with a political party and exercise pressure within that party, which reinforces the position of political parties in European politics. By far the largest pressure groups are the trade unions, which in most countries organize between one quarter and three quarters of all employees (see Table 6.2). Employers' associations (as business organizations are called in Europe) have an even higher density among corporations and individual businessmen.

The link between organized interests and political parties is a mutual one. Parties promote themselves as the "natural" representative of specific interests in parliament and the government. They even reserve seats in parliament for prominent interest group leaders (social democratic parties for trade unions leaders, Christian democrats for farmers and small business). With the notorious exception of trade union funds to support social democratic election campaigns, pressure groups as a rule do not contribute to the parties' election funds. For that reason, and due to the greater secrecy in private contributions to election funds, political action committees (PACs) are unknown in Europe.

The close contacts between the major interest groups and political parties reduce the role of publicity in competing for parliamentary or governmental attention, as well as the need of lobbying in the corridors of the parliament. Because of these contacts (and due to party discipline), there are no pressure group ratings or press listings of individual voting records in the parliament. If an organization wants a change in government policy or wants to focus attention on its members' misfortune, it will contact its representatives within its party first and they will discuss further tactics, like talking to the press or representatives of other parties. However, everything is done in conformity with the principle of "party allegiance comes first." In short, neither the government nor the parliament is an open market where all kinds of pressure groups compete for influence. Some pressure groups have preferential access to political parties and to the government, while others do not. An open market for influence with equal chances of a willing ear (at least in principle) is sometimes called "pluralism." However, that term is often also used in a wider sense, as synonymous with civil society. Proponents of a pluralist open market reject preferential treatment as a violation of pluralism, or even of democracy.

ONE OF EUROPE'S FAVORITES: BUSINESS-LABOR-GOVERNMENT TRIPARTISM

Employers (business) and trade unions are among the most privileged groups. In many countries, formal meetings are held between the national government, national employers associations, and trade union confederations at least once or twice a year. These tripartite contacts are called "corporatism" if they include frequent cooperative meetings.

Did we not meet that term before, as part of the Christian democratic ideology? Indeed, the term is derived from earlier Catholic ideas about trade union/employer cooperation in order to prevent increasing state power and reduce labor conflict. Fascist dictators in the 1930s (Italy and Portugal, not the German Nazis) forcibly imposed this kind of cooperation after first eliminating the social democratic or communist unions and creating state-controlled unions. Neglecting this negative overtone of the term corporatism, political scientists now use the term again as a neutral concept, because the countries in which this new form of corporatism prevails are stable democracies. The organizations involved in corporatism still do not like the term, because in their view, it continues to have the connotation of too much integration in the state and too much (forced) mutual cooperation. Even when they actively engage in "corporatist" contacts, business and trade union leaders underline the "non-corporatist" nature of their organizations.

In its new and democratic form, corporatism refers to the conscious involvement of a small, select number of national organizations in the formation of government policies. It implies a preferential treatment of a few organizations in national politics in order to guarantee the acceptance of these policies and to facilitate their implementation. The tripartite business/trade union/government contacts that constitute a necessary ingredient of corporatism developed following the economic crisis of the 1930s and World War II. They were motivated by the need to reconstruct the devastated nations in a common effort, not to be interrupted by major labor conflicts, and to secure trade union participation in social and economic state policies, as a compensation for union pledges of voluntary wage restraint.

Corporatism is based upon a tradition of multiemployer collective bargaining for industrial branches, economic sectors, or even nationwide. Collective bargaining has gradually created a sense of mutual trust among employers and unions, as well as a willingness to share responsibility for the national economy and social well being of the population. The attitude is expressed in the widely used term "social partners" for employers and unions.

Corporatism has developed mostly in the smaller Germanic nations (Scandinavia, the Low Countries, and the Alpine Countries). Its rise has been attributed to a combination of economic and political causes, including the small size and economic vulnerability of these nations, the numerical and organizational strength of their trade union movement, and the close relationship between the trade unions and the social democratic party. While economic vulnerability has stimulated the idea of a "common effort to survive," the nationwide force of the trade unions allowed them to impose restraint upon both affiliated and nonaffiliated workers. Corporatism emerged when social democrats entered government power. Social democratic participation in government encouraged the trade unions to refrain from action that would hinder economic and social policies, such as large strikes or too high wage demands. It also stimulated business to compromise with the unions, if only to prevent further reaching social democratic state policies. Once a tradition, corporatism easily survived changes in government composition, because it is also rooted in the orientation toward political consensus in these nations and in the opportunities for opposition groups to influence the government. Although European trade unionism is often set against American (nonpolitical) "business unionism," the participation of trade unions in corporatism actually means that they are more business-minded (toward national business, not separate companies) than U.S. trade unionism.

Corporatism takes different shapes. The Scandinavians prefer regular—up to weekly—tripartite contacts. The Low Countries and Austria have established special tripartite councils for these contacts, like the Social and Economic Council in Holland and the *Paritätische Kommission* (Joint Committee) in Austria. Hardly a week passes in which the trade union and employers' leaders do not meet with each other and government ministers in a formal meeting or in a more informal setting like conferences and receptions. Frequent contact does not mean total union-employer agreement. Unions are only willing to moderate wages if employers create jobs; employers want to confine tripartite talks to a small range of topics in order not to reduce enterprise flexibility; and governments are now under pressure of budget deficits. They are no longer able to facilitate compromise by means of additional funds for social security, employment policies, or tax deductions as a compensation for wage moderation. Despite these setbacks, several of the smaller corporatist countries have served as international models of domestic cooperation and successful social and economic policies.

Although corporatism may be at home in the smaller Germanic nations most of all, other European countries have also adopted elements of corporatism. Tripartite meetings and councils have been established throughout Western and Central Europe, but their success does not match that in the smaller Germanic nations. In the course of the 1990s, mounting unemployment has served as a motive to call special tripartite "employment conferences," which may result in formal "employment pacts" in a number of non-corporatist countries. In those talks, the trade unions promise to moderate wage claims and accept flexible forms of employment.

Employers promise to create more jobs and expand training facilities. The national government's main function is to facilitate compromise, preferably by offering tax facilities, training funds, and active employment policies, as well as to integrate the conference results in new legislation if the partners so wish. Table 6.1 reveals the problem of such pacts, like the participation in the negotiations of organizations that then refuse to sign.

Tripartite consultation is confined to the major federations and excludes minor organizations. It presupposes strong national federations. These peak organizations should be able to speak on behalf of their members and be capable of imposing wage and price restraint upon their member organizations and upon the rank and file. The "closed circuit" of selected organizations is generally regarded as the primary disadvantage of corporatism. Only a few organizations, not subject to much outside control, prepare and implement state-endorsed or even state-financed policies. This objection is not considered as very serious in the countries involved. Often, one or two national trade union confederations and employer's associations

Table 6.1. Some Examples of Tripartite Employment Conferences and Agreements

Country	Year	Subject	Comment
Bulgaria	1990	Reform Policies	One of the first tripartite pacts in Central Europe, before a tripartite council was set up.
Poland	1993	Reform Policies	Concluded at the time the independent trade union movement Solidarność dominated the government, but under pressure of actions by the Solidarność locals.
Czechia	1994	Wage Policies	The last in a series of annual pacts on reform policies; due to government disinterest no more pacts were concluded.
Portugal	1996	42 hours working week	The largest (communist) trade union confederation took part in the negotiations but refused to sign the agreement.
Italy	1997	35 hours working week	Under pressure of the communist party, which preferred legislation, the national government refused to sanction the agreement.
France	1997	35 hours working week	Right after the conference, the government imposed the 35 hours week by law, in spite of fierce employer resistance during the conference.
Ireland	1997	Developing Social Partnership	This "Partnership 2000" agreement provided for wage moderation, more overall social participation and less social exclusion. New for Western Europe was the participation of a number of social-aid organizations in this project.
Germany	1998	Unemployment	Exceptional effort in Germany, called *Bündnis für Arbeit* (Coalition for Employment), and the participants failed to reach agreement.

predominate, and in addition, it is the government that decides participation and exclusion. Table 6.2 shows the strength of the trade union movement in a number of countries.

Table 6.2. Trade Union Strength

Country Millions	*Density (%)*	*Largest confederations with members in millions*	*Comment*
Sweden 8.9	91	Social democratic 2.2 Social democratic 1.3	Highest trade union density in Europe, with one dominant general confederation and an office workers confederation.
Hungary 10.2	60	(Post)communist 1.0	Six new and smaller trade union organizations are also represented in the tripartite council.
Belgium 10.2	52	Catholic 1.4 Social democratic 1.1	The only country in which the Catholic trade union organization outnumbers the social democrats.
Italy 57.5	44	(Post)communist 5.0 Catholic 3.5 Social democratic 1.8	The three confederations cooperate especially at the local level. Large numbers of strike days, including political strikes and other actions.
Austria 8.1	41	Social democratic 1.6	Only one confederation. Very low number of strikes and no political strikes at all.
Poland 38.6	34	(Post)communist 1.0 Catholic 1.0	Catholic Solidarność has not been able to replace the former communist trade unions.
Great Britain 58.8	33	Social democratic 7.3	Highly decentralized trade unions, without real power for the national peak organization. Many short strikes but no political strikes.
Germany 81.9	29	Social democratic 9.8	The confederation is dominated by *IG Metall* (3 million members). Low number of strike days, no political strikes.
France 58.2	9	Radical social democratic .6 Communist .6 Social democratic .4	Europe's most divided trade union movement. Trade unions prefer mobilization of strikers to permanent membership. Frequent political strikes.

Density: Members as a percentage of all wage earners. (Post)communist means former communist and engaged in a process of ideological reorientation. U.S. trade union density stands at 14 percent.

Sources: ILO: World Labour Report 1997–98; most density figures for 1995.

The selection for tripartite talks between the government, employers, and unions may seem a foregone decision. In most countries, national trade union confederations are treated by the government as representatives of all workers, despite the fact that they only organize a minority of all workers. The government then artificially creates a power balance, in which one or a few nationwide organizations are allowed to represent a category of people, independent from their actual rate of representation, as expressed in trade union density. The idea is based upon the power balance in multiemployer collective bargaining. The protagonists of corporatism argue that the alternative to this power balance might not be a "pluralist" open market for influence, but a preferential treatment of big business, which has more facilities at its disposal for informal contacts with members of parliament and government officials. In their view, unequal treatment under corporatism actually provides more opportunities for equal business and labor influence than a pluralist open market would.

The impact of tripartism on government responsibility before the parliament is hardly felt as a disadvantage. The government takes on a lot of obligations that can only be prevented or stopped by dismissing the cabinet, and in this case, the government can always cancel the promises it has made. A more recent objection is that corporatism imposes clumsy procedures upon any changes in corporate strategy and affects flexibility. Time is spent on talking about change instead of introducing change. National employers' federations sometimes use this argument as a motive to decrease the contacts.

Advantages of corporatism are the enhancement of political legitimacy (the general acceptance of government and its policies) and political effectiveness, because state policies can count on the support of the major organizations that are involved or affected. Corporatism also contributes to political stability. In the countries involved, it is not regarded as a political activity, but as an effort to remove social and economic policies from the sphere of politics—as a form of depoliticization.

A different approach to integrate trade unions and employers associations is to appoint their leaders as ministers in the national government. In cabinets dominated by social democrats, ministers of social affairs are often recruited among trade union leaders. In liberal or conservative governments, ministers of economic affairs come from business ranks.

FROM DOCTORS TO STUDENTS: OTHER PRESSURE GROUPS

Doctors on strike? Yes, in Europe doctors may go on strike. Sometimes, even students may go on strike, but with fewer results.

Corporatism implies frequent contact between the national government and the major organizations that are active in "the field." It is the strongest form of government/pressure group contact. In a weaker form, such contacts are a common phenomenon throughout Europe in almost all policy fields. Organizations engage in regular and sometimes also formal contacts with governments in order to influence state policies, while governments seek contacts with "the field" in order to enhance political legitimacy and secure the implementation of policies. The establishment of such formal contacts often leads to the emergence of "networks" of politicians, government officials, civil servants, and leaders of pressure groups. Such "networking," as it is called, does not necessarily mean closed circuits, in which there is hardly room for newcomers. Networks need not even be permanent, as is the case in corporatism, but may change with the nature of issues at hand, and in addition, ad-hoc "issue-networks" may be formed. Most networking is something in between corporatism with its strong and formal links between government and organizations, and lobbying. In contrast to lobbying, it still involves some kind of official government recognition (and selection) of specific organizations as representatives of "the field." In Europe, networking is more valued than lobbying mainly because of this greater amount of government initiative in selecting the organizations with which it wants to talk.

While corporatism in social and economic policy is most developed in Germanic Europe, networking is widespread throughout Western and Central Europe. It is most developed in agriculture, health care, and even in education. In agriculture, farmers' organizations, agricultural workers, and the food industry all play a role. In health care, national medical associations, coordinating bodies of hospitals, and public and private insurance companies are involved. In education, peak organizations of the schools and universities, teachers' organizations, and even the student movements participate. In France, agricultural networking almost amounts to corporatism, and this is one of the few fields in which corporatism functions in that country. However, frequent actions by French peasants—destroying truckloads of Spanish fruit or British meat imports that undermine their own marketing opportunities—show that it is not generally accepted.

More than in social and economic policy, the background of networking (or even corporatism) in these policy fields is the fact that there never has been an open market for the supply and demand of products and services. Either the national government exercises a strong degree of control, as in health care, or the European Union does, as in agriculture. If a kind of power balance has been achieved between the organizations involved, and at least a minimum degree of mutual trust, national government may even try to leave some of the decisions and their implementation to these organizations. In that case, networking resembles corporatism, with similar advantages (de-politicization) and disadvantages (closed circuits). Like America's American Medical Association (AMA), medical associations would probably be even more powerful if the government did not construct an artificial power balance by supporting or even imposing public or private health insurance and by having the insurance companies act as a counterbalance during tripartite sessions. By way of exception, doctors may even go on strike, refusing to comply with the outcome of such corporatist talks or with changes in their state-regulated pay rates.

Due to the importance of national education for national unity and for imposing specific values and norms, corporatism in education is limited. Governments are more reluctant to leave education to a representative forum than social and economic policies. In Catholic countries, educational policy has implied a confrontation with what is probably the single most important pressure organization next to trade unions and employers: the Catholic Church. By way of contrast to corporatism, which implies strong networks and serves the de-politicization of political issues, Catholic Church political activities are often displayed outside formal networks and easily result in polarization between pros and cons. This polarization is partly due to the nature of issues on which the Catholic Church speaks out. In addition to education, it is concerned with ethical and family questions, and even more with sexual attitudes and sexual behavior, which is its favorite field of expertise. However, its preaching in this field has less and less effect. The Protestant and Orthodox Churches have been far more modest in aspiring for such an ethical watchdog role in society and politics.

Since the 1960s, a new kind of pressure group has made its appearance. The 1968 student revolt and youth protests targeting the Vietnam War triggered the rise of radical protest movements—labeled "new social movements"—as opposed to traditional social movements, like the trade unions. In contrast to the traditional pressure groups, the new social movements at first rejected formal organization and preferred to continue as a flexible movement without old-fashioned hierarchy and bureaucracy. Many also refused any form of integration in formal networks, since that would amount to "manipulation" by the state.

Lasting examples of these new social movements are the feminists, the gays and lesbians, the environmentalists, and small so-called autonomous trade unions. The environmentalist movement emerged out of the antinuclear energy movement. It started with attacks on nuclear sites and sit-down actions aimed at preventing the dumping of nuclear waste. Some of the actions led to violent clashes with large police forces. Other movements have not survived, like the peace movement, which succumbed with the end of the cold war. A form of spontaneous protest that has dwindled is occupying empty houses in the larger cities as a means of protest against (and to solve) housing shortages. Only in Berlin do such radical protesters (*Autonomen*) still form a sizable movement, sometimes engaging in violent clashes with the police.

The new social movements have had some impact on European politics. They have reduced the domination of closed circuits and changed pressure politics in the direction of more open networks or even of a pluralist open market in which smaller organizations and more radical movements are heard, too. Well-established pressure groups have taken more distance to political parties and have stressed the relationship with their "base" instead, a partial shift from elite politics to the grassroots. Some trade unions have even given up "their" seats in parliament as part of social democratic fractions. This more open and more pluralist competition for influence has also changed the social movements that continue to exist. They have abandoned mass actions and have accepted integration in consultation networks, which by now are much less formal than before, due to the new social movements. The change to a more open television coverage of national politics has also stimulated this shift toward more open politics. Organizations and movements that feel neglected in formal consultation increasingly turn to television channels to express their grievance, to the dismay of the more established pressure groups, which advocate restraint in that respect.

THE COMMERCIAL REVOLUTION: THE MASS MEDIA

At the burial of former French President François Mitterand in 1996, his illegitimate daughter, whose existence had been a secret until then, showed up. In reality, it was a public secret, since the French press knew that Mitterand had such a child but did not write about it. German Chancellor's Helmut Kohl's longtime *affair* with his secretary was another public secret that was hardly ever written about. While in Great Britain such love affairs with or without consequences would have made great headlines, on the European continent they are not blown up too much. The advantage of the continental attitude is that prominent politicians have a private life, too. For that reason all leading politicians expressed their sympathy with U.S. President Clinton during his Lewinsky affair. A disadvantage is that corruption scandals including sex are not easily revealed either. In 1998, a woman published a book on her affair with the former French Secretary of State, who still held the post of chairman of the Constitutional Court. She had been paid by a foreign company to "stimulate" him to buy armament. Was this still a private sex affair or was it corruption? While the French did not know, in most other countries this would have been regarded as a (potential) form of corruption. In Great Britain, similar cases became public scandals and resulted in the resignation of the minister involved. In France it takes more to resign.

Only in Great Britain, and to some extent in Germany, a "tabloid" press exists that hardly pays any attention to political and social developments and highlights personal human features and crimes. In Great Britain, it focuses on royalty (front page) and sex (the famous "page 3"), and preferably a combination of both. (They have been lucky these days.) On the continent (as in the United States) Lady Di was more of a topic in weeklies specializing in royalty and television stars than in daily newspapers. However, the tabloids' focus pays. The most unscrupulous British tabloid papers have the widest circulation of all European newspapers. (*The Sun* and the *Daily Mirror* taken together have a circulation of over six million copies, more than the total European quality press taken together.) They are very conservative, and Tony Blair's success in getting some of them on his side during his 1997 election campaign was a big surprise.

In contrast to the British tabloid press, the continental press has always made a strict separation between critically following politicians and following policies. Scandals in royal families or involving leading politicians have mostly passed without notice as private affairs, which a responsible press does not write about. The reluctance to write about personal scandals has to do with the fact that parties rather than individuals count in continental politics. It is also motivated by the fact that until the 1970s, political leaders were regarded and treated as men of authority, addressed with "Your Excellency," and interviewed only by leading journalists in a humble way with a list of proper questions. Since that time the reluctance has decreased, but newspapers still try to maintain a low profile in these personal matters. Moreover, particularly in Latin countries, a minister having a mistress is no news, only a minister without is. The main political functions of the press then, are to write about living and social conditions, to promote public discussion, to explain state policies, and occasionally to unravel a case of corruption.

Most European nations possess a nationwide press, consisting of one or two leading quality newspapers, like *The Times* and *The Guardian* in Great Britain, *Le Monde* in France, *El País* in Spain, and of a number of more popular national newspapers. In most countries, these popular newspapers devote most of their attention to national and international political, social, and economic matters. The quality press and the more popular national press often represent a variety of ideologies, but they are independent from parties of pressure groups. A "party press" consisting of papers strongly linked to political parties—or even published by parties—existed until the 1960s, but these newspapers either succumbed or became more independent, with the exception of a few remaining communist newspapers.

All continental countries, including the smaller ones, also possess a wide network of regional newspapers, some of which enjoy a local monopoly position. Almost all the regional newspapers have a conservative or conservative-liberal outlook.

As is the case in the United States, a free press has been one of the pillars of European democracy. Governments do not attempt to monitor the press, except in Central and Eastern Europe under communism. That situation contrasts with television and radio channels. For a long time European television stations used to be either public or state-sponsored private organizations. The British Broadcasting Corporation (BBC) was by far the most independent one. On the continent, the government monitored the public channels in a stricter way and the ruling parties always took care to nominate their own people for leading functions. In many nations, state control still exists, but its impact on television is now limited. The spread of commercial television stations has completely changed the media landscape in Europe. In most countries, people can choose from a series of such stations, in addition to the few public channels. The commercial stations are more popular, however, because of their soaps, soccer matches, and the combination of Oprah, Ricki, and Jerry, who are on the screen throughout Europe. In most countries, cable television now also offers the opportunity to look at a number of foreign stations, including Cable News Network (CNN) and the BBC, whose news coverage and political debate are internationally appreciated. With the occasional exception of a soccer match on a foreign station, when many people watch, most foreign stations are mainly popular among intellectuals.

The spread of international commercial broadcasting networks—for which Luxembourg is a popular seat due to its early tolerance of commercial television—has contributed to the "Americanization" of political programs, focusing on people rather than parties or ideologies. Increasingly, politicians are also invited as guests in popular programs like quizzes and live shows. Increased attention to the "human feature" in politics has reduced the traditional efforts to keep silent about personal scandals; they might be disclosed by CNN anyway. Gradually European politicians have adjusted and have come to learn and appreciate the right way to behave in front of the camera.

Increasingly, commercial mass media have become a political issue by themselves, since in some countries they are highly concentrated in a few hands, which is regarded as a threat to the free flow of information. This concentration used to be a problem with regard to the national press and regional newspapers, but commercial television has made it even more acute. The worst example has been Italy, where media-tycoon Silvio Berlusconi has used his media position to promote his role in national politics, and vice versa. At present, government influence in television channels is waning, due to the penetration of national markets by commercial television stations and by foreign channels. This decline does not apply to most of Central Europe and all of Eastern Europe, where national governments continue to control television networks and impose a preferential treatment of government over the opposition.

REGIONAL VARIATIONS IN CIVIL SOCIETY

Pressure politics and in the nature of civil society show great variations throughout Europe. Great Britain is closest to the United States. Corporatism, national consultation, compliance with tripartite agreements, and even formal networking run counter to the preference of a pluralist open market for influence and the appreciation of rank and file initiative in voluntary organizations, including the trade unions. In short, corporatism and networking are not regarded as being very democratic, and are more or less absent. Most organizations try to serve themselves, without state support or state funds. Of all European nations, Great Britain is most attached to "self-help." The trade unions share this preference and hardly ever request labor legislation, and as a consequence, political strikes are rare. Prominent exceptions have been long miners' strikes against mine closures. Pressure groups linked with the party in power exercise influence; the others wait their turn or compete on the pluralist open market for influence. Mass media have also enjoyed more freedom than on the continent.

In Germanic Europe, Civil Society consists of nationwide organizations that are to some extent backed by the state. Conflict is reduced by the integration of important organizations in corporatist institutions or meetings. Corporatism in the smaller nations has a profound base in multiemployer bargaining, in which the number of participating organizations is limited and the degree of compliance with the outcome is high. Conflict between labor and government in the form of political strikes is rare. In several countries, there has not been a single political strike since World War II (see also Table 6.2). The absence of political strikes applies also to Germany, where corporatism is less developed. Collective bargaining is regionally decentralized in Germany and the national umbrella organizations have less power, which makes it harder for them to conclude binding agreements with the government. Moreover, sheer size ensures Germany and the other large European countries a stronger position on the world market and reduces the need for corporatism.

In mass media, the public channels in Germanic Europe have often been linked to more than one political party or civil organization, or they have been formally independent. The state has remained at arm's length, except for financial control.

In Latin Europe, Civil Society is more state-oriented. Employers' associations and trade unions prefer to deal with the national government rather than with each other: Even cooperation within the ideologically split trade union movement— between the various national confederations—has often been difficult. The corporatist de-politicization of issues is possible only in a few policy sectors. In social and economic issues, governments must reckon with hard confrontations with unions and/or business. Political strikes against government policies occur frequently and are considered by the organizing unions as "victories of the working class," at least if enough participants show up. The festive nature of these actions is shown by the fact that they are also called to celebrate the start of labor-friendly governments. Tripartite councils have been short-lived or inactive for long periods. The organizations do not want to tie their hands, since they like to be free to use any opportunity to trip up each other or the national government. Occasional tripartite conferences have been more successful.

In Latin Europe, the state has often exercised more direct control over public broadcasting agencies, for instance by means of politically motivated nominations. Especially during the Fifth Republic, French public television used to bias its news in favor of the president.

In Central Europe, Civil Society is still in the making after forty years of communist rule. Under communism, autonomous organizations did not exist, with the exception of Hungary and Poland. In Hungary, the communist power monopoly was gradually relaxed during the 1970s and 1980s. Independent local trade unions emerged and even some independent candidates made their entry into the communist-dominated parliament. As a consequence, the Hungarian transition process to democratic Civil Society has been a more gradual one than in other Central European nations. In Poland, the Catholic Church regularly spoke out on political issues, and in 1980 Solidarność emerged as the first independent nationwide trade union in Central Europe.

In the Central European command-economies, business organizations did not exist, except for small enterprise that was in private hands. Trade unions functioned as "transmission belts" of the communist parties, transmitting party orders to the workers and ensuring worker compliance with communist priorities. In most of Central Europe the communist trade unions have transformed themselves into more democratic organizations. Newly arisen so called "new" unions, like Solidarność in Poland challenge these transformed "old" unions, but in most nations the old unions continue to dominate trade unionism. In some cases, they have even been able to retain all trade union assets, including holiday resorts. Under communism, these holiday and other provisions, for instance housing, motivated many workers to join the unions, sometimes resulting in trade union densities of over ninety percent, to drop rapidly during the 1990s. (See Table 6.2) In other countries the assets have been divided among old and new unions.

One of the problems in the Central European process of creating a Civil Society is that it is done more from above by former party leaders, than from below, by "real" private initiative. Since most Central European governments are coalitions, the trend in Civil Society is probably one toward networking and corporatism, however, rather than to pluralism British style. A number of countries are now experimenting with tripartite councils or regular tripartite meetings. One of the more successful examples is the Hungarian "National Reconciliation Council," which has served for ten years, although under different names. Despite the large number of organizations represented (seven at either side), it has played an active role in advice on labor bills, and in preventing and solving labor conflicts. A main problem in Central European corporatism is the weak development of business associations. The privatization of enterprise has just begun and many large enterprises are still in state hands. Private enterprise is mainly small enterprise, which is difficult to organize. Outside social and economic policies, networking is still limited.

In most of Central Europe, the state monopoly of mass media has been continued to some extent, particularly in television stations, which are still monitored by the national government. Since the end of communism, this state control is no longer undisputed. In 1998, the Bulgarian state television decided to stop a popular satirical program as a presumed danger to political stability, but the announcement motivated street fighting between protagonists and opponents. The countries that are oriented most toward Western Europe, like Czechia, Hungary, Poland, and Slovenia also enjoy more freedom in this respect.

In Eastern Europe, communist rule has lasted seventy years—far longer than in Central Europe. The national governments continue to monopolize power in most aspects of social life and Civil Society is still in its infant stage. Just as competing political parties are missing, hardly any independent interest organizations exist. The communist unions have almost disappeared from the scene, and business associations have still to arise. Once in a while, spontaneous strike committees, for instance in Russian coal mining, evolve into a kind of temporary trade union movement but most of them are short-lived. In this part of Europe the state controls most of the mass media. State domination of Russian television stations is shown by President Yeltsin's decision to cancel all programs during his clash with parliament in 1993. By doing so, he was able to prevent a television broadcast of a speech by his main opponent.

LOCAL GOVERNMENT AND POLITICS

Only some European political leaders were active in local politics before becoming national politicians, notably French President Jacques Chirac, who was mayor of Paris, and Russian President Boris Yeltsin, who was mayor of Moscow. Even more exceptional is a shift from regional politics to national politics. This kind of promotion is almost totally confined to Germany, a federal republic. Like U.S. Presidents Clinton, Reagan, and Carter, Chancellor Gerhard Schröder was state governor (of Lower Saxony), while his predecessor Helmut Kohl had been state governor of Rhenania-Palatine. Helmut Kohl's three previous social democratic contestants were also state governors.

Most national political leaders in Europe already had a job in a nationwide organization before becoming party leader or assuming office as prime minister, for instance, in their party or a national pressure group. Their career patterns are in accordance with the prominence of the different levels of politics in Europe. Local politics is not very important, and regional politics even less, except in federal nations like Germany and Switzerland. In combination with the smaller number of voluntary associations, this weakness of local and regional politics and government reflects the predominance of national politics in Europe, when compared to the United States. Local politics is also less of a discussion topic: Politics in Europe is national politics.

Europeans do not elect their sheriffs. That office should, in their view, not be a political one, since it might easily become a source of friction between the various ideological groups. Police officers should not be responsible to the voters but to local government, and local government to national government. This reluctance to elect local officers is only one of the examples of the lower degree of local autonomy (and grass-roots democracy) in Europe, compared to the United States. However, all nations possess some form of local government. Local autonomy dates back to the Middle Ages when autonomous towns enforced "town rights" from feudal overlords or kings. The document in which such town rights were granted is now often the pride of the local museum. Absolutism and the rise of the nation-state affected this position, but local decision making did not disappear completely. Since the nineteenth century, a certain amount of local autonomy is laid down in many constitutions (see Table 6.3).

The degree of local autonomy varies greatly among the European nations and there is no direct relation between country size and degree of local or regional autonomy. Some of the smaller nations are federal systems, like Austria and Switzerland, while some of the larger nations, like Great Britain and France, are relatively centralized. Despite the variation in degree of local and regional autonomy, some uniformity exists in the tasks local communities perform. Typical local activities include the administration of public utilities like water, electricity, gas supply, subsidized housing, building permits, local roads, cultural facilities like libraries, theaters, and museums, primary education, and social assistance. In order to perform these tasks, local government relies both on its own financial sources and on national leverage. Local financial resources consist of local taxes

Table 6.3. Regional and Local Units

Country Millions	Regional government	Local government	Comments
Russia 147.0	a) 21 autonomous republics b) 10 autonomous *okrugi* 50 *oblasti*; 6 *kray* 2 *goroda* (cities)	Five different types of local units, over 30,000 in total.	Just as under communism, this is a federal system, with 21 republics. In the complex system of regional government, the autonomy of the regional units varies a lot, sometimes even more within than among the different categories. The two special-status cities are St. Petersburg and Moscow.
Germany 81.9	a) 16 federal *Länder* b) 426 *Kreise* and 117 *kreisfreie Städte* (cities)	16,043 *Gemeinden*	Federal nation since 1948. The 117 larger towns and cities have a kind of regional-unit status. Local autonomy varies among the 16 federal *Länder*.
France 58.2	a) 22 *régions;* b) 96 *départements*	36,763 *communes*	Centralized nation. The regions do not have any general competencies
Italy 57.5	a) 20 *regioni,* b) 94 *provincie*	8,074 *communi*	Five regions enjoy a special status, with almost as much autonomy as in federal systems.
Poland 38.6	49 *wojewodztwa*	2,483 *gminy* 39,277 *solectwa*	The number of *wojewodztwa* will be reduced to 14, and new regions (*powiaty*) introduced. *Gminy* are urban districts, *solectwa* rural districts.
Holland 15.5	12 *provincies*	636 *gemeenten*	The number of local units has steadily decreased over the last twenty years.
Hungary 10.2	19 *megyek* 22 *megyei varos* (towns) *fovaros* (capital city)	195 towns 2,913 villages	As in Germany, many towns have regional-unit status. The capital Budapest enjoys special status.
Slovenia 2.0	No regional units	180 *obshini*	The introduction of regional units is planned.

Column 2: a) highest regional authority; b) lower regional authority. All numbers refer to the late 1990s.

and user payments for local services. In contrast to the United States, property taxes are not very popular in Europe. Most local taxes are based on income or enterprise profit; sometimes they consist of an additional levy on top of national income taxes. These local tax resources only cover a small portion of total local community expenditure. Most local funds are provided by the national government by means of unspecified grants or earmarked funds (categorical subsidies for specific projects and activities). There is no clear relation, however, between dependence on state funds and local autonomy. Even in countries where communities are financed almost totally by the national government, a considerable degree of autonomy may be enjoyed because countries may prefer a comprehensive national tax system for reasons of efficiency or control.

In Western Europe, local government functions have gradually expanded during the last decades. During the 1960s and 1970s, this increase in number of local tasks had to do with the expansion of the welfare state. In the course of the 1980s and 1990s, decentralization has become a popular means for national governments to reduce the state deficit. They shifted state services to local authorities without a corresponding transfer of funds. Moreover, decentralization was often accompanied by an expansion of government rules on local government competencies. The consequence has not been greater local autonomy, but a form of mutual dependence of local and national government. Tension has arisen between the two, because the communities are confronted with an expansion of their tasks without a proportional rise in funds. The communities have sought a solution in the form of a rise of user payments for local public services.

In most countries, larger urban centers enjoy special status, with more autonomy than villages and small towns. Within big cities, neighborhood councils have come to gain some popularity as a means to increase grass root initiative and control.

Decentralization has also expanded the functions of regional units. In the larger countries, regional units include a layer of large regions and a layer of smaller provinces or counties. This combination amounts to a four-tiered structure: national, regional, provincial, and local. The smaller countries posses only one regional layer in the form of provinces, and the structure of these nations is a three-tiered one: national, regional, and local. Only the smallest nations, like Iceland, Luxembourg, and Slovenia do without any regional units and have a direct relation between national and local government. In Slovenia there is an ongoing debate about the possible introduction of regional units (see Table 6.3).

The functions of the regional units overlap with those of the local government and include larger-scale, state-supervised services like regional planning and infrastructural works, secondary education, and health care. The regional units also often monitor local government.

The way in which local and regional democracy function is similar to national politics. In Great Britain, one party dominates the elected local council. On the continent, several parties make up the local and regional councils, and they often form coalitions. The mayor is either elected by direct local vote or by the council.

Europe shows great variations in community size and local politics. In Germanic Europe, most local units have well over 10,000 inhabitants. Smaller communities were merged in the course of the 1970s in order to improve management of the increasing number of welfare state services and utilities. An example of this extension of scale was the reduction of the number of Swedish municipalities by several thousand. In Germanic Europe, the post of mayor is often more an administrative than a political one.

In Latin Europe, the average community size is still under 10,000, and more than in Germanic Europe the mayor is a political figure. This stronger political nature (politicization) of local government is one of the reasons that local communities in Latin Europe were not merged during the 1970s. Any attempt in that direction met with loud local opposition, with the mayor himself conducting the protest choir. This more pronounced political nature of local government does not imply more local autonomy. Actually, the small size of the localities in Latin Europe reduces their autonomy when compared to Germanic Europe. Latin mayors may also play a role in national politics, for instance, when they combine their post with a seat in the parliament. In contrast to the "normal" career pattern of national political leaders, many French politicians are town mayor and member of Parliament at the same time. This *cumul* (accumulation) *de mandates* has been very frequent in France and has given the communities a voice in national politics. On the other hand, France has always been a highly centralized state, in which state supervision over local government is exercised by the prefects of the 96 *départements*. Since the early 1980s, the country has joined the general decentralization movement. The prefect (head of the *département*) is no longer the chairman of the regional council, but merely a kind of state commissioner with reduced powers.

Great Britain and Ireland have by far the largest local communities, with an average size several times those in Germanic Europe. Whereas on the continent, national governments imposed cuts in local budgets by shifting tasks to that level without additional funds, the conservative British governments of the 1980s and early 1990s did it the other way. They considerably reduced the range of local services and imposed stricter political and financial control—an attack that was aimed specifically at Labour-dominated local councils. The conservatives also tried to change from property tax to a flat-rate individual "poll-tax." The lack of fairness in the new system aroused a storm of protests, and after some years the government gave in and returned to the former system of property tax, but the new "council-tax" retained some elements of the individual poll tax.

In Central and Eastern Europe, local and regional autonomy used to be very limited under communism. In the last ten years, new forms of local government have been introduced without a uniform pattern. In some countries, reforms have consisted of a merger of local and regional units; in others, such units have been split up. Russia has the most complex system of regional units. It has made a great step toward more regional autonomy by a transfer of power from Moscow to the regions, and the direct election of the regional governors. The reforms have offered the communist opposition the opportunity to block reformist policies in the regions they dominate. Increasing regional autonomy in Russia is also due to the lack of central decision-making power. In order to compensate for that absence, the national government has concluded a series of bilateral "power-sharing agreements" with the most important regional units. The agreements especially deal with fiscal facilities.

FEDERALISM

Until World War II, federalism was exceptional in Europe. Throughout European history there existed a number of federations and confederations, like various confederations of German states. The process of nation building and the long tradition of absolute royal power in some countries did away with regional autonomy. The only long-standing example of federalism is Switzerland, the oldest federal nation in the world. Since World War II, federalism has gained some popularity, partly under U.S. influence. Germany and Austria adopted a federal political structure; later Belgium and, to some extent, Spain followed. As the examples show, federalism has not been confined to larger nations, but also exists in a couple of small nations. While the German federal *Länder* on the average have about the same number of inhabitants as U.S. states—around five million people—the average size of the Swiss cantons is only 250,000 people. Interestingly, Germany includes three "city-states," in the form of *Länder*, which consist of one city only: Berlin, Bremen (actually two cities), and Hamburg.

In contrast to Switzerland and the United States, all the postwar federal systems have been federalized from above, rather than as a "bottom up" initiative of the participating units. German federalism was introduced to serve a number of purposes. It aimed at reducing the fear of a strong German state in the surrounding countries, preventing a new dictatorial takeover of the whole state (as happened when the Nazis seized power), and providing more opportunities for democratic "grass-root" initiatives. The borders between the sixteen German *Länder* follow historical frontiers but the formerly dominant state of Prussia, throughout the ages the core of the German Empire, has been split up (and part of it is Polish territory by now). The *Länder* enjoy great autonomy, which extends to education and the nature of local politics. Since the 1970s, Belgium has gradually adopted a federal structure and split the country into three regions, Dutch-speaking Flanders, French-speaking Wallony, and the bilingual capital Brussels. In all these federal systems, the national Senate (the upper house of Parliament) represents the constituent political units, as in the *Bundesrat*. (The Germans do not call that institution a Senate, because that term refers to the city-governments of the three city *Länder*, including the *Berliner Senat*.)

Unlike federalism, a number of nations grant special rights to distinct regions, because of their minority culture. This form of regional autonomy has often been established by a powerful country after it had conquered or acquired neighboring states or regions, such as Scotland (Great Britain) and South Tirol (Italy). The most prominent example of this type of regional autonomy is Russia. European Russia, officially named Russian Federation, contains twenty-one autonomous republics, most of them located on the edges of the country like the Caucasian region (including rebellious Chechenia) and one on the Finnish border (Karelia). Almost all these republics have less than one million inhabitants each, compared to over one hundred million in Russia properly speaking, the real center of power in this "federal" country. However, due to the growing power of the normal provinces (*oblasti*), the country has increasingly become a truly federalized country, with a lot of autonomy for the various types of regional units. The Commonwealth of Independent States (CIS), in which most independent states that sprang off the Soviet Union voluntarily cooperate, bears some similarities to this system, although it is more loosely structured and the participating states have the formal right to leave. Like the former Soviet Union, CIS is heavily dominated by Russia (the Russian Federation), by far the largest member state.

In these forms of regional autonomy, the borders between the participating units coincide with language borders or other lines of division. As the fragile new Bosnian nation shows, such a split up along major lines of social division may increase rather than reduce tension, especially in case the participating units compete for power. In Germany, this potential conflict between the *Länder* is a minor problem—to the relief of the neighboring countries. By far the most populous of the sixteen states in Germany is Rhenania-Westfalia (with nineteen million inhabitants it is larger than any of the smaller European nations). Not only does it contain the largest concentration of industry in Europe, the Ruhr Area, but also a sizable nonindustrial population, and Protestants as well as Catholics. This living together of various groups within each state (crosscutting cleavages!) is typical of U.S.-inspired federalism. It allows the growth of mutual understanding among various religious (and language) groups within each state. The resulting sense of community reduces the amount of mutual conflict. In multilingual Switzerland, almost all cantons are single-language units, but conflict is prevented by the existence of religious crosscutting cleavages. Protestant German-speakers make up its majority but the country also includes Catholic German-speaking cantons, as well as Protestant and Catholic French-speaking cantons.

The latest example of a federalist development, Spain, is gradually moving from regional autonomy for minorities to a full-fledged federal system. It has granted more autonomy to the three language minorities, Catalonia (the largest language minority in Europe), Basque country, and Galicia than to the other regions. Most of these *comunidades* speak Castilian (Spanish), but a few have developed or rediscovered regional languages since that time. That differentiation of regional tongues decreases the impact of language as a highly contentious line of division.

The development of the European Union and the consequent weakening of national boundaries, as well as its focus on regional policies, have contributed to a growing regional consciousness of minority groups. This interest in minority culture has increased the popularity of federal structures. Even more than in Western Europe, the countries of Central and Eastern Europe, with their many minority languages, may constitute a breeding ground of federalism, although the first attempt in Bosnia has not been very successful so far. Some protagonists of European unification regard the European Union as the definite federal system in Europe, a multinational unity of a large number of ethnic groups, which live together in peace under some kind of federal authority. Opponents of the European Union see this European federalism as a danger to national independence and try to stop it by all means.

7

Public Policy in Europe

For a couple of years, Holland has come to serve as the latest model of social and economic policies. The Dutch Model or "Polder Model" combines relatively smooth policy-making procedures, including corporatist agreements, with a high level of state expenditure for social policies, but also with a strong devotion to make the national economy more competitive by increasing labor flexibility. The combination of policy making and policy content is called "policy style." In the Dutch consensus-based and integration-oriented policy style (which is common to most of the smaller Germanic nations), the national government has been pivotal in arriving at union-employer compromise. The unions have moderated their wage claims and given up their resistance to job flexibility in the form of part-time jobs. Employers have consented in more extensive labor protection of flexible jobs and in an expansion of training facilities. The national government has shifted toward more active employment policies and implemented cuts in social security spending. The results of this tripartite consensus building have been a reduction of unemployment to four percent in 1998, far below the European Union's eleven percent unemployment rate, and a steep increase in the number of flexible (part-time and temporary) jobs. However, critics can point to the fact that almost all flexible jobs are occupied by female employees and that the Dutch performance was reached after a long period in which women were in actively banned from the labor market—until they were needed to fill the flexible jobs.

POLICY STYLES IN EUROPE

Policy making in Europe requires a lot of deliberation and even negotiating. Unlike federal policy making in the United States, these processes do not primarily take place between the executive branch and the parliament (especially in the case of a hostile majority in Congress) or among congressmen (in the case of logrolling). Policy making negotiations in Europe take place first of all within coalition cabinets, and in corporatist countries also between the cabinet, employers' associations, trade unions, or other prominent pressure groups. Once the cabinet has taken a decision, and business and trade unions have not raised too serious objections, there is not much room for a lot of amendments that especially serve local constituencies of the members of parliament, let alone for logrolling.

Within this overall pattern, policy styles in Europe reveal a great deal of variation. The divergences are related to differential paths toward democracy, which was a course of gradual reform in some nations and one of great and revolutionary upheaval in others. The composition of the political spectrum and the nature of the party system also influence policy styles. It makes quite a difference whether most big parties favor a gradual or a revolutionary course, and if one or two major parties exist that are located close to the center of the political spectrum. The nature of civil society is yet another determinant of the way policies are made. In corporatist nations, governments need to build in some latitude of compromise in their proposals, in other countries they enjoy more freedom to decide by themselves. The variations in political history and political system lead to pronounced variations in policy making, in particular between the three parts of Western Europe: the Germanic nations, the Latin countries, and Great Britain.

All smaller Germanic nations share a tradition of gradual and often relatively uncontested political and economic reform, and of smooth adaptation to changes in international political and economic conditions. This reformism has a long history. Most of the smaller Germanic nations already followed a gradual course toward the introduction of parliamentary democracy. The main interruptions of political life, forcing social and political changes, have been the two world wars and revolutions elsewhere. The prevalence of large social democratic parties, and in some nations big Christian democratic parties that maintain links with the labor movement, has fostered a policy style of gradual reform. The type of civil society, with corporatism as one of its main ingredients, has contributed to a policy style of small steps. Although gradualism does not exclude radical changes in policy, changes do not take place overnight. They are the result of a number of small steps.

Due to the prior consultation of employers' associations and trade unions, most social legislation is not very disputed under the corporatist system of mutual consultation. Bills that meet with a hostile reaction of the "labor market parties" or "social partners" are adapted or even withdrawn. Moreover, labor legislation mainly sanctions what has been negotiated before between trade unions and employers, and it often confirms and extends what has already become current practice in a number of firms or sectors. In this system of "bargaining before legislation" labor protection is a matter of politics only as a second resort. Government policies in this area are adaptive rather than innovative. An exceptional policy area in which legislation has sometimes been used to force a breakthrough is employee participation in enterprise decision making. At times, this subject constitutes a hotly debated issue, which prohibits business/trade union compromise.

Germany has also become used to a policy style of gradual reform. Before World War II and under the Nazis, the country often implemented radical ("final") solutions to economic and social problems, but since then even the term radical by itself has gotten a bad meaning. The German hostility toward any form of extremism has been motivated by the horrifying examples of the Nazi period and the postwar communist domination of East Germany. The millions of immigrants who were expelled from Poland and Czechoslovakia after the war, who blamed communism rather than Nazism for their fate, reinforced the trend toward moderate conservative policies that abhor radical solutions. The position of the Christian democrats near the center of the political spectrum has also contributed to this new gradual reform. However, German policies still refer to grand theories and all-encompassing schemes to a greater extent than in the rest of Western Europe.

Policy making in Latin Europe is intended to implement new ventures in social and economic life and consequently it is also more contentious. The Latin European countries had in common a less gradual course toward democracy. France is the only long-standing democracy; in the other states democracy was introduced later and interrupted by fascist dictatorships. The distance between left and right has been greater than in Germanic Europe, with communist-dominated labor movements opposing conservative parties that have long dominated the national government. Corporatism is also less at home in this part of Europe because of the more adversarial, if not overtly hostile, relationship between business and the trade unions. Moreover, in France, the sovereignty of the State over social and economic issues is more of a principle than in other countries, and corporatism is rejected as an infringement upon that sovereignty. Trade unions and employers regularly call in the state to support their conflicting positions, and social measures have often been introduced under the pressure of political strikes and trade union demonstrations or during long trade union/employer stalemates. The absence of more permanent corporatist consultation and compromise imposes fewer limits to government initiative than in Germanic Europe. Consequently, labor legislation and social policies may sometimes be more of a break with the past. However, since labor legislation is often passed under the threat of trade union action and in face of strong employer opposition, it sometimes seriously strains political life, and worse still, it is hardly observed by employers. They consider such measures as a form of state indulgence under illegitimate trade union pressure. Of course, employer noncompliance calls forth new union actions to pressure for state intervention (see also Table 6.1).

Rather than standing organizations that impose organizational discipline, spontaneous individual and collective political action is highly appreciated in Latin Europe. At times such *action directe*, as it is called in France, may "provide the spark" (a typical anarchist expression) for nationwide political action, in the form of a local or national strike or some other protest manifestation. Especially in France, political organizations are preferably called *mouvement* or *front*, to stress their dynamic nature. The result of this prevalence of weak nationwide organizations and a strong sense of collective action is a political process in which periods of great innovation under the pressure of collective action interchange with long intervals of immobility.

As the difference between the Germanic and the Latin pattern of preparing and introducing labor legislation reveals, the amount of social legislation by itself does not say much about labor conditions. While fine examples of labor laws, as in France, are hardly observed, the strongest trade unions (in Scandinavia) often accomplish more without legal support.

In Great Britain, the long tradition of gradual political and social reform, and the absence of any revolutionary movement have resulted in a rejection of all-encompassing ideologies or great schemes German-style. The political culture is one of pragmatic "muddling through" or "trial and error." This does not exclude radical policies. During the 1980s, Conservative Prime Minister Margaret Thatcher (the "Iron Lady") tried with great force to dismantle the British Welfare State and break the power of the trade unions. She also fervently privatized public services, despite the fact that Great Britain was already the most conservative economy with less government intervention than in continental countries. This radicalism is facilitated by the absence of corporatist consultation with trade unions and employers and by Britain's one-party government. Bold steps need not be negotiated among the parties within the cabinet, as is the case on the continent.

In Central Europe, national policy styles are still in the making. Even subsequent governments within one country may display great variations in the way they make public policy. Radical solutions without any consultation with pressure groups may interchange with cautious efforts of reform after intense talks with employers and trade unions. Some of the countries have had periods with a lot of corporatist talks, followed by a complete neglect of tripartite councils by the national government. In the group closest to Western Europe, the policy process at least partly resembles the general Western European system in that one person cannot dominate national politics without much deliberation.

In Eastern Europe, policy making is least deliberative. The presidents dominate the political scene and only at times are they willing to compromise with the parliament, or the other way around. This personal power enables them to introduce radical solutions and bold steps, but it also accounts for rather unpredictable policies, and sometimes for long stalemates with a hostile majority in the parliament. Only Ukraine is heading into the direction of policy making that includes deliberation with the opposition in parliament.

WELFARE IS NOT WELFARE

When in Europe, only a few Americans who pass by the Eötvös-Loránd University in Budapest, the Calouste Gulbenkian Museum in Lisbon, the Pushkin Theatre in St. Petersburg, the *Lycée Molière* in Paris, or the Victoria and Albert Museum in London, would be misled in thinking that all these institutions are named after rich sponsors. Only one is. (Any idea?) In Europe, privately financed museums, theaters, libraries, or ballet schools exist but they are not very common. Most of these institutions are run by the national or local government, and it is local or national government (the state) that often decides about the name of such institutes. If they bear a name at all, other than Royal Museum, Municipal Library, or National Theatre, it is often the name of royal persons (Victoria and Albert), national poets (Molière, Pushkin), scientists (Eötvös-Loránd), or some other celebrities from the nation's history. These persons may have written famous poems, novels, or scientific essays, but only exceptionally did they write the cheque with which the institution was financed, or bequeath their painting collection (Gulbenkian is one of the most prominent exceptions).

The role of the state is not confined to the liberal arts or education. Many Europeans are born in state-subsidized or even state-controlled clinics or hospitals. Their growth and health are regularly checked through state-financed local health centers. They go to public schools (and universities), live in houses that are partly financed by means of state subventions, use public transport to get to their work (or by car, paying over $4 a gallon for gas, which mostly goes toward taxes, and visit cultural festivities in municipal theaters that receive large state and local subsidies. For all these provisions and services, European citizens pay income tax rates that in some countries may take up to fifty percent of their income. They nurture the hope that they will never need state unemployment pay until they will receive their state pension. Finally, after having enjoyed a state pension for a number of years, they die in the same state-subsidized hospitals they were born in.

The great majority of European citizens count on the state for these services and provisions. Only a few (wealthy) Europeans would prefer to do without all this state interference. Even for them, escape from this great amount of state-provided or state-subsidized services is not easy. There are not many nonsubsidized schools, private clinics, universities, or theaters, and even billionaires receive the basic old-age pension. They could move to another country to reduce their tax load. Yet, in search of even less state interference they would have to leave Europe, to the United States for instance.

In addition to Europe's language-based national identity and its parliamentary rather than presidential political system, this all-encompassing welfare state is another basic difference between Europe and the United States. A European nation is more than a collection of taxpayers that would prefer to do without a government. Although the government is blamed almost permanently and for almost anything, most Europeans realize there would not be much social life without it. They are accustomed to some form of authority and see the government as an institution of a higher order than other nonprofit organizations. "The state has to look after it," or "politics should decide about it," are current political expressions, applying to the higher arts as well as to housing and health care. In many countries, social security transfer payments amount to twenty or twenty-five percent of national income. An additional twenty percent is spent on other state policies, as compared to thirty percent for total social expenditure, including social security in the United States.

In espousing these "welfare state" policies, European governments interfere in the free market to an extent unknown in the United States, in particular in education, the housing market, the health care "market," and the labor market. State measures mitigate or compensate for negative effects of the free market and protect the weaker parties: the patients in health care, tenants on the housing market, and employees on the labor market, including the unemployed and other people without an income of their own. Despite the current retrenchments in social policies, state social protection is still regarded as a means to foster social integration, or "social citizenship," which is a core element of national integration.

The welfare state is not simply a social democratic invention. Conservative political leaders in the late nineteenth century already recognized the importance of social integration. It was the authoritarian German Chancellor Otto von Bismarck who in the 1880s broke with the liberal creed that social legislation should remain confined to women and children. He introduced social security for male workers, which was meant to foster national integration and prevent the further rise of the socialist labor movement. The initiative was widely imitated by social liberals and Christian democrats, and resulted in the general start of European social legislation around the turn of the century during a period of fast economic growth. At the end of World War I, a second wave of social legislation accomplished the realization of one of the foremost social democratic priorities: the eight-hour working day. This time, communist and social democratic governments took the initiative. Almost overnight, frightened liberals and conservatives followed, in an attempt to stop the diffusion of the 1917 Russian Revolution. A third sequence of social laws took place at the end of World War II. In that period, the ideas of two British liberal experts were generally acclaimed and adopted. John Maynard Keynes recommended anti-cyclical state intervention in the economy (called "Keynesian" economic policies) in order to foster economic growth, keep unemployment low, and prevent a repetition of the 1930s crisis. In the same vein, William Beveridge advocated an extension of social security to the population at large. It was not until the 1960s, however, that in Western Europe social policies (supported by almost all ideologies) overshadowed other state policies, and the term "welfare state" was used, once again in a time of fast economic growth. In the countries under communist control, the communists introduced their own version of "welfare state."

As this brief historical note shows, war and economic growth have been as important for the expansion of social policies as the rise and the influence of the labor movement. This combination of forces explains why Europeans are more devoted to social policies than Americans. The European labor movement has played a crucial role in politics and the two world wars have had far more impact than in the United States.

THE WELFARE STATE AND ITS REDEFINITION IN WESTERN EUROPE

The Western European welfare state comprises state-financed, income-maintenance expenditure (social security), public education, public health and housing programs, employment policies, and labor protection. European governments undertake great efforts to get or keep people at work, to some extent monitor their labor conditions, and in case the efforts fail they provide social security benefits to those without work and to the elderly. For a long time, Western European governments have even taken for granted that strict labor protection and high social security benefits might move unemployment upward, because they reduce the incentive to recruit new employees or to seek new jobs. On the other hand, social security offers the unemployed a minimum living, so they do not need to accept any kind of work, irrespective of the labor conditions. In contrast to the United States, income maintenance to some extent prevails over job maintenance.

Social security is often regarded as the very core of the welfare state. In many nations, social security is a more extended version of American social security, in others it also includes American welfare. Almost all European nations possess state-financed or state-subsidized systems of social security, which provide benefits in case of illness, work disability, old age, unemployment, and child allowances. The social security benefits are often fixed as a percentage of one's previous wage (earnings-related benefits). If they are not linked to previous personal income, they consist of flat-rate benefits, sometimes linked to the national minimum wage. (In a number of countries a statutory or jointly decided national minimum wage applies.) The basic social security provisions either cover the total population or they apply to employees only, with additional provisions for others. In either case, no distinction is made between "deserving" and "undeserving" poor. The notion of "undeserving poor" hardly plays a role in the European welfare state debate. Either one has paid for the benefits, and for that reason deserves them, or one has been unable to pay, in which case society is to blame as much as the individual. Consequently, food stamps hardly exist in Europe, since they stigmatize the recipients as a special group of people. In Europe, welfare is not a residual category of social services and provisions for undeserving poor. In contrast, welfare refers to prosperity, and the term *welfare state* to a national society on a high level of economic development and a concomitant high level of state social services.

Since the rise of unemployment and state deficits after the two consecutive oil crises in 1973–74 and 1979–80, some speak of a crisis of the welfare state or even about its end. Deregulation, privatization, and liberalization, all intended to encourage more flexibility in producing goods and services, have become the new catchwords of national economic and social policies. Governments have implemented cuts in state budgets and stimulate private business through a reduction of labor protection and social security. Deregulation should make the European economies more competitive and reduce unemployment. At the same time, decline of state control meets the demands of more freedom and personal responsibility in social life. The main thrust of state policies so far has been to reduce the growth of social expenditure, rather than a reduction in absolute spending levels. For that reason "redefinition" of the welfare state seems a more apt term than welfare state crisis.

The redefinition of the welfare state is a difficult process, which regularly gives rise to ardent debate in parliament. While most political parties, including the social democrats, have slowly come to accept the new realities of economic life, the trade unions show less resignation. They are involved in disputes with employers about working time reduction and extension of operating hours, and even more in disputes with national governments concerning the adaptation of labor legislation and social security.

Keynesian economic policies used to consist of the steering of private and public demand ("demand management") and investment by means of adapting tax levels, transfer payments, and public spending to the condition of the national economy. These policies allowed for some inflation, in order to boost the economy and employment. The 1979–80 oil crisis sealed their fate. Keynesian state intervention proved unable to cure growing inflation and rising unemployment ("stagflation") at the same time, and was replaced by promotion of the free market. French President François Mitterand was one of the last believers, but he had to give up demand management within two years. Throughout Western Europe the focus has shifted from "demand management" to technological innovation and cost reduction in the production process ("supply side economics"). One of the means to promote private enterprise is the stimulation of small business. Rules to set up one's own shop, workplace, or service agencies have been relaxed. A second element is the sale of state enterprises. Even public utilities that used to be an integral part of the state sector because of their "natural" monopoly position or their strategic value, like the national railway company and electricity works, are privatized. In countries where public services were used to set the unemployed to work, this policy has been given up. The expansion of the public sector ran counter to the general idea of a smaller state and a leaner budget. Nowadays, governments provide tax reductions or other forms of subvention for companies that hire long-term unemployed or young unemployed workers. New forms of apprenticeship are introduced, which combine paid work with unpaid days of training. Vocational training has even become a new catchword in labor relations and labor legislation.

Rules pertaining to labor conditions are also relaxed in order to bring about more labor flexibility. In most of Europe, social legislation or joint business-union collective agreements stipulate minimum wages and maximum daily or weekly working hours (actual working time in Europe is under forty hours a week). Additionally, state or joint rules cover holidays (in most countries amounting to four or five weeks, partly double-paid as a contribution to holiday costs), parental leave and sometimes also educational leave. National rules also cover working conditions within the enterprise, including health and safety, sexual harassment, trade union representation, and employee participation in company decision making. Employee participation within the enterprise is the task of "works councils," which are elected by the company labor force. The works councils have to be involved in major decisions that affect working conditions and employment prospects. Particularly in Germanic Europe, trade unions monitor this participation in order to prevent the works councils from interfering with the wage agreements they reach with employers' associations. By doing so, the trade unions assist in maintaining labor discipline and raising productivity, one of the common goals of corporatism. In response to the trade union demand of shorter working time as a device to reduce unemployment, companies now ask for extension of operating hours. That demand has made Sunday work an issue in employer-union contacts and in social legislation. (Work on Sundays used to be limited by law in many countries.) This working time flexibility has become one of the main subjects of tripartism (see Table 6.1). Rules on part-time work and temporary work contracts are relaxed, and more opportunities are created for commercial work exchange agencies that specialize in temporary work contracts.

In social security, costs are reduced by lowering benefit levels—from eighty to seventy percent or from seventy to sixty percent of previous earnings— by tightening up eligibility rules and introducing unpaid sickness days, and by stricter observation of these provisions to reduce abuse. In the debate on the welfare state, incentives to work have become a pressing topic, especially the question whether high unemployment pay does not stop the unemployed from job searching. The debate is a more general one than the U.S. debate on the "welfare trap," however, and it pays more attention to the impact of the "poverty trap" on social life of a new "underclass" of long-term unemployed. Their possible "social exclusion" from participation in social life and in civil society has become a major state concern. New ventures in social policies, like community work, are meant to promote re-integration and "social citizenship." Moreover, in several nations, social assistance to those without sufficient income includes small amounts for newspapers, books, and the cinema. Local communities often offer the persons that receive social assistance free entrance to local cultural and recreational facilities. While Europe is learning from the United States in encouraging flexibility and other developments to fight unemployment, in social policies a wide gap continues to separate the two sides of the Atlantic Ocean. In spite of a growing tendency toward precarious employment, Europe persists in social integration by means of social policies rather than by offering insecure jobs that do not prevent social exclusion. Promoting employment, yes, but not to any price.

One of the most hotly debated issues in social security is old-age pensions. With over one third of total social security spending, pensions are by far the largest item in social policies, but retrenchments in this area are hotly contested. They prompted the rise of a short-lived pensioners' party in Holland, motivated political strikes in Italy, and contributed to Helmut Kohl's 1998 election defeat. Due to this opposition, many governments have preferred to look for other sources of saving money, in particular unemployment pay.

LEFT AND RIGHT: DOES IT MAKE A DIFFERENCE?

In a number of cities, famous housing projects can be admired that were constructed during the 1920s by social democratic dominated local councils. The "Karl Marx Hof" in Vienna and the housing estates by the "Amsterdam School of Architecture" still stand as models of twentieth-century architecture; many of the outstanding projects in Berlin were destroyed during World War II.

Such housing projects are one of the visual expressions of differences between left and right in politics. Rightist governments have also initiated housing projects, but they have preferred to leave housing to the free market and to stimulate house ownership by means of tax deductibility of mortgage rent. The left has also promoted such tax facilities, especially for lower income groups. After the war, the German trade union movement established large funds to finance home ownership among its members.

Generally, social democratic priority has not been with state care *per se* but with bringing about more social equality. That goal may be served by state measures that equally apply to all citizens (universal coverage), like flat rate social security benefits, and by provisions that especially cater for the working class or low income groups in general (limited coverage), like compulsory health care for lower incomes. The social democrats have preferred universal coverage, since they are a better expression of national solidarity than provisions aimed at specific groups. Examples are state pensions, which imply solidarity of all those under sixty or sixty-five with all elderly, and national health care insurance, which is an expression of solidarity of the healthy (who pay more than they receive), with the sick and disabled. (And any day one may move from the first to the second category.)

Conservatives and conservative liberals prefer the functioning of the free market to state care but they are willing to make an exception for the poor, who should be helped by support programs that exclusively focus on that group. This preference means that they object less to limited coverage than to universal coverage. Christian democrats have also favored differentiation. They embrace collective initiative by voluntary associations (subsidiarity), but for a wider segment of the population than the poor only, and they have given the family a greater role in social policies. Indeed, while national services, like British and Scandinavian national health care for the total population, are often run by the state, specific health care and health insurance for the lower incomes are often administrated by private foundations under state supervision.

Left and right differ not only in their views on how state money (Americans would say taxpayers' money) is to be spent, but also on how it should be generated. During the nineteenth century, indirect taxes in the form of levies on food products were the main source of state funds. Since poor people spent a larger part of their income on foodstuffs, they carried a relatively higher tax burden (as a percentage of their income) than the middle class. This motivated the social democrats to enforce a change from indirect taxes to direct taxation, on wages and other income. Such direct taxes may even have differential rates for lower and higher incomes, in order to secure a heavier burden for those who can afford it. In that case the tax is called progressive (here we encounter yet another use of that term in European politics), in the sense that higher-income people pay higher rates than lower-income groups. In the course of the twentieth century, such progressive systems of income taxes were implemented throughout Western Europe, with top rates of over fifty percent.

High progressive taxes have a serious disadvantage. They motivate high-income receivers to think of all kinds of escape, in the form of high costs that can be deducted from the tax bill, transferring part of their business to tax resorts (like some of Europe's mini-states), or moving to low-tax states themselves. Moreover, tax deductibility of mortgage rent favors house owners with higher tax rates, since any deduction reduces their tax bill with a larger sum than that of low-income groups who pay lower rates. In combination with problems of control, these disadvantages have resulted in a combination of indirect and direct taxes in most of Western Europe, and now also in Central and Eastern Europe. Moreover, because it is easier to harmonize indirect taxes than direct taxes, the European Union has also stimulated a development toward more indirect taxes. Most countries still oppose uniform European tax rates as undermining one of the last vestiges of national sovereignty.

Table 7.1 summarizes some of the differences in policy priorities and preferences between left and right in European politics that have been discussed in this and previous chapters. (Education will be dealt with subsequently). Due to economic considerations, political opposition, and the need to build coalition governments, neither side has been able to implement its priorities to a large degree.

Interestingly, social democrats have also been more active in implementing cuts in the state budget than conservative and liberal parties during the 1990s. When in opposition, they could fight any conservative savings in public spending as immoral and mobilize protests. When in government, they were forced to reduce the budget themselves, and conservatives and liberals could not oppose such policies. The right could only point to the fact that the left then espoused similar policies to what they had opposed right before.

The differences between left and right visions of the welfare state are to some extent reflected in regional variations. Social integration has been mostly a concern in Germanic Europe, due to the social democratic domination of the labor movement and frequent participation of social democratic parties in the national governments. The goal of social integration has been served both by social legislation and by employer-union agreements. The Germans have coined a special term *Soziale Marktwirtschaft* (Social Market Economy) for the mitigation of the free market by social measures.

The long social democratic domination of politics has given the Scandinavian countries the lead in active labor market policies. Contrary to American popular belief, however, social democratic power in these countries has not resulted in a big public sector consisting of nationalized enterprises (apart from public services like hospitals and schools). Scandinavia is also ahead of Europe in women's

Table 7.1. Left and Right Priorities in European Politics

Subject	Left	Right	Comments
Corporatism	In support, because of the prominent role for social democratic trade unions.	Only interested if it leads to wage restraint	The relationship between social democratic parties and trade unions has fostered corporatism.
Education	Comprehensive schools	Differentiation in school types	The trend toward comprehensive schools has not been successful.
Environment	Sensitive to green demands and willing to conclude coalitions with the greens	Hardly interested, and opposed to any restriction to free enterprise	Green parties now participate in a number of "red-green" coalitions.
Health care	State insurance or state-supervised private insurance with wide coverage	Private insurance; state insurance for very low incomes	Almost all the European countries possess state (supervised) health care insurance systems.
Housing	Social housing estates and cheap mortgage facilities	Mortgage deductibility	Social housing was especially popular following both world wars.
Social security	Universal coverage, with high flat rate benefits or high income-related benefits	Limited coverage, with low flat-rate benefits	Low flat-rate benefits prevail in Great Britain; high flat rate or income-related benefits on the continent.
Taxation	Progressive indirect taxes (income tax)	Indirect taxes (levies)	Indirect taxes are becoming more popular, partly due to the European Union.
Women rights	Sensitive to feminist demands	Against state interference	Feminists have been most active within social democratic parties.

participation on the labor market, in income redistribution, and in social security, including old-age pensions. In social security, social democrats have established stronger equality than is to be found elsewhere in Europe, through high and equal flat rate benefits for all (universal coverage). All these extensive provisions are financed by means of employer/employee contributions and high taxes, in particular direct taxes on personal income.

In the rest of Germanic Europe, including Germany, Christian democratic influence is reflected in greater differentiation in social security entitlement, for instance between wage earners and independent workers, and between manual and nonmanual workers. Moreover, benefits are often related to previous earnings rather than flat-rate amounts. In social security and social policies, the state subsidizes private or, better, collective funds, like social democratic, Catholic, and Protestant foundations. Social security is mainly financed by employer/employee contributions, but also by high taxes that mainly consist of income tax. Table 7.2 provides a survey of social security in Germany, as a prominent example of a European welfare state. It combines the left goal of high benefits with traditional right preferences like differentiation among social groups, earnings-related benefits, and activities by private foundations.

The change toward more flexibility is reflected in the waning interest in the "Swedish Model" of labor relations and social policies, and the wide appraisal of the "Dutch Model," discussed at the beginning of this chapter. The Swedish trade unions pioneered in retraining workers in less productive sectors for jobs in more promising industries, and even more in public services. In addition to the active employment policies, a high degree of wage equality and far-reaching employee participation in the enterprise were among the elements of the widely acclaimed "Swedish Model." For a long time, the active retraining of unemployed workers managed to keep unemployment below two percent, one of the lowest figures in Europe. However, in the course of the 1990s the size of the public services

Table 7.2. Social Security in Germany

Subject matter	*Sickness*	*Nursing care*	*Work accident*	*Unemployment*	*Old age*
Coverage	Wage earners, unemployed, retired, dependent family members	Similar to sickness	Wage earners	Wage earners	Wage earners; on voluntary base: housewives, self-employed
Total contributions	Local differentiation	1.7% of wages	Not uniform	6.5% of wages	20% of wages
Financed by	50% employer; 50% employee	Similar to sickness	100% employer	50% employer; 50% employee	50% employer; 50% employee
Benefits	Medical expenses; 70% of wage during sickness	Care at home or in nursing home	80% of net wage	60% of average net wage, during a period of 6 to 32 months, dependent upon age and contribution period	Amount related to previous wage and period of contribution

For those without sufficient income, including the long-term unemployed (3.5 percent of the total population, one quarter of them immigrants), the local communities provide social assistance (about 1,000 German Marks a month for two adults).

became a source of concern and its function to provide employment for the unemployed was given up. Unemployment increased dramatically from two to over ten percent within two years, and the widely admired Swedish Model lost its appeal. Moreover, business and the social democrats grew apart when the trade unions increasingly attempted to introduce labor reforms through political decision making, which they were unable to carry through by means of joint agreements.

In Latin Europe, social integration has enjoyed less priority. The labor movement has been dominated by communists, who were kept out of government most of the time. Latin social policies are less extensive than in Germanic Europe. This has not only to do with the conservative domination of politics, but also with the lower level of economic development in countries like Spain and Portugal. More than in Germanic Europe, social security consists of state-monitored private insurance funds that offer social security coverage to specific groups of people, and the level of benefits, even in France, is lower than in most of Germanic Europe. In taxation, Latin Europe has always had a larger share of indirect taxes than the Germanic nations, to some extent motivated by the lower propensity-to-pay of its citizens and the greater ingenuity in evading taxes.

In Latin Europe, Keynesian planning was facilitated by the nationalization of basic industries, in particular in France and Italy. Nationalization was carried through immediately after World War II and was intended to generally facilitate state monitoring of postwar reconstruction and economic growth. It resulted in large public sectors (in countries that were governed by conservatives or Christian democrats most of the time). In addition to energy distribution, national railroads, and other public utilities, which used to be in state hands in most of Europe, the public sectors in Latin Europe also included shipyards, oil industries, and even car factories like Renault. In France and Italy, the large state sector served as an instrument of economic policy. In particular, France actively invested in this sector whose enterprises were considered to play a pivotal role in the national economy. An outstanding example was nuclear power. While several other countries gave up nuclear energy or delayed its growth, France increased its number of nuclear power plants, not stopped by a growing green movement. The close link between the state bureaucracy and national enterprises in France also provided the administrative elite from the *Grandes Ecoles* ample opportunities to move from public administration to management functions in the public sector. However, with the exception of energy, most state enterprises are now being privatized. This shift to private business in France has increased the number of shareholders from two to over five million.

Until the recent Europe-wide privatization wave, privatization used to be the monopoly of British Conservative governments. They privatized enterprises that a previous Labour government had nationalized just before. Actually, Labour was the only social democratic party that always put great trust in nationalizing a large part of the economy. In this respect and in social policies, Great Britain is a case apart once again. Labor legislation is very rudimentary and it hardly affects national politics or labor relations. Social integration has never been a major government goal. Labour has hardly been interested in promoting labor protection, since that could undercut the unions' position in social life. Social security is also less developed than on the continent with flat-rate benefits that are much lower than both Scandinavia's flat rate benefits or Germany's differential and earnings-related benefits. (On the other hand, the country has a unique National Health Service.) The result has been greater social inequality than on the continent. People from the continent are often astonished or even appalled by the great disparities in working and living conditions in Great Britain. Working class quarters seem to be a different world from middle class quarters. In Germanic Europe, and less so in Latin Europe, more extensive social policies have mitigated these differences and promoted social integration.

REDEFINING THE WELFARE STATE: CENTRAL AND EASTERN EUROPE

If you wanted to buy something in a Russian shop during the period of communism, you had to pass through a lengthy procedure. First, you had to ask an invariably very unfriendly lady at the counter if the shop had what you wanted, and if you could have a look at it. If you were lucky, you could. If you asked very humbly, you might even have a glance at a similar product, if available, for a quick comparison. Then you had to go back to a separate cashier at the entrance, where you paid for what you wanted. With the receipt in hand, you returned to the counter first to see if your favorite product was still there and second to convince the unfriendly lady to hand it over to you. Often, you had to stand in line three times, first at the counter, then at the cashier, and finally at the counter again, so you were never sure if the product you were going to pay for would still be available when you arrived at the counter with your receipt. If you changed your mind or wanted to buy a second product, you had to go through the same procedure. In communist Central Europe, procedures were a bit simpler, but the waiting lines were just as long. Especially at butcher shops—you never knew if there would be any meat at all left when it was your turn. Some smart people even earned a living as professional liners. For a small fee they would do your shopping, in other words, they would stand in line all day for you.

Scarcity under communism was due most of all to production priorities. Communists were obsessed with the production of investment goods, to build a classless communist society and they neglected consumer goods and distributive problems. Locomotives came first, consumer products second. This gave rise to jokes that Russians were lucky to have so many locomotives since it enabled them to go shopping several hundreds of kilometers away to see if they could find there what they in vain had looked for in their hometown. Failing distribution was a second source of problems pertaining to the allocation of products. Although people were not very poor under communism, and increasing numbers of people could afford a car, the main problem was that there were not enough cars. One could be on the waiting list for a car for ten or more years!

Since the collapse of communism, Central and Eastern Europe have been engaged in epochal economic and social reforms. State retreat in the economy and the development of private business in industry and services require even more state activities than deregulation and privatization in Western Europe. Privatization of public companies in these parts of Europe differs also from related trends in Western Europe. Under communism, almost all large enterprises were in state hands and only in small-scale agriculture and services was there any room for private initiative. An exception was Hungary, where economic state control declined already under communism, small business was allowed to flourish, and the transition to the free-market economy was more gradual. In other nations, privatization had to start from a situation in which most of economic life was still concentrated in state hands at the end of the 1980s.

The pace of privatization is a core political issue, and so is the way in which public enterprises are transferred to private hands. Some countries have opted for a "shock therapy," while others have preferred a more gradual course. Hungary and, even more, Czechia have experimented with "voucher capitalism," by issuing enterprise shares (vouchers) to the enterprise workforce. In other countries, the leaders of the communist parties and state enterprise managers have been able to concentrate wealth in their own hands, in what has been labeled "nomenklatura-privatization." This term denotes the transfer of state property into the hands of the former communist elite (the *nomenklatura*, or "list of names"). Even where the elite has been more scrupulous, the governments do not always have the capacity to monitor the process. In some countries a new Mafia-type entrepreneur has emerged who uses all kinds of illegal means, including violence, to take over. In the worst case, the government has even been helpful to this emerging Mafia. The expansion of the Russian Mafia toward Western Europe is now straining the relations between Russia and the European Union.

Social policies in Central and Eastern Europe are not merely attempts to redefine the welfare state. They are meant to accomplish a complete change in welfare provisions, or even to introduce a real welfare state. Full employment was at the heart of the Central and Eastern European "welfare states," and privatization is also a political issue because of its impact on employment. The state guaranteed job security by obliging enterprises to keep superfluous workers on the payroll. This obligation caused a lot of "hidden unemployment" of workers who were paid, but for whom there was actually no work available. On the other hand, the system had the advantage of preventing social marginalization of unemployed people. The communists always proudly referred to this absence of unemployment and to the consequent absence of unemployment benefits. During the transformation toward a free-market economy, full employment could no longer be secured and unemployment pay has been introduced. However, for the Central and Eastern Europeans who were used to job security, having to apply for unemployment pay is a traumatic experience.

The official absence of unemployment was not the only difference with the Western European welfare states. A second element of income maintenance was the large-scale subvention of foodstuffs, house rents, and fuel, in order to keep consumer prices low. After the collapse of communism, governments have been reluctant to do away with these subventions, if only because they fear widespread discontent and revolt. The governments have to navigate between the International Monetary Fund (IMF), which requires strict budget discipline and austerity packages as preconditions for granting loans, and the International Labor Organization (ILO), which promotes fair labor practices and social policies, but has fewer sanctions at its disposal than the IMF.

A third element of the Central and Eastern European welfare states consisted of enterprise-based social provisions, like health care centers and housing facilities, hailed as communist accomplishments. With the spread of private enterprise, many such institutions are now being transferred to local communities. Where they have survived as enterprise provisions, they form an argument for superfluous workers to ask for the continuation of their job, even with reduced or no pay.

The transformation of these economies, then, requires an unprecedented overthrow of economic and social policies, which makes it difficult to compare Central and Eastern European trends with those in Western Europe, despite the fact that terms like privatization suggest a basic similarity. Living standards under communism were low and many would rather not speak of a welfare state. However, minimum living conditions were secured in combination with strict state control. For that reason, the term "state-paternalistic welfare states" is sometimes used for social policies under communism.

Great disparities exist in the degree of reform, as well as in starting conditions among the Central and Eastern European nations. Czechia and Hungary were already among the most developed countries of the Soviet Bloc, together with the former eastern part of Germany. The Balkan countries were far less developed, despite massive communist industrialization programs. Czechia and Hungary have also made most progress in the adaptation of their welfare policies, helped by government stability during most of the 1990s.

In Eastern Europe, reform has been more piecemeal than in Central Europe. The transformation of the enormous Russian economy is an almost superhuman task and it provides the new Russian Mafia with ample opportunities to settle as "entrepreneurs" or as "protectors" of Western enterprises. The overwhelming majority of people, however, experienced a great loss of income, and, to make things worse, the Russian government has been overdue in wage payment. In some cases the arrears amount to several months of salaries. Even miners' strikes have hardly been effective in enforcing timely wage payment, and strikers have sometimes taken recourse to hunger strikes, in order to impress national and local officials. At times, demanding more loans from the United States and Western Europe seems the only solution for the problems of solvency. However, compliance with the strict monetary conditions set by the IMF adds to the nationalists' (and communists') claim that the government is selling out "Mother Russia" to Western capitalism.

EDUCATION

Cornell, Harvard, Princeton, Yale . . . Neither Europe as a whole, nor any of the European nations have a prestigious Ivy League of universities where you pay a bit more but where the best professors and visiting fellows are waiting for you. In Europe, almost all universities are state financed, with increasing supplements from private research contracts. Professors are mostly paid the same salaries throughout the country and students have to pay the same fee for enrollment in all national universities. It is not individual universities that provide grants, but the national government, independent of the university of your choice. Variations and differences in quality of research and teaching qualities are due to active professors, rather than to differential fees or to a strict selection of students. Great Britain's Oxford and Cambridge are probably the major exceptions to this rule.

As a major agent of economic and social development, and even more as an instrument of social and political integration, education is a core policy area of national politics. In a number of nations, education is also the largest single item on the national state budget. Although more money is spent on social security and social provisions, these provisions are sometimes financed by means of employer and employee contributions that flow into private social security funds (as is the case in Germany).

A number of countries have introduced systems of quality assessment that set minimum standards, not only for university education, but also for primary and secondary schools. Often, final exams are monitored or even organized on a nationwide scale for public as well as private schools. Great Britain is the only country that, like the United States, has a large private education sector, with ample autonomy for the local school boards. It was not until the late 1980s that the conservative government tried to impose more uniformity in school curriculums. In continental Europe, private education is a rather marginal phenomenon, and the overwhelming majority of schools are in public hands. Primary schools are the responsibility of local government, but it is the national government that sets the standards and even the curriculum. Exceptionally, most schools in Holland have been set up by Catholic and Protestant foundations, as part of the pillarization of society. However, all Dutch schools, whether public or private, are totally financed out of the state budget and the state exercises tight control over the curriculum through this financial leverage. In other countries, the Catholic Church has also been a major provider of education, in particular primary schools. In some Latin nations, this Catholic Church responsibility has resulted in "school conflicts" about state control of the remaining Catholic schools. In 1984, a social democratic French minister resigned after failed attempts to extend state surveillance of Catholic schools and under pressure of demonstrations against his proposals.

Despite a century of social democratic pressure, European society is still more of a class-based society than the United States and this is reflected in education. Selection is made at an earlier stage than in the United States, often before entering secondary education. The prestigious grammar schools (gymnasium) are mainly attended by middle and upper class pupils. Universities also enroll less working class students than in the United States. Many countries provide a two-track system in secondary and tertiary education, with a practice- and occupation-oriented track, which is more popular among working class students, and a theory-oriented track. Polytechnics or technical colleges form the highest level of the first track, regular universities of the second one. Efforts that have been made especially by social democrats to do away with the gymnasium and create comprehensive "middle schools" for all pupils, with some differentiation in levels of teaching, have hardly been successful outside Scandinavia. Neither have the attempts in Germany to merge technical colleges and universities into one new institution of higher learning.

A new source of concern in Western European education is the concentration of immigrant children, in particular from Arab and Turkish descent, in some schools, which makes it more difficult to reach national standards and to foster social integration. Especially in big cities, a growing gap separates "black schools," with many children of foreign descent, from "white schools."

In the most federalized countries, Germany and Switzerland, education is left to the federal units. National education policy in Germany is made during meetings of the ministers of education of the sixteen *Länder*. In practice, they often leave decision making to the common educational agency they have set up, but they have been careful in not making this into a federal institution. Incidentally, there have been conflicts about recognition of school diplomas of another German *Land*, when the Christian democrats in Bavaria refused to accept new comprehensive school types introduced by social democrats elsewhere in the nation. Belgian politics reveals the problems of leaving education to lower levels of state authority. In that country, education was one of the last items that were transferred to the competency of the federal communities. At first, Christian democrats blocked decentralization, arguing that it would lead to "red" education in French-speaking Wallony, which is dominated by social democrats. Social democrats also opposed decentralization, since they predicted a monopoly of "papal" education in Dutch-speaking Flanders, where Christian democracy prevails. In another nation that is now federalizing, Spain, tension has arisen between the national government and some autonomous comunidades about the contents of history schools books, which describe the evolution of the Spanish state, without much attention for regional diversity.

LIFE AND DEATH

A president with an illegitimate child, a Chancellor who has a long-standing affair with his secretary, his successor campaigning with his fourth wife . . . in some countries even a gay or lesbian prime minister would probably already be accepted by a majority of the population.

Social and economic issues dominate national politics in Europe, but questions of sexual morals, family values, and the attitude toward termination of life (the vertical line in the spectrum expressing the libertarian-authoritarian opposition in the political spectrum) incidentally make headline stories in the serious press. In these matters Europe has moved to the libertarian side of the United States. This is especially true since the 1970s, due to the influence of post-materialism, the feminist movement, and the youth revolt against traditional authority generally.

Strict rules relating to sexual morals have been relaxed or abandoned. Contraceptives are for sale almost everywhere and restrictions on abortion have been lifted or mitigated during the 1980s and 1990s. Homosexuality is recognized, at least formally, as a way of life, and discrimination of homosexuals is as liable to punishment as any other form of discrimination. Some countries have already provided homosexual relationships with the same or a similar legal status as regular marriage.

It is especially social liberals and social democrats that have forced new openings in this area of policy making during the 1980s and 1990s, under strong pressure of the women's movement. Until that time, women had to seek recourse to illegal abortion or go to specialized clinics in London, that have come to function as international abortion centers. If the left would always be more libertarian than the right, the horizontal and the vertical lines of the European political spectrum would overlap and it would resemble the American spectrum. However, communists have been very strict in their rejection of homosexuality and conservative liberals have been more libertarian than Christian democrats.

Moreover, probably even more than ideology, religion matters in these moral issues. The communist regimes in Central and Eastern Europe were least strict in their abortion policy. That had to do mainly with their rejection of religion and religious morals, but also with their promotion of population growth. (All dictators like to see the number of their subjects grow.) Contraceptives were hardly available, which left abortion as the regular rather than the ultimate contraceptive. For that reason, East German women protested when, after Reunification, the stricter West German laws on abortion were adopted. In Western Europe, the Protestant nations (Great Britain, Scandinavia, Holland, and the Northern German states) are most permissive, while the Catholic nations are strictest, at least in formal rules. Beside the Catholic Church, which does not tolerate abortion at all (whatever the circumstances), hardly any single-issue pro-life movement exists. The Spanish social democrats challenged the Catholic Church by allowing abortion in case of rape and grave health danger. Any further relaxation met with too large of a resistance, which have left the flights to London as a way out for women that do not meet the conditions. In Poland, the Catholic Church used the fall of communism to demand stricter abortion laws. Catholic Ireland was the last nation to abolish the ban on the sale of contraceptives and the ban on foreign travel for pregnant women that were suspected of seeking abortion. The country is now an exporter of contraceptives. With respect to homosexuality, efforts by the French social democrats to improve the legal status of homosexual relations met combined resistance by Gaullists and conservative liberals.

European tolerance extends to pornography and prostitution. In contrast to the American women's movement, its European counterpart has accepted these phenomena as facts of life that can better be tolerated than be made part of the criminal scene. All bookshops that sell magazines have their stock of pornography, and instead of the Bible, the better European hotels offer a choice of "Pay TV," including pornographic films—the first two minutes free of charge. Prostitution is tolerated, cat houses need not hide in the desert, and a few cities even recommend their "red light" districts as tourist attractions.

The greater permissiveness of the left and Protestants in sexual matters is not only an expression of a more libertarian attitude, but also of more women's rights, since it is women, not men, that fall victim to strict rules on contraceptives and abortion. Consequently, a libertarian stance with respect to these issues need not necessarily be an expression of general permissiveness but may be part of public policies to improve the position of women in society. A prominent example is Sweden, which is in many respects Western Europe's most regulated country. In 1999, it made paying money to prostitutes—not prostitution as such—liable to punishment, in a typical effort to erase prostitution once and for all by means of legislation. (One of the effects was to stimulate ferry-crossings to the nearby Danish capital Copenhagen.) Sweden also possesses Europe's strictest laws on alcoholic beverages, which motivate the Swedes to use any journey to a non-Scandinavian country to drink as much as possible.

In drug policies, almost all the European countries possess such strict rules. In practice, however, some nations tolerate the use of soft drugs and concentrate on the hunt for hard drugs like heroin. Holland is most tolerant in this respect, with its legal sale of small quantities of soft drugs for personal use in the Dutch coffee shops, where coffee has now become a side dish. Swiss cities like Zürich experiment with the free distribution of hard drugs or methadon to the local addicts, in order to keep them from stealing. These experiments often meet with hostility by the U.S. government, but the countries involved point to their low addiction and low crime rates.

Europe not only (increasingly) differs from the United States in its more permissive attitude in sexual matters, but also in rules on death. Almost all the European countries have abolished the death penalty, if only under pressure of the Council of Europe, where this is now one of the criteria of admission. Probably the most prominent difference, however, is in the general European ban on firearms. While the ban on the death penalty is not supported by all Europeans, the ban on firearms is. Europeans would not like to be more permissive on this point. To them, firearms are not an instrument of self-protection but of war. They are right, at least when referring to Europe.

8

Supranational Politics: The European Union

Brussels is the "capital" of the European Union and the seat of NATO headquarters, the London "City" is the capital of international banking, and Paris and Milan are centers of Latin culture, including new fashion. Geneva stands for international negotiations and the International Red Cross, Amsterdam for nonconformist youth culture, and Prague is the symbol of Central European revival. Nowadays, a new name predominates in discussions on European trends: Frankfurt, the seat of the Bundesbank that issues the German mark (*deutsch Mark*, DM) and also of the European Central Bank (ECB) that has functioned since 1999.

CATCHING THE EMU-TRAIN: EU POLICIES

The European Union (EU) is currently developing into a full-fledged European Monetary Union (EMU), in which all participating currencies will be firmly linked to each other. On January 1, 1999, the Euro was introduced as an accounting unit in the European Union. By 2002, the Euro will be a real currency and replace the national currencies. With a lot of nostalgia, West Europeans will have to bid farewell to Austrian schillings, Belgian, French, and Luxembourg francs, Dutch guilders, Finnish and German marks, Irish pounds, Italian liras, Portuguese escudos, and Spanish pesetas (see Table 8.1). Together with the transformation of the Central and Eastern European economies this is the second epochal change in current European economic policies.

The German mark, Europe's strongest currency, will be the main base of the European Monetary Union. Since the 1970s, it has already functioned as the core of several formal European systems of fixed exchange rates (before that time the European currencies were linked to the U.S. dollar). The German currency owes its solid rock position to the industrial predominance of that country but even more to the independent position of "Frankfurt" (the German Bundesbank).

German governments have hardly any influence on the Bundesbank's decisions with respect to the interest rate and the printing of new money. One of the first activities of the 1998 Schröder government was to pressure the bank for a reduction of the interest rate, but Frankfurt won and the minister of finance resigned. The bank's independence is due to the great fear of inflation in Germany. In the early 1920s the country suffered from running inflation when even small food items cost millions of marks. That inflation led to great political instability and the Germans are determined not to let that happen again. The leading international position of the German currency forces several of the smaller nations to adapt their currencies to changes in the exchange rate of the mark. The Dutch do so within an hour, even during the night. Consequently, Frankfurt guaranteed a stable currency system in a large part of Western Europe. The new European Central Bank will take over that responsibility, as a kind of European "Federal Reserve System" (Fed). However, the ECB will have less power than the Fed, because the national banks of the participating countries bring in more votes than the ECB as such. France was among the main proponents of the ECB. France hoped that the introduction of the Euro and the establishment of the ECB would finally stop France's second rank position vis-à-vis the German mark and the German Bundesbank. That expectation would come true if the national governments would have a stronger influence on the new institutions than the German government had over the Bundesbank. Germany was more reluctant to exchange its strong and stable mark for an international currency that could be influenced by the French government, or by any government at all. At last, it welcomed the new currency and the new European Bank as new symbols of unity, as long as the independence of the institution was safeguarded.

All EU member states (as well as aspirant members) have been preparing for the EMU. They have undertaken urgent efforts to meet the formal requirements, which include:

- state budget deficit should be under three percent,
- total national debt should not exceed sixty percent of (GNP), and
- inflation should not be higher than one and a half times the three lowest national levels within the European Union.

Since hardly any country met all the criteria, obvious development in the right direction also qualified for admission. In particular, the maximum level of three percent for the state deficit led to hasty cuts in state budgets. French efforts to implement retrenchments in public spending unleashed large strike actions in 1996. Germany, whose membership is indispensable, faced problems in 1997 and thought about selling part of its gold stock to reduce the deficit, but this idea met with opposition from Frankfurt. Frankfurt won.

Currency unity will also terminate the opportunities for national governments to print more money or adapt the exchange rate of the currency as a means to boost the economy. That curtailment of national competencies went a couple of EU members too far (Denmark, Great Britain, and Sweden), and they preferred to opt out. They did not want to give up their freedom in monetary and financial policies but they have left open the possibility of joining EMU at a later stage. The British hesitancy is also given in by the idea that the British pound sterling continues to be a major international currency, one of the last remnants of the British Empire, and by the long-standing position of the London "City" as an international banking center. The European Central Bank, which will serve as the watchdog of Euro stability, does not have its seat in London, however, but in Frankfurt. On this point, the Germans rejected any compromise, since it feared British or French government influence on the stability of the Euro in case the bank is located in London or Paris. Of all EU member states, only Greece failed to meet the criteria for admission to the EMU, but its is trying to catch up. Italy's admission aroused most discussion, since that country has a reputation of consciously stimulating inflation (printing money) as a means to reduce its national debt. The other countries did not want to discourage the energetic efforts of the Italian government to put the country's finances in order and approved its admission, if only grudgingly. The Italian prime minister who accomplished this "miracle," Romano Prodi, is now president of the European Commission, the European Union's executive.

The decision by the European governments to introduce the EMU, establish the ECB, and replace national currencies by the Euro mainly serves as a political symbol of unity. The introduction of the Euro will do away with the troublesome change of money after each border crossing or airplane landing, which used to leave tourists with a lot of francs, pesetas, escudos, or liras after each holiday trip.

The publicity and hype about the introduction of the Euro may easily hide the fact that it is not monetary or economic policies but agricultural policies that have been the core EU activity. During most of the European Union's existence, agriculture absorbed seventy percent of the EU budget; at present that share is still almost fifty percent, and agricultural subsidies continue to be by far the largest budget item. Their main purposes have been to remove internal trade barriers (agriculture has always been the sector most liable to state protection in Europe) and to improve the farmers' standard of living. To serve these goals, EU agricultural policies consist of a system of guaranteed prices for agricultural products far above world market prices, made possible by external tariff walls. Agricultural policy is complicated by the fact that the member states have opposing interests in this field, in particular between the northern states (milk, butter) and the southern members (wine, olive oil). The different interests have to be compromised in long and protracted negotiations that take place each year. The costs of compromise have been high, in the form of a costly, intricate, and arbitrary system of guaranteed prices for farmers, internal prices, and export prices. The high price guarantees for farmers have caused an enormous overproduction of dairy products and wine, resulting in a so-called butter mountain and wine lake. In response, the European Union is now attempting to reduce production by lowering guaranteed prices and by means of production ceilings and national production quotas. (Even a wine lake has its limits.)

The arbitrary nature of agricultural subsidies and guaranteed prices has increasingly become a source of internal EU concern. The debate was started in the 1980s with the British demand of more balance in its national contributions and benefits. Until that time, national imbalances had not been a problem, since the Germans were the largest net payers and did not raise any complaints. The "mad cow crisis" (about an export ban on British cows) intensified the debate on the scope and costs of agricultural policies. From its core policy field and its major source of pride, agriculture has now become the European Union's sick child, and voices are raised to do away with most subsidies. The trade barriers have also strained relations with agricultural exporters. Third world countries have protested about unfair treatment of their exports. Trade disputes with the United States have even resulted in a series of EU-U.S. "tariff wars." At present, the reform of agrarian policies is one of the core elements of "Agenda 2000," which must prepare the EU for its eastward extension. The reforms have been a prominent issue at recent European Council meetings (see Table 8.2). They will probably end the complex negotiations on prices and production quotas.

Twenty years ago, the European Union mainly functioned as a Common Market of agricultural products, and the termination of agricultural policies would have dealt a fatal blow to almost all European cooperation. As the introduction of the Euro shows, however, the European Union's scope has extended from agriculture to include a range of other areas. The gradual extension of the European Union's concerns from one policy area to another is sometimes called "spill-over," one of the most widely used terms in the literature on European integration. Spill-over from steel and agriculture to other policy fields has not been an automatic process but is encouraged by pressure groups that demand European policies. According to some, it is even these groups and organizations (including "Frankfurt") rather than the national governments, that are the real motors behind the current integration process. In addition to agriculture, three policy fields stand out as objects of EU concern: Regional policy, industrial policies, and social policies.

The European Union's regional policy aims to make less developed regions more competitive, in particular by improving their infrastructure (roads and ports). Southern Europe and Ireland have benefited most, and some of these nations even totally classify as regions in need of support. The Irish are not only the most grateful, they have also been most successful in the use of European funds. The country has attracted huge foreign investment and has almost become the European Union's "greenfield." From a position as one of the less prosperous EU member states, it has been able to catch up with the more prosperous members (see Table 8.1).

The European Union's internal market policy in industry and services is probably its most successful accomplishment. It has removed internal industrial and commercial trade barriers, and it has also created more equality in international competition by setting strict limits to financial state support of national industries. This policy has even opened sectors for (inter)national competition that were traditionally monopolized by one public company, like telephone networks and, more hesitantly, railways. An international railway strike in 1998 failed to stop this policy of allowing competition on the tracks.

In social policies the European Union has much less of a record. One of its main concerns has been the removal of barriers to labor mobility, the free flow of people to jobs in other countries. In practice, labor mobility remains severely curtailed by language diversity and great variations in national social security systems. It is still very difficult for people who move to other member states to transfer the collective old-age pension rights they have earned in their country of origin. This "nontransferability" of social security rights, in particular of old-age pension rights, is called the "pension gap."

In contrast to practice in most member states, the European Union's social policies have not included any active employment policies. Unemployment now stands at eleven percent, more than twice the U.S. unemployment rate. The EU can point only to a modest social record in health and safety regulations, equal conditions for women and men on the labor market and in social security, and worker participation in multinational enterprises. These subjects have been covered by a number of European Union Directives, which must be integrated into national legislation. This kind of national application of EU measures is a source of concern by itself, since national governments use all kinds of arguments to postpone the adaptation of their laws. The weak development of social policies has reinforced opposition to the European Union among those who argue that the European Union is mainly an economic instrument serving multinational companies, and that the EMU will only add to the predominance of economic considerations over social aims. Others attribute the relative lack of social policies to the strenuous efforts by the national governments to keep this policy domain for themselves, as one of the main instruments to forge national allegiance toward the national government and the national state.

However, the member states do not have the same interests. The richer northern countries favor some form of social harmonization. They fear "social dumping," in the form of shifts in investments toward the less developed southern countries and an influx of workers from those countries and from Great Britain (disguised as self-employed people not subject to social security regulations). Optimists regard this internal migration as just another version of labor mobility. Pessimists point to the fact that such workers undermine business-labor agreements and national social legislation. Social dumping is one of the major concerns of the European trade union movement. The British position is most at stake, since the country's conservative governments have refused to implement any EU social directives, a step that the Labour government has now undone.

A debate is going on about the possible impact of the EMU on employment. Some fear that the loss of national economic policy instruments will result in an even higher unemployment rate. Others point to the fact that independent monetary policies as a means to stimulate economic growth and employment had already been abandoned in most member states under the previous systems of fixed currency exchange rates.

TOWARD EUROPEAN INTEGRATION

The long lines of trucks waiting at the borders in Western Europe have dwindled and custom officers' uniforms have become museum pieces. Since the early 1990s, a number of EU member states have even abolished all passport controls, at least in principle. One can now travel thousands of kilometers through several countries without any border stop, a unique feature in European history. These are merely the more visible effects of the European Union. National policies in a wide range of fields increasingly have to take into account or even merely implement the EU directives from Brussels, the European Union's "capital" (Luxembourg and Strasbourg are also important seats of European Union institutions). Reference to "Brussels" has also become an effective means to silence opposition toward government proposals. ("We can't help, we are merely implementing European Union directives.")

Most European innovation originates with war. The history of European integration has deep historical roots but the final steps were not made until the end of World War II. In particular the French-German rivalry—one of the backgrounds to both World Wars—was a motive to look for international cooperation. While the United States tried to forge European cooperation as a condition of the Marshall Aid they offered for the postwar reconstruction of Europe, the cold war stimulated the integration of West Germany in Western Europe. The first step toward integration was not taken, however, until France realized that German heavy industry would soon outmatch French industry once again and reduce France to a minor power. Six "founding nations" then set up the European Coal and Steel Community in 1952, as a kind of international coordinating body for these industries. It brought together France and West Germany, joined by Italy and the Low Countries (Holland, Belgium, and Luxembourg). Its purpose was to coordinate the development of coal mining and the steel industry in postwar reconstruction and stop the clumsy system of national protection in coal and steel. To the Germans, the new organization offered a means to integrate in Western Europe as a full-fledged sovereign state. It should allow for the further growth of German industry, as a contribution to German prosperity, and offer France ample opportunities to catch up with the Germans. That would serve French-German *rapprochement* and political stability in Europe.

The 1957 Treaty of Rome extended cooperation to a customs union and a Common Market in agricultural products. Due to the Cold War and the limits that were imposed on German rearmament, the French concern over the German steel industry withered away, and the Common Market in agriculture (called European Economic Community, EEC) soon overshadowed the European Coal and Steel Community. In the Common Market, internal trade barriers in agriculture were reduced and the intricate system of differential prices was set up for food products. A third European agency, Euratom, was to check nuclear energy policies.

For a long time, French President de Gaulle blocked British membership, arguing that Great Britain was not at all interested in Europe and that its participation would be detrimental to efforts of European coordination. France did not give up its opposition until it realized that Germany had become the foremost economic power in Europe. Great Britain was finally admitted in 1973, together with Ireland and Denmark. In the course of the 1970s, regular summit meetings of the heads of government and frequent meetings of foreign ministers became a tradition and provided new impulses to European integration. Even when disagreement predominated, the government leaders sought new fields in which common objectives could be reached (spill-over).

In the 1980s, Greece, Spain, and Portugal joined, which moved the axis of the Community to the less industrialized South. Two diverging trends dominated further efforts of integration. On the one hand, the British Prime Minister Margaret Thatcher started a crusade against "Brussels" as a big and unchecked spending machine, and against political integration as undermining national interests. On the other hand, the 1979–1980 oil crisis and growing competition by East Asian countries stimulated the quest for common economic policies. The president of the European Commission, the Frenchman Jacques Delors, drafted a series of economic and social plans and used the British intransigence to get the continental countries to align. A time schedule was set for the completion of a fully integrated market, not only in agriculture, but in industrial products and services as well. All states except Great Britain also adopted a "social charter" outlining some common social policies. Foreign policy coordination became also a regular item on the agenda of the summits. In 1993, the full open market, which abolished internal border checks, came into effect. The 1992 Maastricht Treaty, which contained the plans for a monetary and a political union, made the formal transition from European Economic Community to European Union. Following "Maastricht," other nations shared Great Britain's reluctance to join a political union, and in national referendums the Treaty was accepted only by small margins.

In the same period, the Schengen Treaty came into effect, which removed the border checks between most member states. At the international airports, special "Schengen" signs allow the citizens of these member states to entry without any passport or luggage check at all.

In the course of the 1990s, Austria, Finland, and Sweden became European Union members. This admission of three highly developed nations moved the axis a bit back to Germanic Europe.

Fifteen out of the nineteen Western European nations are now members of the European Union (see Table 8.1). Only four Western European countries keep aloof. All of them are small-scale national communities that are afraid of losing their traditional values and fear the "import" of the large member states' social problems.

- Far off Iceland, with even less inhabitants than Luxembourg, maintains close economic relations with North America,
- Norway, a society of dispersed local (fishing) communities, and because of its large gas reserves is hardly interested in common economic policies. The country has twice rejected joining the Union in national referendums.
- Switzerland, which refuses any transfer of governmental powers, is now totally surrounded by European Union territory, and
- Malta, also has less inhabitants than Luxembourg. It was a British colony until 1964, and is still enjoying its recent independence.

Several Central European countries are lining up to join the European Union ranks. In 1997, the European Union announced that it would first begin talks with Czechia, Estonia, Hungary, Poland, and Slovenia. According to the European Union, they have made the most progress in the direction of parliamentary democracy and a free-market economy. Their admission will extend the European Union from a Germanic and Latin institution to a partly Slavonic institution. The Greek-speaking republic on the Mediterranean island of Cyprus is another candidate for admission.

THE EUROPEAN UNION'S STRUCTURE

When Europeans talk about state power, they still mean the national state. The European Union is a supranational institution, able to impose decisions on the national member states. However, the European Union is less than a federal union, since it is the member states that make the binding decisions. Is the European Union a state? Because the member states dominate political decision making, the European Union is not a state in the classical sense of a territory with a central authority. Some argue that it is a new kind of state, in which only some aspects of social life are covered by central authority, while others are left to the participating units. In that case, it would be an extreme form of federal state, with very limited federal powers.

Like the member states, the European Union officially acknowledges the *Trias Politica* principle. It has a parliament (the European Parliament), an executive branch (the European Commission), and a European Court of Justice. There is a crucial difference with most member states, however. National politics in most European countries consists of the interplay ("dual power") between the parliament and the government. In the European Union, the national governments of the member states play first trumpet and decide on major policy lines. European Union policies are then worked out in contacts between the national governments (the national executive branches) and the European Union's own executive, the European Commission. This system of decision making means there are actually two levels of European Union policy making, one is "intergovernmental" and consists of meetings of national political leaders. The second is the level of the European Union—as such, the "supranational" level.

The Maastricht Treaty made a distinction in three "pillars" of policy fields, in which the European Union will display activities. The first pillar consists of the

Table 8.1. European Union Member States

Country	Inhabitants (millions)	Government composition in 1999	Votes CM	Seats EP	GNP per capita	Currency
Original member states (since 1952)						
Germany	81.9	Social democrats/ Green	10	99	22.0	German mark
France	58.2	Social democrats/ Communist/Green	10	87	21.3	French franc
Italy	57.5	Postcommunist/ other left	10	87	21.3	Italian lira
Holland	15.5	Social democrats/ Liberals	5	31	22.1	Dutch gulden (Guilder)
Belgium	10.2	Christian democrats/ social democrats	5	25	23.2	Belgian franc
Luxembourg	.4	Christian democrats/ social democrats	2	6	33.1	Luxembourg franc
Joined 1973						
Great Britain	58.8	Labour	10	87	20.5	Pound sterling
Denmark	5.3	Social democrats/ social liberals	3	16	25.5	Danish krone*
Ireland	3.6	Conservatives/ conservative liberals	3	15	20.6	Irish pound*
Joined 1986						
Spain	40.5	Conservatives	8	64	16.0	Spanish peseta
Greece	10.6	Social democrats	5	25	14.0	Greek drachme*
Portugal	9.9	Social democrats	5	25	14.6	Portuguese escudo
Joined 1995						
Sweden	8.9	Social democrats	4	22	20.4	Swedish krone*
Austria	8.1	Social democrats/ Christian democrats	4	21	23.1	Austrian schilling
Finland	5.1	Social democrats/ 4 smaller parties	3	16	20.5	Finnish mark
Total	374.6		87	626		Euro

CM: Council of Ministers; EP: European Parliament; GNP: National income per capita, in thousands U.S. dollars, Purchasing Power Parities. Source: OECD 1998.

* : will not (yet) be replaced by the Euro in 2002.

U.S. population: 270.3 million (on three times the EU-territory); U.S. GNP per capita: 29.3.

EU's original concerns, the internal market policies. The second pillar includes common foreign and security policies ("CFSP"). Despite the efforts in these fields, the European Union is still hardly able to face even a European crisis like the war in Bosnia, due to its internal division, which leads to long debate without any substantial result. (Military action in Kosovo was a NATO affair, not an EU initiative.) The third pillar refers to justice and internal affairs like drug policies and admission procedures for political fugitives. The European Union's supranational institutions mainly play a role in the first pillar, which is the European Union's core field of activity. In the second and third pillar, decisions are in the hands of the national governments and are made at intergovernmental meetings. However, the third pillar is gradually being integrated into the first pillar.

Intergovernmental Decision Making

The European Council, as the summit meeting of heads of government is called, takes the major decisions in all three pillars. The European Council is held at least twice a year, and key decisions require unanimity among the fifteen member states (see Table 8.2). France and Germany dominate the meetings. If they agree on a proposal, it is likely to become European policy; if not, the proposal will be dropped anyway. The French presidents are far less compromising when their economic or political interests are at stake than the German chancellors. Germany more often enjoys the support of some of the smaller nations and is also more sensitive to the needs of these countries. The difference is in accordance with internal policies in France, preferably without compromise, and in Germany, with its permanent coalition governments and federal structure. Moreover, for Germany, the main advantage of European integration is the reduced fear of German political power in the surrounding countries. At the same time, European integration has allowed the country to become by far the largest economic power in Europe. Great Britain has successfully fulfilled de Gaulle's fears; of the three major Western European powers it has been least interested in Europe.

Hardly any coalitions are forged prior to or during the summit meetings, not even between "natural" partners like Sweden and Denmark, or Portugal and Spain. Each nation speaks for itself. The presidency of the Council circulates. Its meetings are held in the chairman's country, preferably in an old *chateau* and under safety regulations that are reminiscent of a medieval siege. The official picture taken of the European council reveals one of the distinctive advantages of a presidential system. As the only Head of State in this company, the French president always occupies a prominent position in the first row, close to the formal Head of State of the host state.

The country that will preside over the next meeting sets targets to be reached in the half year of its presidency. The preparations of the meeting include some nervous travelling to the other member states in order to gain support for the plans by means of "package deals," which offer different benefits for each of the member states. More than results, consensus is what counts. A meeting of the European leaders should always result in agreement, if only about minor points or vague guidelines. Because of the national governments' domination of EU decision making, some prefer to define the European Union as a "transnational"

Table 8.2. Important European Council Meetings

Year	Location	Subjects
1991	Maastricht, Holland	Most important meeting of the 1990s, resulting in the Maastricht Treaty, dealing with the EMU, more political unity, and the new name European Union. The Maastricht Treaty had to be ratified by the member states.
1992	Lisbon, Portugal; Birmingham, Great Britain	Discussion of the political problems, faced by several governments, in ratifying the Maastricht Treaty.
1994	Corfu, Greece	Conflict about the Presidency of the European Commission after Jacques Delors resigned. The question was solved at a later extra meeting in Brussels, where Luxembourg's Prime Minister Jacques Santer was elected.
1995	Madrid, Spain	The final stage of the EMU; procedures for institutional reforms.
1996	Dublin, Ireland	Stability Pact, with sanctions for countries that have large budget deficits after the introduction of the Euro as the common currency.
1997	Amsterdam, Holland	Treaty of Amsterdam, covering more influence for the European Parliament, and final decisions pertaining to the "Stability Pact."
1997	Luxembourg	Extra meeting on unemployment, which is considered to be a national affair.
1997	Luxembourg	"Agenda 2000," with reforms in institutions, in decision-making procedures, and in agrarian policies to prepare the extension towards Central Europe.
1998	Vienna, Austria	Agenda 2000; more equality in contributions by the richer member states (Germany is the largest net payer; Holland the largest payer relative to its GNP).
1999	Berlin, Germany	Election of Italy's former Prime Minister Romano Prodi as President of the European Commission.
	Helsinki	Admission of political fugitives; EU-extension

instead of a supranational institution. Others even call it an "intergovernmental" instrument in the hands of the national governments.

The policy guidelines adopted at the summits are elaborated at meetings of the national ministers. These meetings are called the Council of Ministers. Until the end of the 1980s, the ministers of agriculture were the most frequent flyers to Brussels, or to Luxembourg, where most agricultural decisions were made about tariffs, prices and, later, production quotas. The extension of the policy range since the 1970s has given rise to frequent flights of other ministers as well, of industry and economic affairs, of finance, and of social affairs and employment in particular. In contrast to the prime ministers, who mostly are of age and go to bed in due time, in particular the agricultural ministers' meetings used to last until early in the morning before a package deal has been reached that was acceptable to all member states. Since the late 1980s, the need of nocturnal compromises has decreased because the rule of unanimity has been given up, except for very important matters. In the Council of Ministers, a qualified majority now suffices for most decisions. Qualified does not mean ten out of fifteen votes, since the principle of "one country—one vote" does not apply. In total, the ministers cast 87 votes. The four largest countries (France, Germany, Great Britain, and Italy) have ten votes each, Spain eight, the other countries between two and five. A qualified majority means 62 out of the 87 votes, and they have to be cast by at least ten member states (see Table 8.1). As a consequence, neither a combination of the five larger member states, nor a coalition of all smaller states can overrule the others. In between the Council of Ministers' meetings, the "Permanent Representatives" of the member countries carry on the negotiations. These high-ranking diplomats serve as the watchdogs of their nations' interests, and at the same time they have to keep decision making going.

The Three Branches of the European Union

While the major decisions are made in the European council and the Council of Ministers—both of them consisting of representatives of the national governments—the European Union possesses three truly supranational government bodies. They are the European Commission, the European Parliament, and the European Court of Justice. Their competencies are mainly confined to the first pillar, the internal market.

The European Union's standing executive, the European Commission (EC), has come to play an increasingly active role in all policy fields. It consists of two commissioners from each of the larger and one from each of the smaller member states. Most of them are former ministers in national governments or prominent opposition leaders. (In some cases their appointment was used as a means to get rid of them in national politics.) With monthly salaries of over $ 20,000 (subject only to a low twenty percent "European" tax rate), plus allowances, they are the highest paid political officers in Europe, not counting kings, queens, and a few strong presidents. The EC members are nominated for five years by their governments but they are required to be independent, and they are.

The European Commission sets the agenda of the Council of Ministers, proposes new European legislation (a right called its "exclusive right of initiative"), and executes decisions taken by the European Council and the Council of Ministers. For these purposes, the Commission disposes of a modest bureaucracy, divided into 23 Directorates-General (DGs), whose posts are allocated among the member states, but in a rather informal way. Being less checked by a parliament than most national governments, the EC's activities have displayed a dynamism of their own, leading to very detailed rules, in particular in agriculture, and to complaints about the Brussels bureaucracy. The connotation of a bureaucracy, hardly checked by others, has made the European Union a source of concern rather than pride for many Europeans. While enjoying the fruits of international cooperation, they distrust "Brussels." In particular, former EC President Jacques Delors (a French social democrat) was highly praised by some and criticized by others for his very active role in stimulating new policy fields and "building bridges" among the member states. In 1994, his succession became a major problem when two contestants showed up—the Belgian prime minister and a former Dutch prime minister—both of them Christian democrats. France and Germany together spoke out in favor of the Belgian candidate, Great Britain then felt isolated and supported the Dutch candidate. As a result, agreement was not reached until an extraordinary meeting of the European Council (the Council of government leaders) was called, where Luxembourg's prime minister Jacques Santer was elected, who was expected to have a much lower political profile.

Although it has expanded continuously, the role of the European Parliament (EP) is still rather limited and does not yet match that of national parliaments. Formerly, national allegiance used to dominate in the European Parliament. The introduction of direct EP elections in all member states in 1979 has contributed to increasing prevalence of party allegiance over national sentiment. All major party groups are now coordinated at the European level, with the Christian democrats and the social democrats as the largest ones. The number of MPs varies according to country size, from 99 for Germany, 87 for France, Great Britain, and Italy to 6 for Luxembourg (see Table 8.1). Actually, Germany (with over two hundred times as many inhabitants as Luxembourg) should have gotten over one hundred seats, but one hundred proved to be beyond the psychological limit to some members.

The EP members are still elected under different types of national electoral systems (proportional representation, first-past-the-post). The European Union is now investigating the possibility of introducing one uniform electoral system for these "European elections." The elections for the European Parliament have a very low turnout. This lack of voter interest reflects the large distance between national electorates and "Brussels," as well as the lack of real parliamentary power. European politics is rightly considered far off by many nonvoters, handled by the national governments and the European Commission, and with a very limited say for the parliament. This does not mean that the European Parliament doesn't play any role. In the procedure of decision making, it is active in between the time the Commission prepares the proposals and final decision making by the Council of Ministers. If the parliament rejects Commission proposals, they require unanimity in the Council of Ministers in order to be adopted.

The European Parliament is hampered by the fact that meetings of EP committees ("part meetings") take place in Brussels and plenary sessions in Strasbourg, a French provincial town on the French-German border, some 450 km away. This dual seat forces the members to travel back and force between Brussels and Strasbourg continuously. The French government has never been willing to give up the clumsy role of Strasbourg in European politics, but EP committee meetings, all of them convening in Brussels, have made the Strasbourg plenary sessions into a rather marginal ritual.

The most important confrontation between the European Commission and the European Parliament took place in January 1999. Two EC members, one from Spain and one from France (a former French prime minister), were under attack of nepotism in allocating funds to private contractors. Instead of promising an investigation, the EC rebuked the charges and defended its collective responsibility for EU policies. This prompted EP members, who had rather seen the two EC members resign, to announce a motion of no-confidence ("motion of censure") against the European Commission as a whole. The following days were filled with lobbying by national governments, who did not want a crisis in EU decision making, and by France most of all, in defense of its EC member. Social democrats and Christian democrats were particularly involved, since the two EC members under attack were social democrats, while the EC president, Jacques Santer, was a Christian democrat (and former prime minister of Luxembourg). During the final debate, the leader of the Christian democrats (a former Belgian prime minister) was most active in bringing his party on one line against the motion. As an outcome of all this lobbying, the motion of no-confidence was rejected with 293 votes against and 232 votes in favor. The large fractions were divided; most Germans voted in favor, most French and other Latin European EP members against. Despite this result, the EC's position vis-à-vis the European Parliament was weakened and it had to accept an independent investigation of the allegations of corruption. When that report was published a few months later, the full EC resigned anyway. Former Italian Prime Minister Romano Prodi was then appointed as the new president.

Germans like to compare the relationship between the major European decision making bodies to their own federal institutions. The EC is then compared with the German government, the EP with the *Bundestag*, and the intergovernmental European Council with the *Bundesrat*, the German Senate, in which the governments of the federal states are represented. Although the structure looks a bit similar, the division of power is totally different, since the German government is a real government, while the EC is not. In particular the French and British have always looked with suspicion upon any extension of the EC's power, as a form of creeping German-style federalism.

Although the European Union's judiciary branch, the European Court of Justice, has a limited role, it has been active in interpreting EU legislation and in bringing the member states in line after a common decision. The European Commission or any citizen may bring a noncompliant government before the Court in order to have European rules applied. This new citizen right has introduced creeping judicial review in countries where it did not exist earlier. In other words, the European Court may declare national laws unbinding, because they violate citizens rights laid down in European Union agreements, which now constitute a kind of European Union "Constitution."

The development of the European Union has given rise to a large amount of networking and lobbying between European Union agencies, national governments, national pressure groups, and newly created European-level pressure groups. The European Union has even introduced a kind of tripartism in the form of contacts between the European Committee and an advisory council composed of business and labor representatives, called ECOSOC. This body bears some similarities with business/trade union councils in some of the member states. However, the contacts at the European level stop short of real tripartism, because of the European Commission's lack of real governing power.

Even the member states engage in European Union-wide networking, mobilizing their national citizens at high European Union posts to defend their interests. Great Britain, which lacks such a tradition of networking at home, is worse off, but it is gradually learning how to imitate the Latin nations (the strongest networkers) in that respect. In spite of these hectic activities, pressure group activities in Brussels are more characterized by lobbying than by networking. National pressure groups have established European-level coordinating bodies to represent their interests in the European Union. Large companies and even regional governments have set up their own lobbying offices in Brussels.

A typical problem that plagues efforts of international integration in Europe is the diversity of languages, and the refusal of states to stick to one international language, for instance English or French. English would be the most logical solution, but France stubbornly refuses to accept a second rank for its national language. At European Union meetings the representatives speak their own languages. The eleven national languages of the fifteen member states all are official European Union languages and documents have to be translated into these languages. One third of the European Union's bureaucracy is devoted to that job of translating and interpreting. English and French are often used as working languages, but even that poses problems. English as spoken by Greeks and Portuguese may sound very cute but it is not always clear to the EU professional interpreter's service how to translate it into Finnish or Swedish (or even back into Greek or Portuguese for their less cosmopolitan compatriots).

The decision-making structure and procedures are now the subject of a debate on "institutional reforms" and policy changes, in particular in the agricultural budget. Under the name of "Agenda 2000," the changes must adapt the EU bodies to the expected admission of new members in Central Europe. This extension of the European Union has not been undisputed, of course. In the debate about "widening" versus "deepening," proponents of widening argue that the Central European countries cannot be isolated, since that would create a new gulf between Western and Central Europe. Others fear that the enlargement of the EU might postpone its "deepening" for many years to come, that is, its extension to new policy fields and its function of harmonizing national policies. They prefer a process of deepening prior to widening. Moreover, the lower income Latin nations fear a decrease of the support they get, and Greece has also demanded the status of aspirant-member for Cyprus, as a precondition for any extension in Central Europe.

Institutional reforms include a limited enlargement of the EP from 626 to 700 seats and an adaptation of the number of EC and EP seats for all countries. Not all the smaller countries will then be represented in the EC at the same time, and the larger countries will lose their second seat in that institution. They will be compensated by a change in the number of votes in the Council of Ministers, which will better reflect country size. Moreover, a stricter distinction will be made between official languages (all languages of the member states) and the two working languages, English and French, which will be used in small committees and in the EU bureaucracy.

9

International Politics

St. Petersburg, Petrograd, Leningrad, St. Petersburg . . . the former Russian capital has changed names several times during the twentieth century. Its original, German name was Russified in 1917, and after the revolution its name was changed in honor of the Soviet leader Lenin. After the collapse of communism its original name has been readopted.

Renaming cities, towns, streets, and squares after communist leaders and successes was a common phenomenon in Central and Eastern Europe. By now, the "Lenin boulevard" and the "Revolution Square" have reverted to their previous names. The rise of new nations as a result of the world wars and the end of Soviet power has required still more adaptation in name-giving, because of the use of new national languages. The Ukrainian city of Lviv probably holds the record. In the course of this century its name has shifted from Lvov to Lwow, Lemberg, Lvov, and Lviv, depending on its rulers: Russia, Poland, Germany, Russia, and Ukraine.

The reshuffling of borders and the emergence of new nations have been due to the "power politics" of the major powers. During the nineteenth and early twentieth century, five European powers (Great Britain, France, and the German, Austrian and Russian Empires) decided on Europe's fate. After World War II, two superpowers dominated international politics in Europe: the United States and the Soviet Union. Today only one such power is left, the United States. Since the collapse of the Soviet Union, no European nation is a real power in world politics. International politics is dominated by one single center of power, by one "pole": the United States. In this "unipolar" system even the larger European nations occupy second- or third-rate positions, unable to wage a major conflict without United States consent—a striking contrast with "multipolar" Europe of the nineteenth century and the "bipolar" world during the cold war.

MARKING TERRITORIES IN MULTIPOLAR EUROPE

Great ideas and ideals have been invoked to justify international peace treaties and international warfare. (The most classical war of all, the Trojan War, with

Achilles and Odysseus as heroes, was about women—at least according to Homer.) Religion played a role during the Middle Ages, when the Catholic Church organized and inspired wars. Later, Russian expansion into the Turkish Empire was justified as an effort to save the Orthodox Christians from Islamic repression. Another dominant theme in international relations was the opposition between revolutionaries (like France after the French Revolution) and conservatives, and later between revolutionary communism and democracy. Often, the ideals have merely hidden power politics, which aims at stabilizing or reinforcing national power. Territorial considerations have played an important role in this traditional European "geo-politics," the marking of territories that is common to most animal species, including kings and emperors. While rivers and mountains served as barriers to expansion and as "natural frontiers," open plains invited conquest.

Although it seems long ago, traditional European power politics have had a large impact on Europe as it looks today. With five major powers until World War I, Europe used to be a "multipolar" continent. Apart from contested areas of colonial expansion outside Europe, a few regions have suffered more than once as battlefields between the powers: Belgium and Alsace-Lorraine in Western Europe, Poland and the Balkan Peninsula in Central Europe.

Belgium formed a buffer zone between Great Britain, France, and Germany. For that reason Great Britain in particular guaranteed its neutrality after Napoleon's defeat in 1815. Germany realized that any attack upon Belgium, as an easy way into France, would almost certainly lead to war with Great Britain. So, the position of Belgium as the neutral heart of Western Europe was hardly in dispute, but once a war broke out Belgium became a battlefield, as happened during both world wars.

The second contested region was Alsace-Lorraine, the border region between France and Germany. Germany conquered it in the short French-German War in 1870–1871, then had to give it back at the end of World War I, to retake it during World War II, and to lose it again. The disputed nature of this region in French-German relations was one of the French motives to have the central Alsacian city, Strasbourg, play a role in European Union politics. With Brussels and Strasbourg as the two meeting places of the European parliament, the two traditionally (but no longer) contested regions are now well represented in the European Union.

The disputed territories in Central Europe have been worse off. Poland is situated between Germany and Russia, and its territorial integrity has not been respected by either of the two. Just before the nineteenth century, Poland was partitioned by Austria, Prussia, and Russia, with the latter getting most. On several occasions, national revolts broke out against Russian rule. During World War I, Germany conquered the country. The peace treaty secured its independence, but not for long. In the beginning of World War II, Nazi Germany and communist Russia in close cooperation partitioned it once more. The country suffered more than any other European nation from that war, and most of the Holocaust victims were Polish Jews. After the war, Poland was moved westward under Russian pressure. This partial shift of territory became a new source of friction with Germany, since almost all Germans were expatriated from the new Polish territories. The new Polish nation became part of the safety zone of communist Russia against any new German threat.

The Balkan Peninsula, has also been a region of divergent interests. The basic issue during the nineteenth century was the Russian objective to gain access to the Mediterranean. That position on the Mediterranean would permit it to play a greater role in European politics and allow sea transport during the winter, when the ports in Northern Russia are hardly accessible and only the Black Sea ports are open. The shipping route from the Black Sea to the Mediterranean passed through two sea straits, both of them Turkish territory: the Bosporus, along Istanbul, and the Dardannelles. The Turkish Empire was in decay, however, and seemed an easy prey. The Russian aim to play a role in the Mediterranean was also served by means of cooperation with the Serbs, who were Orthodox Christians like the Russians, and looked for a leadership role on the Balkan themselves once Turkey would have been thrown out. The Russian interest was met with a reaction from the Austrian Empire, which included a number of (especially Slavonic) minorities within its borders and feared nationalist and separatist movements.

The Balkans would never have played so prominent a role in European politics if Great Britain and France were not interested in it as well. British involvement was motivated by the fact that Russia might threaten the routes to the British Indies. This argument gained force after the opening of the Suez Canal. France was looking for colonial expansion in North and West Africa and was determined to meet any challenge to its position as the major Mediterranean power. Later that century, a new contestant showed up: Germany. While Great Britain and France completed their colonial empires, Germany (unified since 1871) was developing strength as a potential colonial power, for which the remnants of the Turkish Empire offered the best opportunities. The expansion of German influence implied conflict with Russia, and eventually posed a danger to British and French colonial interests. Map 9.1 shows Europe as it looked in 1900.

A series of short Balkan crises and Balkan wars destroyed the delicate balance of interests on the Balkan Peninsula. They culminated in World War I. That war started as a conflict between Austria, supported by Germany, and Serbia, and assisted by Russia, following the assassination of the Austrian Crown Prince by a Serbian nationalist. The act took place in the city of Sarajevo, then under Austrian rule, later part of Yugoslavia, and now the capital of Bosnia. In the choice between the lesser evil of the two (Germany or Russia), France and Great Britain took sides with Russia. The war mainly developed into a French-German conflict in the North of France and Belgium, and a Russian-German conflict fought in Russia. At the peace treaties, U.S. President Woodrow Wilson introduced the idea of national self-determination for the Central European peoples, which occasioned the rise of a number of new nations. Several Slavonic language groups were united in the fragile kingdom of Yugoslavia. During World War II the

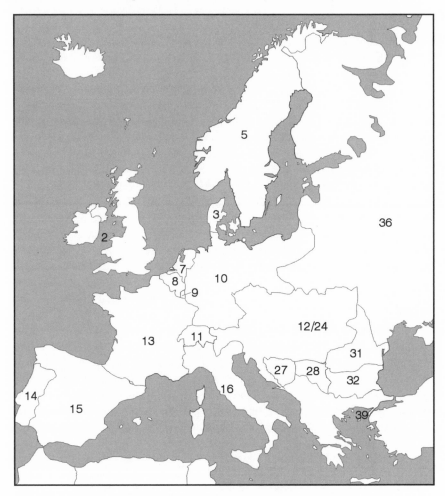

Map 9.1. Europe in 1900. For country names, see Table 1.1.
The following countries were not yet independent in 1900: 1, 4, 6, 17–23, 25, 26, 29, 30, 33–35, 37, 38, and 40.

Balkan Peninsula remained a marginal battlefield. It was invaded and occupied by Germany. Except for Greece, the Balkan Peninsula was liberated by domestic communists (Yugoslavia and Albania) or by the Russians, and under communist rule after the war.

Although some Europeans look back with nostalgia upon the period of empires and European power politics, it resulted in half a century with two world wars, as well as a number of smaller international conflicts. Europe may not have invented war, but it certainly carried the principle to its very extreme in World War II. That war put an end to the role of the Western European powers and started a period in which international politics in Europe was dominated by two centers of power, or two poles, the United States and the Soviet Union. This "bipolar" period lasted over forty years and was characterized by the cold war.

THE BIPOLAR WORLD DURING THE COLD WAR

Suppose you live in Seattle and want to visit close relatives in Vancouver. You have not seen them for some time, since they never got permission to leave Canada. After a lot of formalities and troubles you get a one-entry visa for one week, and the journey can start. You pass the U.S. customs office and before arriving at the Canadian border, you pass a fence of barbed wire, a mine field, watchtowers with armed soldiers, and a second fence with soldiers and dogs. You have to stay in the car while waiting two to four hours for the border check, or they will send you back, without any chance of another visa. Finally, it is your turn. Armed policemen scrutinize your car, both inside and also, with mirrors, under it. All presents that had been wrapped with care are opened with force. The border police may even tear open the seats in search of hidden merchandise. Protests will only cause a delay of at least one hour. Finally, they are done with you and you drive into Canada, angry as well as relieved. Soon you enter upon another group of dogs, guns and policemen. This time a quick glance in your passport suffices. Although you are prepared for the return trip, it will be worse than you expected. Policemen need even more time to look for fugitives that might be hidden in the car. It is hard to realize how lucky you are: You may leave that country again; your relatives are stuck there.

The Iron Curtain was like that (see Map 1.2). In East Germany barb wire, mine fields, and watchtowers were not enough. Automatic rifle installations were added to kill any moving object along the border. The pretext for this show of terror was to keep out "capitalist agents" from the West but the actual purpose was to deter (and kill) those who tried to escape to the Free World.

The cold war between the "Free World" and the Soviet Union broke out when Soviet Russia imposed total control over Central Europe. Following World War II, Stalin claimed a Soviet "sphere of influence," to prevent another surprise attack by Germany. Soviet influence implied control of these countries by the national communist parties, which in turn were subordinated to the Soviets. The United States opposed such a division of Europe but grudgingly saw communists under Soviet control take over in Central Europe. The only two communist countries able to claim national autonomy were Yugoslavia and Albania, since they had not been "liberated" by the Russian army.

The American Marshall Plan, which provided reconstruction funds and tried to enforce international economic cooperation, caused the final breach. Accusing the Americans of enforcing the subordination of their economies to American capitalism, the Soviets compelled Central Europe to refuse the aid. At the time of the communist "takeover" in Central Europe, tension between the Allies also mounted in Germany, which had been divided into four occupation zones. The

Soviets sealed off their zone, in order to hide growing suppression of noncommunists and the removal of German industry to Russia. The western allies (United States, Great Britain, and France) merged their zones and initiated the foundation of the Federal Republic of Germany (West Germany). In response, the Russian zone became the German Democratic Republic (East Germany), a part of the Communist Bloc. This completed the division of Europe. Berlin, located within East Germany, was split. The Western part remained under the administration of the western allies, while East Berlin became the capital of East Germany. The division of Berlin became the symbol of Europe's fate. (Although West Berlin formally remained under allied control, in practice it was governed as just another West German federal state.)

At first, the guiding Western principle in the East-West conflict was the "containment" of communism, in particular by the most powerful Western nation, the United States. After the beginning of the cold war, both the Free World and the Communist Bloc established the principle of mutual military aid to the partners in case of an attack by the other side. Western Europe and the United States set up the North Atlantic Treaty Organization (NATO), under American leadership. Most Western European countries became NATO members. When West Germany joined NATO in 1955, the Russians integrated their half of Europe in the "Warsaw Pact," which all communist countries had to join, except for Yugoslavia. During the cold war, NATO never took recourse to military action. The Warsaw Pact provided the Russians with the instrument to crush the 1956 Hungarian revolt and the 1968 Prague Spring, and to threaten Poland with military intervention in 1956 and 1981. All of these anticommunist and national movements were ascribed to "capitalist agents" from the West. The 1956 Hungarian revolt marked the beginning of a period in which the cold war temperature rose a bit. To the great disappointment of the Hungarians, the Western World did not interfere, which amounted to a *de facto* recognition of Russian control over Central Europe. The new paradigm of East-West relations was called "peaceful coexistence" in which capitalism and communism would show their advantages before the eyes of the increasing number of independent nations outside Europe.

The construction of the Berlin Wall in 1961 closed the last hole in the Iron Curtain, a first explicit communist recognition of their failure in the peaceful "competition" with the West. The wall sealed off East Berlin from West Berlin, leaving only a few official openings, like "Checkpoint Charlie" where foreigners could pass to East Berlin. The wall completed the military safety provisions at the Iron Curtain. Only high-ranking members of the communist parties and retired people were allowed to travel to the West, the elderly on the condition of giving up their old-age pensions.

During the cold war, international politics were simple. The total division of Europe and the "arms race" of nuclear weapons between the United States and the Soviet Union left hardly any room for autonomous international action within Europe by other states. Former great powers like Great Britain, (West) Germany, and France were dependent upon U.S. military force to defend their country against any Soviet attack, despite regular French claims of autonomy in that respect. The claims were based on the small French arsenal of nuclear weapons (*force de frappe*), developed in the 1960s. An advantage of this bipolar world was that it prevented regional conflict within each bloc (and even more, their escalation into a major war). National conflicts were absent on the Balkans. In the Soviet bloc all major decisions were made in Moscow, and Yugoslavia was held together by President Tito, who used the country's international position in between the two blocs as a motive to impose a highly authoritarian dictatorship. The integration of Greece and Turkey into NATO prevented armed conflicts between these two sworn enemies. The outcome was forty years of peace, be it heavily armed and not the kind of peace most of Central Europe had hoped for.

The cold war dominated the functioning of the United Nations, which was established in 1945. All European countries became members, except for both parts of Germany, which were refused membership, and Switzerland, which feared international obligations that might affect its abstinence in international political affairs. Within a few years, the start of the cold war split the United Nations into a Western bloc, led by the United States, a Communist Bloc ruled by Moscow, and a number of neutral countries. The latter increasingly came to operate as a bloc by themselves, and was referred to as the group of "neutral and nonaligned nations." Most of its members were Third World countries but a few European nations were active in this group, communist Yugoslavia most of all. The Yugoslav President Tito became one of the leaders of the group of the nonaligned nations. A few Western European countries, Finland and Austria, were obliged to be neutral as a result of postwar treaties. Sweden voluntarily opted for such a course, partly in order not to isolate Finland.

The tragic split of Europe ended in the late 1980s when the Soviet Union collapsed. Spontaneous revolts terminated the communist regimes in Central Europe, and the Berlin Wall was broken to pieces, which proved to be the start of a fast movement toward German Reunification. The Warsaw Pact was never heard of again, but NATO has survived. The end of Soviet domination has allowed the emergence of nationalist disputes on the Balkan Peninsula. The region has lost its strategic importance, however. Colonial empires have disappeared, the Suez Canal is no longer used for oil transports to Europe, and Turkey is in firm command of the Sea Straits between the Black Sea and the Mediterranean. The larger European nations, the former great powers, have nothing to defend there, except the protection of minorities, as is the case in Kosovo.

EUROPE IN THE NEW UNIPOLAR WORLD

Europe maintains very intensive relations with the United States, as a junior partner in almost all fields except old culture. In defense, Europe is still dependent on the United States for its protection, although it is no longer clear against whom. In foreign affairs, the European Union is far from united and has hardly any answer to crises in Eastern Europe, like the Bosnian war. It was the United States, not the European Union, that brought the Serbs, Croats, and Bosnians to the bargaining table, where they concluded the Dayton agreement. It was also American diplomacy that tried to stop Serbian military action in Kosovo, followed by NATO intervention under U.S. leadership. Although Western European investments in the United States are catching up, Europe is also a junior partner in economic power, as it is in technology and science. In popular culture, the United States dominates the movie industry and television broadcasting. At times France has called for protection of European culture against the United States imports, but unsuccessfully so. Europe has no answer to American movies, soaps, talk shows, and Mickey Mouse. The most popular French comics heroes are Asterix and Obelix, who fight in first-century France for independence from the Roman Empire, but the recreation center near Paris inspired by their adventures was no match for Eurodisney.

Once in a while, economic relations between the European Union and the United States are strained by the European Union's high external tariffs for agricultural products, which affect United States exports. Incidentally, a "tariff war" between the European Union and the United States has to be prevented or solved. Europe's relations with the rest of the world to some extent continue to be influenced by former colonial ties. Table 9.1 lists the colonial empires, in the order of the size of their colonial empires in 1945. Some of the remaining overseas territories are now considered to be integral parts of the European nations concerned. As the table shows, decolonization involved warfare against national liberation armies (called terrorists by that time).

The British Commonwealth, which comprises former British colonies, is by far the largest postcolonial international community. Except for the United States, most of the larger English-speaking countries are members. Attachment to royalty and discussing cricket serve as common bonds. France has tried to set up a similar network of French-speaking countries. Most of its members are small states in North and West Africa. With less pomp and pretensions, Spain still tries to act as the cultural center of the Hispanic world, which includes some twenty Latin American countries. While these language-based international communities mainly focus on common culture, the French pursue more active goals in their relations with the former French colonies. A number of Caribbean and Pacific Islands have been integrated into the French nation, and France remains involved in its former territories in Africa, most of them small states. Occasionally it has sent troops to "protect" or evacuate French citizens during a popular revolt or to interfere directly in national politics in its former African colonies. The smaller Western European nations maintain less close relations with their former colonies. The most obvious exception is Denmark, still ruling over Greenland. Central and Eastern Europe did not have any colonies. The Soviet Union maintained intense contacts with many Third World countries, but these relations have been affected by the demise of Soviet power.

The cultural and political bonds are only the more visible expression of a more general Third World dependence upon the Western European (and North

Table 9.1. Colonies that Gained Independence after World War II and Remaining Colonies or "Overseas Territories"

Colonial Power	Continent	Colonies, with year of independence and if independence was gained during a liberation war (W); remaining colonies or "overseas territories" in italics.
Great Britain	Africa	Sudan 1956, Nigeria 1960, most of East Africa 1960s
	Americas	Jamaica 1962, Guyana 1966, Caribbean Islands 1960s, *Falkland Islands*
	Asia	India 1947, Pakistan 1947, Burma 1948, Malaysia 1957, Hong Kong (to China 1997), Cyprus 1960W
	Europe	Malta 1964, *Gibraltar*
	Oceania	Many Pacific Islands 1970s; a number of other *Pacific Islands*
France	Africa	Morocco 1956, Tunisia 1956, most of West-Africa 1960, Madagascar 1960, Algeria 1962W, *Reunión*
	Americas	*French Guyana, French Antilles*
	Asia	Cambodia 1953, Vietnam 1954W, Laos 1954
	Oceania	A number of *Pacific Islands*
Holland	Americas	Suriname 1975, *Dutch Antilles*
	Asia	Indonesia 1949W
Portugal	Africa	Guinea Bissau 1973W, Angola 1974W, Mocambique 1975, Cape Verde 1975, *Madeira, Azores*
	Asia	Goa (to India 1961), East Timor (to Indonesia 1976), Macao (to China 1999)
Belgium	Africa	Congo 1960
Italy	Africa	Libya 1951
Spain	Africa	Spanish Sahara (occupied by Morocco 1976), *Ceuta, Melilla, Canary Islands*
Denmark	Americas	*Greenland*

European countries are listed in rank order of the size of their colonial empires in 1945.

American) economies for their exports and for mounting import credits. In particular, the African economy is based on exports of unprocessed foodstuffs, whose import quantities and prices are, to a large extent, determined by the importing countries and whose trade is handled by American or European multinational companies. Only the (predominantly Arab) oil-producing nations in North Africa and the Middle East have been able to set their own export prices and have gained economic independence. European relations with this part of the world are rather uneasy. The European economy is partly dependent upon the undisturbed oil flow from the Middle East, mostly in the form of crude oil processed in Europe. The "old continent" is trying to regain some of the cash flow to the Arab countries by attracting orders for infrastructural works, construction, and industry in the Middle East. The economic relations between (Western) Europe and the Middle East have intensified contacts but not contributed to mutual understanding. Most Arab countries were British or French colonies until the 1950s, but nowadays they have loosened their relations with Europe and turned to their common Arab and Islamic culture. Within Europe, the religious and other customs of Muslim immigrant workers, especially relating to the rights of women, are a source of friction with the native Europeans, who have just become used to gender equality. The recent spread of Muslim fundamentalism in North Africa and the Middle East has increased this tension.

Europe is more cautious in the response to this Muslim fundamentalism than the United States, since it does not want to endanger its oil imports and its agricultural and industrial exports. For that reason, most European nations are reluctant to interfere directly in Middle East affairs. European support of the American war efforts during the 1991 Gulf War against Iraq was an exceptional expression of European unity in safeguarding its own interests rather than leaving this uneasy job to the United States. With the exception of the French role in Africa, the same reluctance applies to the rest of the Third World.

As this short survey shows, Europe's role in world politics is limited. At times, Russia attempts to regain some of its lost power in international relations. It is in a weak position, however, because it can no longer count on the support of Central Europe. Moreover, it is hardly capable of offering substantial financial support to Third World countries, and it has been forced to ask itself for U.S. and Western European financial help. Two other former European powers, Germany and Great Britain, no longer aspire an independent position in world politics.

Germany is conscious of its role in both world wars and its Holocaust past. It is sensitive to any suggestion that it would like to become a major power again. Even its participation in United Nations peacekeeping missions has been a source of debate in the German parliament. Despite its reluctance to become active again in international politics, it is now seeking a permanent seat in the United Nations' Security Council. (At present the five permanent seats are occupied by the United States, Russia, China, France, and Great Britain.)

Great Britain is still a nuclear power, but gave up its position as an international power in the late 1950s under pressure of decolonization and the cold war. With France it intervened in Egypt in 1956 when that country nationalized the Suez Canal, but that failed attempt was its last international "adventure." In 1982, it fought a short war with Argentine concerning the Falkland Isles off the Argentine Coast. That action was not regarded as an effort to resume "great power" status but as an exceptional (and successful) attempt to prevent a foreign invasion of territories inhabited by Britons who claimed state protection. The costs of the armaments race during the cold war was another motive to leave all international initiative to the United States, and not to expand its nuclear arms force. Almost without exception it supports international U.S. initiatives.

France is the only European country apart from Russia to have its own nuclear force (*force de frappe*). It takes more distance from U.S. actions and it is proud of its status as a second-rate international power. For that reason it is not very interested in common European Union initiatives in international politics. The differences in interests between the three former Western European powers are reinforced by variations in focus: Great Britain is interested in its Commonwealth, France in (Northern) Africa, and Germany in Central and Eastern Europe, just as in the old days of European geopolitics, but less harmful this time.

The smaller European nations, including all of Central Europe, do not pursue an active international policy at all, apart from foreign policy in dealing with their neighbors. In Central Europe, that policy is often based on the existence of language minorities in the neighboring countries, and in some nations also on the search of security against Russia.

A DIVIDED CONTINENT IN SEARCH OF UNITY

Europe is not a unity. Within the new unipolar world dominated by the United States, Europe has become a multilayered continent. It is no longer a multipolar continent, since there are no major European powers. Rather, it now consists of several groups of nations at various levels of economic and political development without a real center, but with Western Europe at the top. The different levels could also be represented by a number of concentric circles with the European Union in the center.

The division within the European Union between very rich and less rich member states does not affect national positions in European Union policymaking. In EU foreign policy, Greece, the second lowest income member, is often most vociferous, especially regarding EU relations with Balkan countries, Turkey, and the Middle East.

Central Europe constitutes the second layer or circle. Almost all Central European nations want to join the European Union. National income per head, even in the richest nations of this group, is lower than that of the low income EU member states, Portugal and Greece. In political development and in level of economic development, Central Europe falls apart into three different groups. Czechia, Hungary, Poland, and Slovenia are on the brink of formal negotiations for admission to the European Union. They have made the most progress toward democracy and they are also the most prosperous Central European countries. They are already urgently adapting national legislation in a number of policy fields to European Union standards. This "privileged" position also applies to Estonia, one of the Baltic countries.

The second Central European group consists of nations that would like to join, but are at a longer distance from the European Union in political and economic terms. In some of these nations, like Romania and Bulgaria, communists have ruled for some time during the 1990s and they have halted economic and political reform and refrained from any aspiration to join the European Union. Two of the three Baltic nations are in this second group, and so is Croatia.

The third group in Central Europe is too far off in levels of political and economic development to arouse any European Union interest in their admission.

Moreover, in most of these nations the political regimes by themselves do not show any interest, either because they want to play a role as a regional power, like Serbia, or because they are still busy with sheer survival, like Bosnia and Albania. Europe's poorest countries are all in this third group.

Eastern Europe constitutes the bottom layer of Europe, or the outermost circle. Although Russia at times aspires a leading position in world politics, it faces big internal political and economic problems. International isolation by the United States and the European Union is one of its greatest fears, which shows its vulnerability and its dependent position, at least in economic conditions. From a world power, it has become a marginal nation in Europe, but one that still could pose a threat to Western and Central European safety. The two other Eastern European countries share most of these problems.

The hierarchy of layers or circles is not just an expression of Western European chauvinism. It is also felt in Central and Eastern Europe. Most Central European countries are looking forward to European Union membership or at least some kind of formal relationship with the European Union. Countries that have not been invited for preliminary negotiations to that order have expressed their disappointment and nurture the hope that they will be next in line. In Eastern Europe, joining the European Union is out of the question, but formal links and financial aid are not. The fear of international isolation that exists in these countries also reveals the awareness of a marginal position.

The same hierarchy is even more visible in the membership of European international organizations. See Table 9.2, which lists the international organizations with predominantly European members.

Central Europe does not have any international organization of its own. The only international organization dominated by a nonmember of the European Union is the Commonwealth of Independent States (CIS), in which most states that formed part of the Soviet Union cooperate, with the exception of the Baltic States. However, CIS is not a real community.

Two organizations mainly serve international security: NATO and the West European Union (WEU). NATO includes most Western European nations, as well as the United States and Canada. The European countries that were formally neutral during the cold war and for that reason did not join (Austria, Finland, Ireland, and Sweden) now participate in some of its activities. Three Central European countries, Czechia, Hungary, and Poland, joined NATO in 1999, in order to guarantee their safety in case of renewed Russian expansionism. Russian opposition to NATO's expansion in Central Europe points to the country's isolation in case most European nations join a military alliance that can only be aimed at keeping Russia in check. The organization itself tries to emphasize its nature as a device for multipurpose cooperation instead of merely a military alliance and its role in peacekeeping. Its latest military operation has been the action against Serbia in 1999.

Most European Union members are also members of the second organization that is devoted to international security, the Western European Union

Table 9.2. International Organizations with Predominantly European Members (except EU and CIS)

International Organization	*Year, Seat*	*Members*	*Aims*
North Atlantic Treaty Organization (NATO)	1949 Brussels	West Europe: almost all nations Central Europe: Czechia, Hungary, Poland Other: USA, Canada, Turkey	Security, protection against Russia
Western European Union (WEU)	1954 Brussels	West Europe: almost all nations are (Associate) members or observers. Central Europe: 10 Associate Partners	Security, peacekeeping.
Organization for Economic Cooperation and Development (OECD)	1961 Paris	West Europe: Almost all nations Central Europe: Czechia, Hungary, Poland Other: USA, Canada, Australia, Japan	Economic cooperation
Council of Europe	1949 Strasbourg	Almost all European nations	Cultural exchange, human rights
Organization for Security and Cooperation (OSCE)	1975 Prague	Almost all European nations, USA, Canada	Dialogue on international security

(WEU). This organization, seated in Brussels, was established in 1954 to make German rearmament acceptable to France and to serve as a kind of European "inner circle" within NATO. It has never been very active, however. France developed its own nuclear weapons, Germany was reluctant to display initiative in matters of international security, and the smaller nations preferred a close relationship with the United States. Increasingly, the WEU tries to become the European Union's military arm and act as crisis manager in Europe, but a small and local police force in Bosnia has been the main result until now.

In addition to these organizations of collective security, a number of other international organizations exist in Europe. Arguably the most important is the Organization for Economic Cooperation and Development (OECD), established with the goal of promoting cooperation in economic policies. A precursor of the OECD started under U.S. pressure at the time of the Marshall Plan. Since 1961 the organization possesses its current name and has extended its membership from Western Europe to include the United States, Japan, and other industrialized countries outside Europe. One of its most influential activities is the publication of annual reports on the economies of the member states. Although the national governments are involved in the preparation of the reports, these publications serve as authoritative references in defending or opposing the national governments' economic policies. Recently, Czechia, Hungary, and Poland, have joined. They are the same countries that have also joined NATO and eagerly await their admission to the European Union.

Only two international organizations have a European-wide membership. The first one, the Council of Europe, is dominated by Western Europe. Most Central and Eastern European countries joined, or better, were admitted, in the course of the 1990s. Human rights are the main concern of the Council of Europe, which is seated in Strasbourg (a very international town). It was established in 1949 as a Western organization to look after human rights and cultural exchange. It has drafted over a hundred conventions in these fields. One of the latest topics has been the abolition of the death penalty, which has now been achieved in most of Europe. The admission of Central and Eastern European countries was not without problems. The Russian application led to a discussion about the value of an international organization for human rights that includes Russia. The country was admitted under the condition that it would ratify a number of the Council's conventions. Serbian and Croatian membership has also been an issue, because of their support of war atrocities during the Bosnian war.

This leaves us with the only international organization that has encompassed all of Europe from the very outset, the Organization for Security and Cooperation in Europe (OSCE), which has its seat in Prague. It started as a device to promote mutual contacts between the two blocs in Europe during the cold war. The OSCE has survived the end of the cold war and is active in the field of human rights and economic "East-West" cooperation in Europe. It has even become the leading international agency in Bosnia, where it monitors elections and arms control measures.

Most European governments are convinced of the advantage of joining these European organizations, and the European Union most of all, as a means to prevent international isolation. There is only one European country to which the rule that absence in international organizations implies a marginal position does not apply: Switzerland. Europe's richest country, Switzerland, is now a non-European Union island within EU territory. It has not joined all of the other international organizations either. It is very reluctant to join anything that would affect its sovereignty and has consistently refused to accept international obligations.

EVEN GOOD NEIGHBORS HAVE THEIR QUARRELS

A few miles off the coast of country "Mainland" lies an island, "Archipelago," which belongs to another country. In between the coast and the island are two rocks, inhabited only by a few goats. In 1995, a Mainland boat got into trouble near the rocks and asked its own port for help, rather than the authorities on the Archipelago island. This resulted in the exchange of angry diplomatic notes between the two nations about the sovereignty over the rocks and the extent of both countries' territorial waters. One month later a Mainland journalist raised his national standard on the rocks, which was taken down the next day by

Archipelago. New angry notes followed, and battleships from both sides were sent in. It was only after U.S. mediation that the ships were withdrawn again.

This conflict is not situated in East Asia but in the Mediterranean, at the fringe of Europe. Relations between Greece ("Archipelago") and Turkey ("Mainland") are like that. Apart from nations that have problems with their neighbors over the treatment of national minorities, Greece has worst relations with its neighbors. Its relations with Turkey have seriously affected the relationship between the European Union and Turkey, which is already strained by EU criticism of the lack of rights for the Kurdish minority. Since the European Union supports the Greek position, the United States has to be called in for mediation. Sometimes it looks as if Greece and Turkey, both NATO partners, are on the brink of a war, but the Greek armed forces are no match for the Turkish army, and violence remains verbal. The long lasting conflict was intensified in 1974, when the Turkish army occupied the part of Cyprus that is inhabited by Turks, in order to prevent the island from joining Greece. That action has resulted in the division of the island between the Greek majority, which claims to be the one and only Republic of Cyprus and the Turkish part, with United Nations peacekeeping forces in between.

Greece and Turkey quarrel over almost anything imaginable, except over national minorities. Disputes about the treatment of national minorities in neighboring countries are now mainly a problem in Central Europe, and they are increasingly solved by means of bilateral agreements. There are a few other sources of international tension in Europe, even among European Union members, but they have not involved any overt hostilities other than exchanging angry diplomatic notes. Table 9.3 lists major disputes, but without conflicts over national minorities. Minor issues between most European nations are not included either. Such quarrels often concern the exact frontier line, overland routes, fishing in other nation's territorial waters, and the location of polluting industries close to the border (national borders are a favorite site for nuclear plants).

In most of Europe, relations between neighbors are also affected by the "Big Brother complex." European nations are hardly interested in smaller neighbors, but invariably nurture some resentment against bigger ones, if only because of wars that were fought centuries ago. Feelings are often not very strong, and they consist of resentment rather than hostility, sometimes even mixed with secret admiration for the big neighbor's achievements, roughly similar to the attitude of Canadians toward the United States. This kind of feeling explains why there are so few coalitions in the European Union between neighboring countries and why nations that are easily grouped together do not maintain close contacts.

A few examples follow: to the Portuguese, Spain is the big brother, not to be trusted since it conquered Portugal in 1581; for Spain, France serves as a model in many respects, but also as a despised big brother, since the conquests of Napoleon two centuries ago; for the French, Germany is the big brother. Since World War II, the French have actively pursued French *grandeur* by means of

Table 9.3. Major Regional Disputes in Europe (except Concerning Minorities)

Country	Country	Issue	Comment
Ireland	Great Britain	The position of Northern Ireland	Possibly solved since the 1998 Good Friday Agreement.
Spain	Great Britain	Gibraltar, which is claimed by Spain as Spanish territory	Spain rejects a referendum in Gibraltar because of the many British who live there.
Spain	France	Too tolerant an attitude toward Basque separatists	To some extent solved by increasing cooperation in fighting terrorists.
Greece	Macedonia	Greece argues that the name Macedonia also applies to the northern part of Greece	Macedonia is now called "Former Yugoslav Republic of Macedonia."
Greece	Turkey	Almost any subject; including uninhabited rocks in the Aegean Sea, shipping in the Aegean Sea, and the unity of Cyprus.	Greece was part of the Turkish Empire for several centuries and had a long history of national revolts.
Slovakia	Hungary	The Gabcikovo dam in the Danube	Hungary abandoned the project and now fears its environmental impact.
Russia	Ukraine	Use of the Black Sea ports	Most ports are Ukrainian territory; agreements have provided for Russian shipping rights.

European unity, which includes Germany ("If we can't beat them, let them join us"). The Germans lack such a complex. They are all of Western Europe's and most of Central Europe's big brother. Russia is Central Europe's other big brother, but this does not mean that big brothers are always large countries. Sweden occupies such a position for the Danes and Norwegians, Czechia for the Slovaks, and Serbia for some Balkan nations. The Big Brother complex is a fine topic to start a conversation in Europe; just ask what they think of the nearest bigger country. Remember, however, that it does not always work. Austrians have hardly any hard feelings about the Germans, and despite its size, Italy does not serve as a big brother at all. All its neighbors look to the North (Germany) instead of to the South.

10

Europe by Region

WESTERN EUROPE

The historical note in chapter 1 listed what the European countries, in particular those in Western and Central Europe, have in common, starting with Greek culture. Even if countries have turned their back to any of these traditions, for instance to absolutism, they have been influenced by them. The big four Western European nations Great Britain, France, Germany, and Italy have made the greatest contribution to the shaping of European politics. They have not only influenced each other, but also the smaller nations. The small countries had their share in the making of European society but on a smaller scale, and they have been more open to influence of the four larger nations. Germany (81.9 million inhabitants), France (58.2 million), and Italy (57.5 million) have probably had a larger impact on European society than Great Britain (58.8 million).

This chapter offers a brief discussion of all nations by groups. The emphasis is on sources of division, the process of nation building, and some basic features of the political system. Concepts that were used and explained in the previous chapters are applied here without further explanation (see also Appendix A). In this chapter, Greece is discussed as part of the Balkan Peninsula.

The British Isles

Both in Great Britain and Ireland, almost everything is different from the European continent. Great Britain preceded the continent in a great number of political developments. It reached political unity before most continental countries and put an end to royal aspirations of absolutism more than one century before the French Revolution, and without any bloodshed. The Industrial Revolution also went off in Great Britain. Nation building, democratization and the industrial revolution succeeded each other with decades or even centuries in between, which allowed the British to address these problems in a reformist way. In political reform toward parliamentary democracy and industrialization, the country for a long time served as an example for other European nations. Since World War II it has abandoned any pretensions of being a great power, and due to its deviant system of parliamentary rule and its slackening economy, it has also lost its position as a pilot for Europe.

Despite its multinational nature, with Scotland and Wales beside England, Great Britain is one of Europe's least politically divided societies, in which language and religion are no great issues. Northern Ireland is a case apart, but it is formally not a part of Great Britain (together with Great Britain it makes up the "United Kingdom"). Region is becoming more important because of a growing gap between the richer South and the less prosperous traditional industrial areas in Northern England and Scotland, which vote Labour and were neglected by the conservative governments of the 1980s and early 1990s. Social class is by far the strongest political issue in Great Britain but it is less disruptive than on the continent.

Ireland (3.6 million) was under British rule until 1921. The country has adopted several political elements from Great Britain, like the legal system and the civil service. It also shares with Great Britain the absence of political conflict. The Irish speak English and attempts to reintroduce the older Irish language have not changed that situation. Religion is not a source of division, either. Ireland is the only Catholic country in which religion is not a political issue. Religion pervades social life and politics, but the Catholic Church enjoys an uncontested position as a national institution because of its role in the liberation struggle against Great Britain. Even social class is not much of an issue, and the country does not have a big social democratic party. The country differs from Great Britain in its continental pattern of coalition governments and recent tripartite agreements.

The "Big Three" of Continental Western Europe

Italy heavily influenced European culture (Roman Empire, Catholic Church, Renaissance) until the last centuries, when it lost its prominent position. Until national unification in 1870 it was divided among a number of city-states, like Venice, and other independent units, since that time it has been united, but heavily divided. The high degree of internal division in Italy has left France and Germany as the two actual continental powers in Western Europe.

France has been a leading nation since the Middle Ages in politics (Louis XIV; Napoleon) and also in arts and culture. During the eighteenth and nineteenth centuries, French was the international language in Europe. Since the 1789 French Revolution, important social movements, like the 1830 and 1848 revolutions and the 1968 student revolt, broke out in Paris and spread from there to other countries. Despite the fact that the country is second to Germany in economic power, it has always claimed a leading political role, to some extent based on its primacy in culture. The country considers itself as the only remaining European Great Power in international politics, after Great Britain gave up that pretension and the Soviet Empire collapsed, and with Germany in a less prominent international role since World War II. Its pilot role is not confined to politics. Paris functions as the cultural capital of Latin Europe, a position without counterpart in Germanic Europe.

Germany was a power during the Middle Ages as the "Holy Roman Empire," but did not become a political unity until 1871. Since that unification, its aspirations to join the ranks of Great Britain and France as a Great Power were among the causes of the two world wars. After World War II, it has regained its position as Europe's largest economy, but it has also maintained a low political profile, without any new aspirations to play a leading role in international politics. It has embraced the European Union as a way to prevent its economic power from posing a threat to the surrounding nations.

In contrast to Great Britain, national politics in these three countries have been characterized by incidental or more frequent shocks in the form of insurrection, revolt, or even revolution. During the last two centuries, France has been an empire twice, a kingdom twice, and a republic five times, with great variations within each of these forms. Neither Italy nor Germany was unified until the 1870s. Each changed from a kingdom or empire to a republic, passed through a fascist or Nazi stage, and became more a regular parliamentary republic after World War II. In 1989, Germany was reunified, and around that time the traditional system of Italian politics broke down.

The changes in political system are to some extent the result of internal division. In France, the French Revolution was not only a contest between royalists and republicans, and between moderate and radical republicans, but also between Catholics and anticlericals. To the latter it was the victory of the French nation, uniting all Frenchmen, over the Church. The contrast between Paris and the rest of the country was another issue during the revolution, and it has played a role in politics since that time. The issue of social class has, to some extent, incorporated some of the other lines of division, with a labor movement that has a strong anticlericalist outlook. The social cleavages contributed to the instability of governments under the Fourth Republic (1944–1958), which prompted the introduction of the (semi)presidential system in the Fifth Republic. Despite the differences in political orientation, many Frenchmen do not make a strict separation between the State, as the highest national authority, and the state as a nation state, and they accept strong state authority in national politics. More than in the rest of Western Europe, the state is involved in a large range of economic and social activities, and internationally its main aim is to pursue French *grandeur*. The privatization of the large public sector is now reducing the role of the French State.

The main line of division in Germany is now the one between the West and former East Germany. Communist East Germany was the most industrialized country of the Soviet bloc, but its outdated industries have totally broken down under the pressure of international competition. This new divide has to some extent supplanted the former dominant line between the Catholic states in the South, like Bavaria and Baden-Württemberg, and the rest of the country, where Protestants are more willing to vote social democrats. As a source of division, social class has lost part of its saliency after World War II, when the social democrats left their Marxist ideology in favor of more social equality for the population at large. (It had already left its revolutionary zeal in the beginning of the century.) Although trade union participation in the supervisory council of large enterprises, the so-called codetermination, has been a hot political issue, it has also tended to reduce the distance between trade unions and business, and more generally between left and right. That distance is greater than in the smaller nations with their tradition of tripartism, but smaller than in the other large nations.

Italy is one of the most divided countries in Europe, with lines of division between the highly developed north (Milan, Turin) and the less industrialized south, between Catholics and anticlericals, among regions that display a high level of regionalism, like Sicily, and between the labor movement on the one hand and middle class and business on the other. Surprisingly, political principles are easily overcome to attain some kind of common arrangement. Italians have the best reputation of preaching one thing and practicing another, and for that reason the worst reputation in political morals. Corruption is more at home here than in any other Western European country. Even the Italian communist party, which was the largest of its kind outside the Soviet bloc, used to be looked upon with mistrust by the other communist parties, since it did not meet the latter's high international standards of dogmatism and authoritarianism. In spite of all sources of division, the prominent role of the family provides for a high degree of social cohesion in social life, both with positive effects, in the form of social cohesion, and negative consequences, like nepotism.

Scandinavia

Scandinavia is Europe's closest knit group of nations. Mutual bonds are helped by easy communication. The Scandinavians understand each other without having to take recourse to English (except for the Fins, who speak a non-Germanic language, but many of them also speak Swedish). Mutual cooperation in the Nordic Council and the sense of common identity, however, do not lead to great uniformity in international conduct. Differences in that field are also due to variations in national history. Sweden and Denmark have long been European powers, while Norway was under Danish and Swedish rule and Finland a part of the Russian Empire until the early twentieth century. As a relatively young nation, Norway is most nationalist in the classical sense. Sweden shares the Norwegian distance to Europe—any new referendum on EU membership might easily lead to a "No" vote, as the two referendums in Norway did. Denmark is more European-minded, but only Finland wholeheartedly joined the European Union as an expression of its belonging to Europe. Finland has the most problematic past, with a civil war at the time of World War I, and annexation of parts of the country by the Soviet Union during World War II. Hundreds of thousands of Fins then fled to Finland—over ten percent of the total Finnish population. After World

War II, the country was obliged to be neutral and have good relations with the Soviet Union, but it was part of the "free world."

Scandinavia stands for success. Since World War II, Denmark (5.3 million), Norway (4.4 million), and Sweden (8.9 million) have come to enjoy the status of success stories, and later Finland (5.1 million) joined them. Political development has taken place without great political conflicts and in spite of their marginal geographical position in Europe, off the main trade routes, these countries have become very prosperous welfare states. In both respects they have served as models for other European nations.

National identity has been shaped by low population density (even flat Denmark is less densely populated than mountainous Switzerland), and by the prevalence of small towns and small-scale production (although Sweden is home to a number of multinational companies). Joining the European Union has also been a highly contentious issue because these countries feel a bit apart from the rest of Europe and fear loss of sovereignty.

Despite the existence of a Finnish minority in Sweden and a Swedish minority in Finland (concentrated on a few islands off the Finnish coast), the four nations are typical examples of language-based nation-states. Religion is not a source of division either, since national Protestant (Lutheran) churches enjoy a monopoly position, without political power. The urban-rural line of division gave rise to parties of independent farmers, who oppose the influence of the national capitals. (The landed nobility has only played a marginal role in this part of Europe.) Notwithstanding the decline of the agricultural labor force, these parties continue to attract electoral support that is based on their position in between the social democrats on the one hand, and conservatives and liberals on the other. In contrast to Christian democratic parties in other countries, the farmers' parties do not attract many working class votes, which reinforces the position of social democracy as the almost exclusive working class representative. Social democrats have governed most of the postwar period, either by themselves or in coalition with the farmers' parties or social liberals. It was also in this part of Europe that democratic corporatism was initiated, at the time other countries endured the Catholic or the fascist variants of corporatism.

Long periods of social democratic participation in government have resulted in relatively egalitarian societies with extensive social policies, but without a big public sector. In order to single out the Scandinavian welfare states, a "Scandinavian Model" has been distinguished, characterized by active labor market policies in Sweden and Norway and strong egalitarian social security rights throughout the region. The differentiation that prevails in other countries between social security rights for manual workers, white-collar workers, and the self-employed, has been abandoned to a large extent. In Denmark and Sweden the trade unions are actively involved in social security payments, which contributes to the high trade union density. Denmark's economy is the least government regulated.

During the 1990s, the Scandinavian countries have lost part of their glamour. In Sweden and Finland unemployment has risen to normal European levels, and in Denmark new nationalist parties have been successful in elections.

The Low Countries

Holland (15.5 million), officially named The Netherlands, and Belgium (10.3 million) have a lot in common, including a former colonial empire. Like Holland, the northern part of Belgium (Flanders) speaks Dutch. The two national economies are highly trade-oriented, with the large ports of Rotterdam in Holland (the world's largest port) and Antwerp in Belgium handling freight to and from Germany. In politics, the two nations share a long tradition of Christian democratic domination of coalition governments, with either conservative liberals or social democrats as partners. In Holland, the tradition was not broken until 1994 when social democrats and liberals took over in a "purple" (red-blue) coalition. With tiny Luxembourg, the two nations have also engaged in formal cooperation since 1944. This Benelux (*Be*lgium, *Ne*therlands, and *Lux*embourg) served as a forerunner of the European Union, on a much smaller scale. However, the differences between the countries are just as pronounced as the common features, which has tended to reduce Benelux cooperation.

Holland is water: canals, rivers, and the sea. During the seventeenth century, the country was a leading maritime power. At home, the struggle against the water (one quarter of the country is located below sea level) has fostered a spirit of cooperation. Holland is the only country in which the Protestant-Catholic divide has not been addressed by decentralization or federalism, as in Germany or Switzerland. Protestantism has shaped national culture but in the course of the nineteenth century, the Catholic minority began to build up its own network of organizations, in order to enforce a greater voice in national affairs. That was the beginning of the pillarization of Dutch society. Due to the trade tradition and the strength of religious affiliation, class divergence has never been a contentious issue. Religious tolerance in the form of pillarization reinforced the culture of compromise, which has survived the disintegration of the pillars in the 1970s.

Belgium lacks a glorious past but it was one of the first industrializing nations in Europe, with industry concentrated in French-speaking Wallony. The language division coincides with the contrast between a trade-orientation in Dutch-speaking Flanders and heavy industry in Wallony, and to some extent also with a religious split. While Flanders is still traditionally Catholic, Wallony has been influenced by France, and is dominated by anticlerical social democracy. The divergence between the two parts of Belgium explains the problematic position of the capital Brussels. It has become a French-speaking city within Flemish territory, but the social issue separates it from Wallony. The large Walloon working class votes social democracy; the French-speaking Brussels *bourgeoisie* and middle class embrace conservative liberalism. Coalitions are supposed to contain both Flemish and Walloon parties, but that representation of both "communities" makes building cabinets a very intricate process in Belgium. While Flemish social democrats may be willing to participate in government, the Walloon social democrats may not, or the other way around.

Luxembourg (.4 million), the third partner in Benelux, is Europe's smallest nation in surface and its third smallest in population. Luxembourgers even joke that it is possible to make a cycle tour—through Belgium, France, and Germany—around their country in one morning. Originally, it was one of the German states within the loosely structured German empire, but during the last two centuries its history has been more linked to that of Belgium. Most inhabitants are bilingual, and speak French and Letzeburgian, which is a regional variation of German. Luxembourg is the most prosperous EU member. It has used its position in between France, Germany, and the densely populated Low Countries well. It is the home of a number of commercial television stations and its allows for low-tax banking accounts.

The Alpine Nations

Austria (8.1 million) and Switzerland (7.1 million) stand for mountains and skiing. Both countries are situated on the old transit routes from Northern Europe to Italy. Mutual relations are limited. While Switzerland has an international orientation, Austria looks to Germany.

Switzerland is situated in between Germany, France, and Italy, and these three languages are also its own national languages. However, neither of the three parts of Switzerland identifies with one of the big neighbors. The Swiss nation has an old and strong national identity, which is based on its smallness and age-old neutrality toward the larger countries. It has been able to preserve its territorial integrity even when all surrounding countries were occupied by the Germans. Austria is a German speaking nation, the remnant of the multinational Austrian Empire that was dissolved right after World War I, which left Vienna as the oversized capital of a nation without national identity. Integration into Germany was one of the options under discussion but national identity has grown since World War II.

While Austrian neutrality was imposed after the war, Swiss neutrality has a long history and implies keeping far from international obligations. This reluctance to engage in international affairs has made Geneva, its most beautifully situated (and French-speaking) town, the location of international organizations like the Red Cross, the ILO, and the prewar precursor of the United Nations. (The country is not even a UN member.)

Both countries are now federal nations, but with a different background. Switzerland is strongly federalized, with a small federal bureaucracy. The "cute" little capital Bern is only Switzerland's fourth Swiss city. Austria's federalism is a more recent (postwar) innovation, and it is less encompassing.

In Switzerland, all major political parties participate in the national government on a permanent basis and the posts of prime minister and Head of State rotate among them. This depoliticization of national politics is compensated to some extent by the extensive use of nationwide referendums, a modern version of the traditional village meeting that was one of the earliest expressions of popular democracy. Austrian national politics has been more divisive, with overlapping sources of division: Urban social democracy in the capital, rural Christian democrats in the rest of the country. In the late 1990s, the two big parties have come closer to each other, due to the change of the third party from conservative liberal to one of Europe's most successful racist parties.

The Iberian Peninsula

Together, Spain (40.5 million) and Portugal (9.9 million) colonized almost all of Latin America until the nineteenth century. Located in the Iberian Peninsula, they have been relatively isolated from the rest of Western Europe during the last centuries (since the break up of Spanish imperial rule over other parts of Europe, including the Low Countries, in the seventeenth century). In both countries, the Roman Catholic Church has been a dominant force in social life. During the twentieth century, fascist dictatorships, supported by Catholics, have ruled for forty years, until they collapsed almost simultaneously in the 1970s. Nowadays, the two countries are catching up with the rest of Western Europe.

The differences in political culture are just as overwhelming as the common features. Portugal has its face toward the sea. With Great Britain and Holland, this has been one of Europe's leading seafaring nations. Portugal is also truly a nation-state. All citizens speak Portuguese and all Portuguese-speakers in Europe are based in Portugal (although some 200,000 live as immigrant workers in and around Paris). During the nineteenth century, British interests dominated the national economy and were also influential in politics. As a consequence of the international orientation, authoritarian rule was less harsh than in Spain. It was followed by a short-lived communist-inspired revolution in 1974. Since then, the social democrats (calling themselves socialists) and conservatives (calling themselves social democrats) have alternated in government. The Portuguese president has more power than Heads of State in the rest of Western Europe—except France.

Spanish politics has always been more landlocked. At an earlier stage than the other colonial powers, its was interested in political control of its colonies rather than in mere trade-oriented political hegemony. At home, Spain has been busy with the political integration of the coastal regions, like Catalonia, Basque Country, and Asturias, by force if necessary. Integration has been hampered by the fact that Spain comprises minority tongues, a well-organized Catholic elite movement (*Opus Dei*) and staunch anticlericals, regions that are richer and more internationally oriented than the political center, and an action-oriented labor movement, concentrated in the industrial regions. Traditionally, Spanish politics has been characterized by a lack of compromise between these groups. In contrast, the transition toward democracy has been very successful and peaceful, partly due to very moderate social democratic governments under Felipe Gonzalez that were in power for fifteen years.

CENTRAL EUROPE

The Baltic Nations

The three Baltic countries—Estonia (1.5 million), Latvia (2.5 million), and Lithuania (3.7 million)—have shared two centuries of Russian rule. They were granted independence at the end of World War I, but incorporated in the Soviet Union during World War II. Many Russians were then settled in this region as industrial workers and civil servants. Since 1991, the three countries have enjoyed independence again. In Lithuania, the Soviet Union at first responded with small-scale military action and the threat of an economic blockade, but in 1991 it gave in and accepted Lithuanian independence.

Despite this longstanding common fate, the Baltic nations are not only the least populated group of nations but also the least cohesive one, and mutual relations are limited. While most Scandinavians can speak their own language at common meetings, the Low Countries manage with Dutch and the Alpine nations with German, the Baltic peoples do not understand each other's language. They have to speak English or Russian (grudgingly) in order to communicate. Estonian is close to Finnish; the other two languages belong to a different group. Like the Low Countries and the Alpine countries, the Baltic nations do not share a common religion, either. The Lithuanians are Catholic, in Estonia Lutheran Protestants form the majority, and Latvia is mixed in this respect. The three countries had also different early histories. While Estonia and Latvia were oriented toward Germany and Scandinavia, Lithuania once had a large empire that stretched over parts of Russia and Ukraine, and it maintained close relations with Poland.

The process of nation building that is going on proceeds best in Estonia. It is facilitated by the relations with Finland, which has also been under Russian rule for some time. Nation building is most problematic in Latvia. It has a thirty-percent Russian minority, and even in the national capital Latvians are a minority. The country has only naturalized people that were already in the country before 1940 and has excluded all Russian immigrants from citizenship. Russia has raised complaints; the Russian minority itself has not (yet) been very active. Some of them even prefer their Russian nationality since that permits travel to Russia without expensive visa. Since the Russians live scattered over the country, federalism would not provide a solution. The three countries have introduced parliamentary systems with a strong presidential thrust. Authoritarian presidents dominate national politics, in particular in Latvia and Lithuania. With envy, these countries look at Estonia's selection for admission talks with the EU.

Poland and Western Central Europe

Poland, Czechia, Slovakia, and Hungary have been close to Western Europe or even part of Western European culture for a long time, and all of them are traditionally Catholic. Three of the four countries in this group speak a Slavonic language, the Hungarian language has non-European origins. The countries have resumed the contacts with Western Europe. Czechia, Hungary, and Poland have already joined NATO, and are also in the first group of candidates to join the European Union.

Of all Central European nations, Poland (38.6 million) is by far the largest, and also the one with the most eventful history, due to its position in between Germany and Russia. In the sixteenth century it was a vast country, during the nineteenth century it was divided among the Prussian (Germany), Austrian, and Russian Empires and disappeared from the map. It was reestablished following World War I, partitioned once again by Germany and Russia during World War II, and in 1945 got its present frontiers. Large numbers of Germans in the newly acquired western part had to move to Germany, which left the country without any substantial minorities.

Poland has a long history of popular revolt. Communism was highly unpopular, if only because of its Russian origins. Under communism, the country feared a Soviet invasion twice, in 1956 and 1980. Communist rule remained a bit less strict than elsewhere in the Soviet bloc, with relatively independent centers of higher learning and a strong Catholic Church. The position of the Church was reinforced when in 1978 a Polish Cardinal was elected—Pope John Paul II. Politics in the 1990s have not been very stable but less unstable as the number of prime ministers (almost one each year) might suggest.

Czechia (10.3 million) had a glorious past as a kingdom with Prague as a center of European culture, but later it was integrated into the Austrian Empire. Following World War I, it was united with Slovakia as an independent nation, but in 1938 was forced to cede the Sudeten region (with a large German minority) to Germany. After the war, this region was returned to the country and many of the Sudeten Germans fled to Germany. The country does not have a tradition of revolt; even the 1968 Prague Spring was initiated by communist leaders rather than by a grassroot movement. The change toward democracy was also nonviolent, with a leader of the underground human rights organization Charta 77, Vaclav Havel, as new president. Since the division of Czechoslovakia in 1993, the country contains hardly any minorities and has easily regained its position as the most "westernized" nation of Central Europe.

In contrast to Poland, Czechia, and Hungary, which can boast of a glorious past, Slovakia (5.4 million) does not even have a history as an independent state, and it is also the only country in this group with a sizeable (Hungarian) minority. Until the formation of Czechoslovakia, it had been under Hungarian rule for centuries. As the junior partner in Czechoslovakia it had to play second fiddle, but also received large subsidies from the central government in Prague. After the collapse of communism, the Czechs refused to meet the Slovak wish of national emancipation, and Slovakia broke apart, at the time the two parts were ruled by opposing governments (rightist in Czechia, leftist in Slovakia). Between 1993 and 1998 the country was governed by an authoritarian leader who limited civil rights and suppressed the Hungarian minority.

Hungary (10.2 million) had a glorious medieval past before it was conquered by the Turks and later ceded to the Austrians. After a national revolt in 1848, the Austrians slowly recognized the position of Hungary as a junior partner and changed the Austrian Empire into the Austro-Hungarian Empire. The territories under Hungarian authority were populated by Croats, Romanians, Slovaks, and Ukrainians. Following World War I, it had to hand over more than two-thirds of its territory to these (new) nations. Since that time relations with neighboring countries have been affected by the treatment of the Hungarian minorities there. Hungary itself is ethnically homogenous, with the exception of a Roma minority. Roma people also live in the surrounding Balkan countries. After the 1956 anti-Soviet revolt, Hungary introduced economic reforms that made it the most consumer-oriented society in the Soviet bloc. Due to these initial changes, the transition toward a free-market economy and democracy has been more gradual than in the rest of Central Europe.

The Balkan Peninsula

The Balkan Peninsula is Europe in a nutshell. Everything that makes European politics intriguing and intricate, and tragic at times, is to be found here. On a 700-kilometer trip (San Francisco–L.A, or Boston–Washington) from the old cultural center of Dubrovnik in Croatia through Albania to the Greek port of Thessaloniki, you will pass (if not stopped by warfare or closed frontiers) through Catholic, Serbian-Orthodox, Muslim, and Greek-Orthodox countries and have to read five languages, written in three different alphabets. The first country you pass (Croatia) is aspiring to join the European Union, the second (Serbia), a communist dictatorship, the third (Albania), a noncommunist authoritarian system short of a dictatorship, the fourth (Macedonia), a fragile democracy-like system, and the last one (Greek), a EU member. Moreover, the region has its share of language minorities.

Until the nineteenth century, a large part of the Balkan Peninsula was under Turkish (Muslim) rule, with the Serbs and the Greeks most active in organizing national revolt. Some of the nations, like Bulgaria, looked to Russia for assistance. New borders were drawn at the end of World War I when the Austro-Hungarian Empire fell apart, soon followed by the disintegration of the Turkish Empire. After World War II most countries changed into communist dictatorships, except for Greece, which became part of Western Europe. Because of its pioneering role as the cradle of European civilization, it was allowed to join the European Union in 1981.

While the Balkan Peninsula is Europe in a nutshell, former Yugoslavia was the Balkans in a nutshell. That country consisted of three culturally highly different parts: Slovenia and Croatia (Catholic, Latin alphabet) in the North, Serbia and Macedonia (Orthodox, Cyrillic alphabet) in the South, and Bosnia in between, dominated by Muslims.

Former Yugoslavia's first part, Slovenia (2.0 million) and Croatia (4.7 million), belonged to the Austro-Hungarian Empire for a long time. Slovenia is closest to Western Europe. It was Yugoslavia's richest region, and a stronghold of liberal opposition against Serbian radical communists during the last days of communism. Serbian military intervention following the country's declaration of independence was confined to one bombing raid. Nation building in Slovenia is helped by the absence of large minorities, and economic and political reforms have been more successful than in the rest of former Yugoslavia. This small country is now heading toward EU membership. Its southern neighbor, Croatia, consists of a long and narrow strip of land along the coast (Dalmatia)—which was influenced by Italy as much as by Austria—and of an interior part (Slavonia), which borders on Hungary and was under Hungarian rule for a long time. The inland region contains Hungarian and Serbian minorities. The existence of this Serbian minority prompted Serbia to resist Croatian independence. After the short war, most of the Croatian Serbs fled to Serbia, which left only a small Hungarian minority to be taken into account in national politics. The short war with Serbia in combination with the Croatian involvement in the Bosnian civil war, have reinforced authoritarian politics.

The second part of former Yugoslavia consists of Serbia (10.6 million) and Macedonia (2.0 million), which have long been dominated by the Turks. Serbia was not only a center of anti-Turkish revolt, but also active in fighting Austro-Hungarian attempts to expand in this part of the Balkans. World War I broke out when a Serbian nationalist killed the Austrian heir to the throne, who was on official visit in Sarajevo (now the Bosnian capital). Russia was its natural ally against both enemies and also assisted it in its efforts to become a regional power. Serbia dominated Yugoslavia as it existed between the world wars as well as Tito's communist Yugoslavia. Officially, the country still upholds the claim of being federal "Yugoslavia," with Serbia and tiny Montenegro, which is inhabited by Serbs, as the remaining parts of the federation. The country supported Serbian minorities in Bosnia and Croatia but suppressed the Albanian minority in it own Kosovo region, which prompted military intervention by the NATO in 1999.

Macedonia is a rather artificial political unit. Until World War II, many Macedonians regarded themselves as Bulgarians, and Bulgarians thought the same way. National identity was reinforced when Macedonia became one of Yugoslavia's constituent republics. Due to the close links with Bulgarian language and culture, the cultural borderlines between Macedonians and Bulgarians are not very clear. Despite this problem of national identity, and the large Albanian minority within its own borders, Macedonia had a relatively smooth record of political and economic reforms during the 1990s. The large influx of Albanian fugitives from Kosovo in 1999 threatened the fragile ethnic balance between Macedonians and Albanians.

The third part of former Yugoslavia, Bosnia (4.4 million), is located in between the other two parts. It is inhabited by Muslims, Serbs, and Croats. With the Albanians, these Muslims are the only people outside present day Turkey that adopted the Muslim faith when they were under Turkish rule. Since the 1995 Dayton agreement, which made an end to the Bosnian Civil War, Bosnia consists of a Muslim/Bosnian Croat republic and an autonomous Bosnian Serb republic. Both parts are artificial states. In the first part, cooperation between Croats and Muslims is uneasy; in the second part the Serbs would prefer to join neighboring Serbia. The division makes the republic as a whole also highly fragile, and in fact, the two units operate separately.

The other nations on the Balkan Peninsula show just as much variation in language, religion, other sources of division and recent developments as former Yugoslavia. Albania (3.5 million) speaks a non-Slavonic language and is the only Islamic nation in Europe since the adoption of that religion under Turkish rule. Both before and under communism, this was one of Europe's most isolated countries. Clinging to harsh Stalinist communism, it had hardly any relations with Western Europe, and soon broke off relations with its big neighbor Yugoslavia and with the Soviet bloc. One single communist dictator held the country in his iron grip for forty years. Dictatorial power shifted hands after the end of communism, without great reforms in political structure or political decision making. Political violence easily breaks out and has already prompted many Albanians to flee to Italy. The country is now trying to deal with the large influx of Albanian fugitives from Kosovo.

Although Romania (22.7 million) is by far the most populous Balkan nation, its role in European history has been a modest one. It is the biggest European country without a glorious past as a regional, maritime, or colonial empire. One half of it was long under Turkish rule, the other half was controlled by Hungary and still contains a Hungarian minority. The two parts were united at the end of World War I. As the only Central European nation that speaks a Latin language, the country has enjoyed special French interest. Within the Soviet bloc, Romania remained the most Stalinist type of dictatorship, in which the dictator had to be hailed officially as the "Genius of the Carpathian Mountains." As a consequence, like Albania, Romania had to build up democracy and Civil Society from scratch after the collapse of communism. This development is hampered by the wide gulf between the national capital and the countryside, including mining communities.

Moldova (4.5 million) is probably the most artificial new state in Central Europe. For the greater part, it consists of a region (Bessarabia) that Romania had to cede to the Soviet Union at the end of World War II. The Russians added a small stretch of land to it, which was inhabited by Russians, and made this Romanian/Russian combination one of the constituent republics of the Soviet Union. Since independence in 1991, the country has not been able to develop as a real nation. In the former Romanian part, there are recurrent movements to join Romania, since many people regard their Moldovian language as no more than a regional variation of Romanian. The Russian speaking part is occupied by a separatist movement, which is supported by Russia.

Bulgaria (8.4 million) has maintained close contacts with Russia, based on a similar language and culture, and on Russian support against Turkish rule during the nineteenth century. Moreover, the country does not border on Russia, which reduced the threat of Russian conquest. Due to this relationship with the Russians, the communist political system was hardly contested, but regarded as a way of modernizing the country. The communist leaders closely observed all guidelines from Moscow, and their obedience was never challenged by any popular revolt. In Bulgaria live several minority groups, including Turks. Incidentally, their suppression has caused an emigration movement from Bulgaria to Turkey, and strained relations with that country. Although Bulgaria also regards the Macedonians as Bulgarians, it has recognized the new state of Macedonia without any reservations.

Greece (10.6 million) has been lucky when compared to the other Balkan nations, even apart from being the cradle of European civilization. First, only small minorities live along the northern borders, and the country is homogeneous with respect to religion. Second, conflicts with other Balkan nations have been limited, due also to the fact that Greece, more than its neighbors, has its face toward the sea. The only remaining obsession is Turkey, by which it was long dominated. Third, the spirit of Western European Enlightenment has influenced the country's culture more than that of the surrounding nations. To an even higher degree than in the Latin nations, civil society is state-oriented, and the importance of the family has reinforced political clientelism and the prominence of popular leaders. At times, this personal political appeal and the quarrels with its neighbors make it look more like a Balkan nation than a Western European country.

EASTERN EUROPE

Although Russia once pretended to be the true heir to the Roman and the Byzantine empires (with Moscow as the "third Rome"), and claimed to protect the Christians in the Turkish Empire, Russia has always been treated with disdain or been neglected by the rest of Europe. That marginal position was due to the long domination of the country by the Mongols, at the time the Renaissance spread over Western and parts of Central Europe. The country missed this reappraisal of humanitarian ideals. Later, occasional British and French support of the Russian Czars was not motivated by any real interest in Russia, but by fear of German expansion.

Russia itself was often not very interested in Western Europe, either, since it had only suffered attacks from that side. Indeed, the large Russian plains proved a fatal attraction for many a Western European ruler, who then was defeated by the enormous distances, the severe Russian winter, and Russian troops. Germans, Swedes, the French under Napoleon, and the Germans once again during World War II shared this fate. The Russians themselves could continue their own expansion for over 10,000 kilometers in barren Siberia. The efforts to gain access to the Mediterranean Sea were partly given in by the need of easier sea transport to the ports on the Asian end of Siberia. In Europe, Russia became a power to be reckoned with during the nineteenth century, after it had conquered Finland, the Baltic States, and Poland. By that time the Ukraine, which had been a large empire of its own in former times, was also incorporated into the Russian Empire.

The 1917 Russian Revolution changed Russia's position in Europe. The Soviet Union became a central concern for the rest of Europe as a formidable threat of the existing order to frightened conservatives, and as the "Land of Hope and Glory" to communists all over the world. The communist glorification lasted even during Stalin's reign of terror. Thousands of communists came to see the great achievements of "socialism in one country" and to hail Stalin as their leader. During the 1920s, the country became the site of enormous social upheaval, with the collectivization of agriculture into collective farms and the forced industrialization under five-year-plans, which prescribed the industrial and agricultural output to be achieved—whatever the costs. Man-made famine and the suppression of opponents took millions of lives, and during the 1930s even high-ranking rivals of Stalin were condemned in fake "show-processes" and killed in concentration camps.

During World War II, the country was devastated by the Germans. The Soviet Union then demanded Central Europe as its own buffer zone between Germany and the Russian border. After Stalin's death in 1953, political terror became less intense and some limited economic reforms were carried out, but the communist power monopoly was not given up and democratic rights were still absent. Mikhail Gorbachev's campaign in the late 1980s to introduce more openness (*glasnost*) and political reform (*perestroika*) dealt the fatal blow to Soviet communism. The Soviet bloc fell to pieces and so did the Soviet Union.

Of today's three Eastern European nations, Belarus (10.3 million) has never been a state of its own. It was either under Polish or Russian rule, and it is now one of Europe's most artificial new nations. The country still lacks a national identity. In contrast to a number of new Central European nations, this delay is not due to the existence of minorities, but to the determination of the communists that have remained in power to undo the separation from Russia. Belarus has already concluded several agreements of merger with Russia. However, each time the Russians were afraid of the prohibitive costs of assisting the Belarussian economy, and they disliked the Belarussian president's power aspirations.

In Medieval times, the Ukraine (58.8 million) was a large empire, but since then it has been under Lithuanian, Polish, and eventually under Russian rule. The country is close to Russia in culture and language, but in contrast to Belarus it has introduced many symbols of national independence. Nation building in this huge country, Europe's second largest in territory, poses many problems, especially in the form of economic and cultural differences between the western and the eastern parts of the country. The West has traditionally been subject to non-Russian influence from Poland and Hungary. The East contains the important centers of heavy industry, but also a Russian minority. Ukraine has a better record in democratic politics than Russia or Belarus. It has introduced a presidential system, in which the reformist president Leonid Kuchma faces a communist-dominated parliament, but without the regular showdowns of force that have paralyzed Russian politics. Moreover, Kuchma's coming to power in 1994 was the only democratic change of the guard in Eastern Europe during the 1990s. He was prime minister, and with success challenged his President.

Russia (247 million, 215 million in the European part, West of the Urals) is facing huge problems of economic and political transformation. Interestingly, the end of the Soviet bloc favored its international economic relations. It allowed the sale of oil and gas at world market prices instead of low "communist prices" to the former communist countries. This price increase of fuel is one of the causes of economic problems in Central and Eastern Europe. The Russian advantage only to some extent compensates for the enormous problem of industrial restructuring in this vast country, in which almost all industrial equipment, except for space missiles, seems outdated. To most Russians, there is hardly anything positive to point at, except personal freedom, but many Russians care less about this innovation than about the loss of economic security.

While all other new nations can focus popular attention on fostering national allegiance, Russia has to do so on the basis of something lost. As the big loser of the 1990s, it has been forced to give up its communist empire and its position as a superpower beside the United States. Additionally, it lacks a strong central government. The existence of a number of minorities, including millions of Muslims, and almost permanent movements for autonomy in the Caucasian mountains (Chechenia), may well reinforce the feeling of a power vacuum. The result could be a Russian position at the margins of Europe, or new aspirations to reestablish a Slavic Empire.

OTHER COUNTRIES

Iceland (.3 million) is Europe's least populous and most remote nation. The country has long been under Danish rule. Although it did not gain full independence until 1944, it boasts of the oldest parliament in the world, which has survived for over one thousand years. It is a small-scale society of fishermen, which is close to Norway in social life and culture, but with its own language. Iceland maintains strong relations with the Scandinavian countries but in a marginal position. Economically, it is more oriented toward North America.

Malta (.4 million) is located at the other end of Europe, but it shares its nature with Iceland as a small insular nation state, its late independence, the appreciation of their small-size national communities, and the consequent reluctance to join the European Union. Malta has long been in the possession of the Catholic Order of the Knights of St. John, but until independence in 1964 it was a British colony for one and a half centuries. Both Maltese (a Semitic language) and English are official languages. Maltese-speaking Labour voters predominate in the South, English-speaking conservatives in the other parts. Neighboring Italy has strongly influenced Maltese culture, and many people speak Italian as well. The conservative party is now seeking close relations with the European Union, but not full membership.

The six mini-states (Andorra, Gibraltar, Liechtenstein, Monaco, San Marino, and Vatican City) are part of Europe's political folklore. With the exception of Gibraltar, which is a British colony, they are remnants from medieval and feudal times. None is a real nation, and culturally, they form part of their bigger neighbors. Four of the mini-states serve as tax resorts. While most of them have nonelected Heads of State, San Marino claims to be the oldest republic in the world. (Of course, the Swiss think differently.) Gibraltar's parliament consists of fifteen members, Monaco's has eighteen, and in the best of European traditions, some of these states are governed by coalition cabinets. With the exception of Vatican City, all states have their foreign relations administered by the neighboring country (or the colonial power), but they participate in some international European organizations.

Although they are normally not included in surveys of European politics, two other countries require discussion: Turkey and Cyprus.

Turkey (63.5 million) has only a small bridgehead in Europe, with Istanbul (one of the biggest European cities) as a bridge between Europe and Asia. After the collapse of the Turkish Empire, the country introduced massive reforms. It changed to a secular state and shifted from the Arabic to the Latin alphabet. However, Islam has survived as the religion of the overwhelming part of the population. The country has a large Kurdish minority in the East, but Kurds are regarded as "Mountain Turks" without minority rights. Turkey is a member of most European organizations and also aspires after EU membership, but runs up against general opposition, with the Greeks as the loudest protesters. Moreover, the European Union's reservations are based on the country's sheer size (it would be the second most populous EU member), its Muslim culture, the recurrent role of the army in national politics (officially, as the watchdog of secularization) when parliamentary politics breaks down once again, and the treatment of the Kurds.

Cyprus (.7 million) is inhabited by Greeks—who make up a large majority—and Turks. It is located close to the Turkish coast, and was part of Turkey until the end of the nineteenth century when it became a British colony. After the bloody struggle for independence, which was combined with a movement to join Greece, the country gained independence in 1960, soon followed by the stationing of United Nations armed forces to prevent ethnic hostilities. In 1974, the island was de facto divided when the Greek part moved closer to Greece and the Turkish army occupied the northern part, mainly inhabited by Turks. Most Greeks then left that part of the island. The Greek Cypriots part do not accept the division and, supported by Greece, are looking for EU membership—for the island as a whole.

Appendix A: Scientific Terms

Alignment   Stable individual or group voting for a political party.

Americanization   Growing prominence of personal over party campaign-
of elections   ing, accompanied by a loss of ideology.

Catch-all parties   Political parties that abandon part of their ideology in
order to win votes outside their original group of sup-
porters. Especially used for social democratic parties in
their attempt to "catch" middle-class voters.

Civic nationality   Nationhood based on citizens' rights for all inhabitants
and citizen participation in civil society.

Civil law   Codified legal rules that do not leave much latitude of
interpretation by courts, as opposed to common law.
Prevails throughout continental Europe.

Civil society   Constellation of active voluntary organizations that pursue social and cultural policies for their members inde-
pendently from government, and act as pressure groups
in contacts with the government.

Class identification Sense of belonging to a specific social class.

Clientelism   Gaining political support by offering favors in return, in
the form of jobs, benefits, permits, etc.

Closed circuit   Close contacts between the government and selected
pressure groups that exclude other groups, as happens in
corporatism.

Common law   Set of legal rules that are not strongly codified and
leave more room for interpretation by courts than civil
law. Common in Great Britain (and the United States).

Consensus model   Political system in which the government constitutes a
coalition of a number of parties and also allows for
influence by the opposition and by pressure groups, in

	order to minimize conflict. Especially common in the smaller Germanic nations.
Corporatism	Active participation by a few select pressure groups in social and economic policy making. These close contacts with the national government are especially pronounced in the smaller Germanic nations.
Cross-cutting social cleavages	Lines of division that do not overlap and, hence, provide citizens with loyalties to different groups. The multiple loyalties weaken the intensity of conflict between the groups.
De-alignment	Decline of stable individual or group voting for a party.
De-politicization	Removing a subject out of the political realm by having experts or the pressure groups involved prepare the decisions. Corporatism is an example.
Deregulation	Reduction of state supervision and regulation of social and economic life, especially common since the early 1980s in Western Europe and since the early 1990s in Central and Eastern Europe.
Dual power	Two organizations or institutions exercise almost equal power, for instance the parliament and the government. Characteristic of most parliamentary systems.
Ethnic nationality	Nationhood based on a common belonging to one ethnic group or on a common language.
First past the post system	Electoral system in which each voting district elects only one candidate. Common in Great Britain.
Floating voters	Voters that regularly shift from one party to another.
Frozen party system	Constellation of political parties in which all major parties have existed for decades, and hardly any new big parties have arisen since. Applies to most of Western Europe.
Gerrymandering	Changing the borders of voting districts in order to carry more districts.
Intergovernmental	International decision making by national governments, rather than by an international agency. The European Council (not the European Commission) is an example.
Legitimacy	Acceptance of a political system, a government, or state measures as legitimate (just) by the population.
Majority system	Same as first past the post electoral system.
Nation-building	National integration of the population in a country into one nation.

Networking   Frequent and stable contacts between the government and pressure groups intended to give the pressure groups more influence and to enhance the legitimacy of public policies.

New social movements   Protest movements that emerged during the 1960s around new issues like feminism and environmentalism. Some of them have become political parties.

Nomenklatura-privatization   Privatization of state enterprises in Central and Eastern Europe in which the former communist elite (nomenklatura) is able to get hold of many enterprises, often combined with clientelism.

Parliamentary system   Political system in which an elected parliament exercises supreme political authority, and has the right to remove the executive from office.

Pillarization   Division of social life into blocs of people, based on religion or ideology, which reduces the number of contacts between the groups involved and prevents mutual conflict.

Pluralism   Political system in which all kinds of groups and organizations are able to express their demands. Sometimes confined to such a system in which the pressure groups compete for influence on the government in an "open market" of influence—as opposed to corporatism.

Plurality system   Same as first past the post electoral system.

Polarization   Strong degree of conflict between two or more groups of people or political parties that nurture exclusive loyalties to their own group.

Policy style   Combination of policy making procedure and the contents of public policies.

Presidential system   Political system in which the head of the government is elected independently by popular vote and cannot be removed from office by the parliament.

Privatization   Sale of state enterprises to private capital owners.

Proportional representation   Electoral system in which each voting district elects a number of candidates and parliamentary seats are allocated in proportion to the number of votes each party wins.

Public administration   Organizational structure with well-defined tasks, strict hierarchy, and loyalty to the government, established to execute the government's decisions.

Public management   New trend in public administration, in which its structure is more similar to that of private companies, and

	with more room for independent decision making by the government agencies involved.
Re-alignment	Shift toward alignment (stable voting patterns), after a period of de-alignment.
Residual state	A state that only exercises limited functions that cannot be left to the free market. Contrasts with welfare state.
Second ballot	Second round of elections in which only the candidates compete that gained most votes during the first round. Common in French elections.
Secularization	Declining impact of religion on political and social life. Affected Western European politics since the 1960s.
Semi-presidential system	Political system in which the parliament and the president are elected independently and the prime minister is accountable to both of them. Exists in France and Eastern Europe.
Separation of powers	The parliament, the executive, and the judiciary enjoy great mutual autonomy. In contrast to the United States, this is not very common in Europe.
Spill-over	Extension of public policies from one area to another in the European Union.
State	Both a national political unit (country, nation), and its political authority.
State paternalistic welfare state	Communist "welfare state" without any participation by independent voluntary organizations nor any enforceable rights for the population.
Subsidiarity	In Catholic social doctrine: leaving state activities to organizations of those who are affected. In the European Union: leaving activities to the member states.
Supranational	Decision making by international organizations whose decisions are binding upon the members.
Trias Politica	The existence of three branches of government: the legislative, executive, and judicial branch. Common in both parliamentary and presidential democracies.
Tripartism	Frequent contacts between the peak organizations of business and trade unions with the national government. Corporatism is the strongest form.
Voucher capitalism	Enterprise ownership by employees in some Central European countries, accomplished through the distribution of vouchers (shares) during the privatization process.

Welfare state   Political system that devotes a large part of public spending to meeting social needs and offering a high level of social services and income-maintenance policies, either by the state or by state-supervised civil organizations.

Westminster model   Parliamentary system in which only two major parties compete for power and the winning party monopolizes the government. Exists in Great Britain.

Appendix B:
The European Nations

Country	Capital	Size	Pop.	Rank	Language	Religion
Western Europe						
British Isles						
1. Ireland, IRL	Dublin	70.3	3.6	21–29	English	C
2. Great Britain, GB	London	242.5	58.8	11–3	English	P
Germanic Europe						
3. Norway, N	Oslo	323.9	4.4	8–27	Norwegian	P
4. Sweden, S	Stockholm	450.0	8.9	5–19	Swedish	P
5. Denmark, DK	Kopenhagen	43.1	5.3	29–23	Danish	P
6. Finland, FIN	Helsinki	338.1	5.1	7–24	Finnish, 6 Swedish	P
7. Holland, NL	Amsterdam	41.9	15.5	30–10	Dutch	P/C
8. Belgium, B	Brussels	30.5	10.2	33–16	57 Dutch, 42 French	C
9. Luxembourg, LUX	Luxembourg	2.6	0.4	37–36	French/ German	C
10. Germany, D	Berlin	357.0	81.9	6–2	German	P/C
11. Switzerland, CH	Berne	40.0	7.1	31–21	German, 19 French, 8 Italian	C/P
12. Austria, A	Vienna	83.9	8.1	21–20	German	C
Latin Europe						
13. France, F	Paris	544.0	58.2	3–4	French	C
14. Portugal, P	Lisbon	92.3	9.9	19–17	Portuguese	C
15. Spain, SP	Madrid	506.0	40.5	4–7	Spanish, 16 Catalan	C
16. Italy, I	Rome	301.3	57.5	10–5	Italian	C
17. Greece, GR	Athens	132.0	10.6	14–12	Greek	O

Column 1: Country names and codes. Column 3: Size in square kilometers. Column 4: Population in millions. Column 5: First figure for rank in size, second for rank in population. Column 6: Language minorities in percentage of population. Column 7: Religion: C: Catholic, M: Muslim, O: Orthodox, P: Protestant. Religious minorities of over ten percent between brackets. Data for Russia apply to European Russia only.

Sources: The Europa World Year Book 1998; The Statesman's Yearbook 1998–1999.

Country	Capital	Size	Pop.	Rank	Language	Religon
Central Europe						
18. Estonia, EST	Tallin	45.2	1.5	27–35	Estonian, 29 Russian	P/(O)
19. Latvia, LV	Riga	64.6	2.5	24–32	54 Latvian 33 Russian	P/(O)
20. Lithuania, LT	Vilnius	65.3	3.7	23–28	Lithuanian, 9 Russian, 7 Polish	C
21. Poland, PL	Warszawa	312.7	38.6	9–8	Polish	C
22. Czechia, CZ	Prague	78.9	10.3	20–13	Czech	C/(P)
23. Slovakia, SK	Bratislava	49.0	5.4	27–22	Slovak, 11 Hungarian	C
24. Hungary, H	Budapest	93.0	10.2	18–14	Hungarian	C
25. Slovenia, SLO	Ljubljana	20.3	2.0	36–34	Slovenian	C
26. Croatia, HR	Zagreb	56.5	4.7	25–25	Croatian, 6 Serbian	C/(O)
27. Bosnia, BiH	Sarajevo	51.1	4.4	26–30	44 Serbocratian, 31 Serbian, 17 Croatian	M/O/ (C)
28. Serbia, YU	Belgrad	102.2	10.6	17–10	Serbian, 17 Albanian	O/(M)
29. Macedonia, MK	Skopje	25.7	2.0	35–33	Macedonian, 23 Albanian	O/(M)
30. Albania, ALB	Tirana	28.7	3.5	34–31	Albanian	M
31. Rumania, R	Bucharest	238.4	22.7	12–9	Rumanian, 7 Hungarian	O/(C)
32. Moldova, MD	Kishinev	33.7	4.5	32–26	Moldovian, 14 Ukrainian, 13 Russian	O
33. Bulgaria, BG	Sofia	111.0	8.3	15–18	Bulgarian, 10 Turkish	O
Eastern Europe						
34. Belarus, BY	Minsk	207.6	10.3	13–15	Byelorussian, 13 Russian	O
35. Ukraine, UA	Kiev	603.7	51.5	2–6	Ukrainian, 22 Russian	O
36. Russia (Eur) RUS	Moscow	4,030.0	115.0	1–1	Russian	O
Other						
37. Iceland, IS	Reykjavik	103.0	0.3	16–38	Icelandic	P
38. Malta, MT	Valetta	0.3	0.4	38–37	English	C
39. Turkey, TR	Ankara		63.5	–	Turkish, Kurdish	M
40. Cyprus	Nicosia		0.7	–	Greek, 25 Turkish	O/(M)

Further Reading

(International and comparative literature only)

CHAPTER 1: INTRODUCTION

Collections of Nation-Studies

Almond, Gabriel A., Russell Dalton, and G. Bingham Powell. 1999. *European Politics Today*. New York: Longman. Contains general chapters on European politics, the European Union, and a number of nation studies, mainly of the larger countries.

Campbell, Colin, Harvey Feigenbaum, Ronald Linden, and Helmut Norpoth. 1995. *Politics and Government in Europe Today*. Boston: Houghton Mifflin. Covers the European Union, Great Britain, France, Germany, and Russia, with chapters on Scandinavia and Eastern Europe.

Colomer, Josep M., ed. 1996. *Political Institutions in Europe*. London: Routledge. Advanced-level survey of most Western European countries.

Hancock, Donald M., David P. Conradt, B. Guy Peters, William Safran, and Raphael Zariski. 1993. *Politics in Western Europe*. Basingstoke: Macmillan. Discusses Great Britain, France, Germany, and Sweden.

Roskin, Michael. 1995. *Countries and Concepts: An Introduction to Comparative Politics*. Englewood Cliffs, NJ: Prentice Hall. Covers Great Britain, France, Germany, Russia, and non-European nations, including chapters on recent issues in these countries.

General and Cross-National Surveys

Bailey, Joe, ed. 1998. *Social Europe*. London: Longman. 1998. Discusses a wide range of political, social and economic trends in Western Europe.

Budge, Ian, and Kenneth Newton. 1997. *The Politics of the New Europe: Atlantic to Urals*. London: Longman. Cross-national and thematic introduction, with links to poltical science theories.

Gallagher, Michael, Michael Laver, and Peter Mair. 1995. *Representative Government in Modern Europe*. New York: McGraw-Hill. Cross-national introduction to (Western) European politics, with links to political science theories.

Holmes, Leslie. 1997. *Post-Communism: An Introduction.* Cambridge: Polity Press. Survey of the transition process in Central and Eastern Europe, including international politics.

Rhodes, Martin, Paul Heywood, and Vincent Wright, eds. 1997. *Developments in West European Politics.* Basingstoke: Macmillan. Advanced level discussion of recent developments in national politics.

Rose, Richard. 1996. *What is Europe?* New York: Harper Collins. A very accessible discussion of European politics, including recent history, the process of democratization, and international politics, relating them to political science theories.

Steiner, Jurg. 1995. *European Democracies.* London: Longman. A very accessible comparative survey of national politics, based on short nation reviews.

Historical Surveys

Calvocoressi, Peter. 1991. *Resilient Europe: A Study of the Years 1870–2000.* London: Longman. A short history of internal and international politics.

Davies, Norman. 1996. *Europe: A History.* Oxford: Oxford University Press. A detailed history of European politics, society, and culture from ancient culture to recent times.

Heffernan, Michael. 1998. *The Meaning of Europe: Geography and Geopolitics.* London: Arnold. A history of the meaning of Europe from the Middle Ages to the European Union.

Moore, Barrington, Jr. 1974. *Social Origins of Dictatorship and Democracy: Lord and Peasant in the Making of the Modern World.* Harmondsworth: Penguin. A very influential distinction between the various courses that have led to democracy and dictatorship.

Therborn, Göran. 1995. *European Modernity and Beyond: The Trajectory of European Societies 1945–2000.* London: Sage. Advanced-level, detailed description of long lasting social trends in recent Western European politics.

Urwin, Derek W. 1997. *A Political History of Western Europe Since 1945.* London: Longman. Survey of postwar developments, especially in international European politics.

CHAPTER 2:   THE MAIN LINES OF SOCIAL DIVISION

Anderson, Perry, and Patrick Camiller, eds. 1994. *Mapping the West European Left.* London: Verso. On the popular support for and internal developments within the labor movement.

Deth, Jan W. van, and Elinor Searbrough, eds. 1995. *The Impact of Values.* Oxford: Oxford University Press. A survey of the determinants of political behavior.

Franklin, Mark, Tom Mackie, Henry Valen, et al. 1992. *Electoral Change: Responses to Evolving Social and Attitudinal Structures in Western Countries.* Cambridge: Cambridge University Press.

Inglehart, Ronald. 1977. *The Silent Revolution: Changing Values and Political Styles among Western Mass Publics.* Princeton, NJ: Princeton University Press. The introduction of post-materialism.

Latawski, Paul. 1995. *Contemporary Nationalism in East Central Europe.* Basingstoke: Macmillan. Survey of ethnicity-based nationalism in a number of Central European countries.

Lipset, S. M. 1960. *Political Man.* New York: Doubleday. A classic book on lines of division in modern society.

Mackie, Thomas T., and Richard Rose. 1991. *The International Almanac of Electoral History.* London: Macmillan.

Smith, Anthony D. 1996. *Nations and Nationalism in a Global Era.* Cambridge: Polity Press. The history and future of (especially ethnic) nationalism.

CHAPTER 3:   LIBERALS ARE NOT LIBERALS:
THE EUROPEAN IDEOLOGIES

Eatwell, Roger, and Anthony Wright, eds. 1993. *Contemporary Political Ideologies.* London: Pinter. A short introduction to the major ideologies.

Gillespie, Richard, and William E. Paterson, eds. 1993. *Rethinking Social Democracy in Western Europe.* London: Frank Cass. Recent trends in social democracy and the social democratic response to neo-conservatism.

Girvin, Brian, ed. 1988. *The Transformation of Contemporary Conservatism.* Beverly Hills: Sage. The relation between the new conservatism and traditional conservatives and conservative liberals.

Griffin, Roger. 1993. *The Nature of Fascism.* London: Routledge. A short introduction, referring to a number of nations.

Hanley, David, ed. 1994. *The Christian Democratic Parties: A Comparative Perspective.* London: Pinter. Discusses Christian democracy in Western European countries.

Kaplan, Gisela. 1992. *Contemporary Western European Feminism.* London: UCL Press. A general survey of the feminist movement.

Luebbert, Gregory M. 1991. *Liberalism, Fascism, or Social Democracy: Social Classes and the Political Origins of Regimes in Interwar Europe.* New York: Oxford University Press. On the impact of various ideologies on Western European politics.

Mueller-Rommel, Ferdinand, ed. 1989. *New Politics in Western Europe: The Rise and Success of Green Parties.* Boulder, CO: Westview Press. A survey of the green movement.

CHAPTER 4:   FROM ELECTIONS TO GOVERNMENTS: THE
LONG WAY

Almond, Gabriel A., and Sidney Verba. 1963. *The Civic Culture: Political Attitudes and Democracy in Five Nations.* Princeton, NJ: Princeton University Press. Classical and very influential comparative survey of political attitudes in the United States, Great Britain, Germany, Italy, and Mexico; later followed by *The Civic Culture Revisited.*

Bartonline, Stefano, and Peter Mair, eds. 1990. *Identity, Competition, and Electoral Availability: The Stabilisation of European Electorates 1885–1985.* Cambridge: Cambridge University Press. Survey of long lasting rends in voter alignment.

Laver, M., and N. Schofield. 1990. *Multiparty Government: The Politics of Coalition in Europe.* Oxford: Oxford University Press. Introduction to theories on coalition formation and a comparative survey of Western Europe.

Lijphart, Arend. 1984. *Democracies: Patterns of Majoritarian and Consensus Government in Twenty-One Countries.* New Haven, CT: Yale University Press. The differences between the British and continental political systems.

Lijphart, Arend. 1994. *Electoral Systems and Party Systems: A Study of Twenty-Seven Democracies, 1945–1990.* Oxford: Oxford University Press. The relationship between electoral systems and the number of political parties.

Reeve, Andrew, and Alan Ware. 1992. *Electoral Systems: A Comparative and Theoretical Introduction.* London: Routledge. An introduction that also discusses the history of electoral systems.

CHAPTER 5: GOVERNMENT AND PARLIAMENT

Blondel, J. and J.-L. Thiébault, eds. 1991. *The Profession of Government Minister in Western Europe.* London: Macmillan. The background and functioning of government ministers.

Farnham, David, Sylvia Horton, John Barlow, and Annie Hondghem, eds. 1996. *New Public Managers in Europe: Public Servants in Transition.* Houndmills: Macmillan. 295 pp. Discusses the transition of public administration to public management in Western Europe.

Gallagher, Michael, and Pier Vincenzo Ulero, eds. 1996. *The Referendum Experience in Europe.* Basingstoke: Macmillan. Nation studies of Western European countries and Russia.

Lane, Jan-Erik. 1996. *Constitutions and political theory.* Manchester: Manchester University Press. On the history and functions of constitutions in Europe.

Lijphart, Arend, ed. 1992. *Parliamentary versus Presidential Government.* Oxford: Oxford University Press. Concentrates on the contrast between the British parliamentary system and the American presidential system.

Page, E. C. 1992. *Political Authority and Bureaucratic Power: A Comparative Analysis.* Hemel Hemsptead: Harvester Wheatsheaf. The role of the bureaucracy in politics.

Setälä, Maija. 1999. *Referendums and Democratic Government.* Basingstoke: Macmillan. A discussion of the value and function of referendums and a survey of recent examples.

Von Mettenheim Kurt, ed. 1997. *Presidential Institutions and Democratic Politics: Comparing Regional and National Contexts.* Baltimore: Johns Hopkins University Press. National surveys of the French and Central and Eastern European (and American) presidential systems.

CHAPTER 6: BETWEEN STATE AND SOCIETY

Batley, R., and G. Stoker, eds. 1991. *Local Government in Europe: Trends and Developments.* London: Macmillan. Survey of developments in a number of Western European countries.

Chandler, J. A., ed. 1993. *Local Government in Liberal Democracies.* London: Routledge. Survey of the functioning of local government in Western Europe.

Della Porta, Donatella, and Mario Diani. 1999. *Social Movements: An Introduction.* Oxford: Blackwell. A general introduction with many European examples.

Einhorn, Barbara, Mary Kaldor, and Zdenek Kavan, eds. 1996. *Citizenship and Democratic Control in Contemporary Europe.* Cheltenham: Edward Elgar. A collection of essays on nationality, citizenship, and civil society in West and Central Europe, advocating the need for a more active citizenship.

Humphreys, Peter J. 1996. *Mass Media and Media Policy in Western Europe.* Manchester: Manchester University Press. Policy concerning the media and the political role of the media.

Kuhnle, S, and P. Selle, eds. 1992. *Governments and Voluntary Organizations.* Avebury: Aldershot. Broad survey of civil society.

Schmitter, Philippe C., and Gerhard Lehmbruch, eds. 1979. *Trends Toward Corporatist Intermediation.* London: Sage.

Slomp, Hans. 1990. *Labor Relations in Europe: A History of Issues and Developments.* Westport, CT: Greenwood Press. A history of European labor relations, including corporatism.

Slomp, Hans. 1998. *Between Bargaining and Politics: An Introduction to European Labor Relations.* Westport, CT: Praeger. An introduction to European labor relations, including corporatism.

CHAPTER 7: PUBLIC POLICY IN EUROPE

Castles, Francis G. 1998. *Comparative Public Policy: Patterns of Post-war Transformation.* Cheltenham: Edward Elgar. A general history of the postwar welfare state, with a wide and analytical focus.

Esping-Andersen, Gösta. 1990. *The Three Worlds of Welfare Capitalism.* Princeton, NJ: Princeton University Press. Influential book on the welfare state with a distinction between a social democratic, a continental-corporatist, and an Anglo-Saxon liberal model.

Esping-Andersen, Gösta, ed. 1996. *Welfare State in Transition: National Adaptations in Global Economies.* London: Sage. Series of updating contributions on the decline or redefinition of the welfare state and current challenges.

George, Vic, and Peter Taylor-Gooby. 1996. *European Welfare Policy: Squaring the Welfare Circle.* Houndmills: Macmillan. A comparative survey of recent welfare state trends in seven Western European countries.

Heidenheimer, Arnold J., Hugh Heclo, and Carolyn Teich Adams. 1990. *Comparative Public Policy: The Politics of Social Choice in America, Europe, and Japan*. New York: St. Martin's Press. A comparison of a range of policy areas in the larger European nations and Sweden.

Katzenstein, Peter J. 1985. *Small States in World Markets: Industrial Policy in Europe*. Ithaca, NY: Cornell University Press. An analysis of the success of the corporatist nations in Western Europe.

Kersbergen, Kees van. 1995. *Social Capitalism: A study of Christian Democracy and the Welfare State*. London: Routledge. Distinguishes a separate Christian democratic model of the welfare state, in addition to social democratic and liberal models.

Pestoff, Victor A., ed. 1995. *Reforming Social Services in Central and Eastern Europe—An Eleven Nation Overview*. Cracow: Cracow Academy of Economics. A survey of recent developments in the Central and Eastern European welfare state.

CHAPTER 8:   SUPRANATIONAL POLITICS: THE EUROPEAN UNION

Dinan, Desmond. 1999. *Ever Closer Union: An Introduction to the European Union*. Basingstoke: Macmillan. An introduction to the history and institutions of the European Union.

Leibfried, Stephan, and Paul Pierson, eds. 1995. *European Socal Policy: Between Fragmentation and Integration*. Washington, D.C.: The Brookings Institution. A collection of advanced level essays on the EU social policy and its impact on national policies.

Lieshout, Robert H. 1999. *The Struggle for the Organization of Europe: The Foundation of the European Union*. Cheltenham: Edward Elgar. The beginning of the European Union, in particular the French and German involvement.

Mazey, Sonia, and Jeremy Richardson, eds. 1998. *Lobbying in the European Union*. Oxford: Oxford University Press. On pressure group politics in the European Union.

Nelsen, Brent F., and Alexander C.-G. Stubb, eds. 1994. *The European Union: Readings on the Theory and Practice of European Integration*. Boulder, CO: Lynne Rienner. A collection of classical texts on the politics and policies of the European Union.

Nugent, Neill. 1994. *The Government and Politics of the European Union*. Basingstoke: Macmillan. A general introduction to the European Union, focusing on the institutions.

Richardson, Jeremy. 1996. *European Union: Power and Policy Making*. London: Routledge. The role of the EU institutions in EU policy making.

Sandhotz, Wayne, and Alec Stone Sweet, eds. 1998. *European Integration and Supranational Governance*. Oxford: Oxford University Press. 350 pp. Discusses the nature of EU decision making in various policy fields.

CHAPTER 9: INTERNATIONAL POLITICS

Booth, Ken, and Steve Smith, eds. 1995. *International Relations Today*. Oxford: Polity Press. Recent developments in international politics.

Carr, E. H. 1995. *The Twenty Years' Crisis 1919–1939*. London: Papermac. Classical work on power politics by the great European powers between the war.

Kennedy, Paul. 1988. *The Rise and Fall of the Great Powers: Economic Change and Military Conflict from 1500–2000*. London: Fontana Books. A broad history of the power play between the great European powers.

Lieshout, R. H. 1996. *Between Anarchy and Hierarchy: A Theory of International Politics and Foreign Policy*. Aldershot: Edward Elgar. Theory-oriented introduction to international relations.

McWilliams, Wayne C., and Harry Piotrowski. 1990. *The World Since 1945: A History of International Relations*. London: Adamantine Press.

Morgenthau, Hans. 1993. *Politics among Nations*. New York: McGraw-Hill. Classical introduction to international relations.

Ray, James Lee. 1998. *Global Politics*. Boston: Houghton Mifflin. A survey of postwar international politics.

Index

Abortion, 20, 32, 41, 69, 73, 120
Absolutism, 8, 50–51, 93, 97, 155
Africa, 9, 28, 36, 42, 141, 146–49
Age, 28, 47
Agriculture, 8, 21–22, 25–27, 86,
125–28, 169. *See also* Farmers
Albania, 4, 13, 17, 20, 30, 77, 143, 150,
165–67
Alignment, 56, 75, 173
Alpine Nations. *See* Austria, Switzerland
Alsace-Lorraine, France, 140
Americanization, 47–48, 56, 90, 173
Amsterdam, Holland, 110, 123, 133
Anarchism, 23, 32, 36, 45, 103
Andorra, 4, 171
Anglican Church, 19, 44
Arabs, 28–30, 119, 147
Aristocracy. *See* Nobility
Asia, 9, 11, 30, 119, 141, 146–47
Asturias, Spain, 162
Austria, 4, 15, 25, 30, 44, 64, 82, 84,
131, 145, 154, 161–62; and EU,
73, 129; federalism, 93, 97
Austrian (Austro-Hungarian) Empire,
8–9, 14, 139–141, 161, 164–66

Baltic Nations. *See* Estonia, Latvia,
Lithuania
Balkan Peninsula, 2, 4, 11, 13, 117, 140,
149, 165–68
Basque country, Spain, 26, 98, 162
Bavaria, Germany, 20, 119

Belarus, 4, 16, 46, 73, 75, 77, 150,
168–169
Belgium, 4, 25, 30, 44, 58, 84, 128, 131,
140, 147, 160–61; coalition gov-
ernment, 49–50, 59, 61; language
division and federalism, 16–17,
44, 97, 119; monarchy, 68–69
Benelux, 160
Berlin, Germany, 12, 29, 63, 68, 87, 110,
144–45
Berlusconi, Silvio, 21, 73, 90
Beveridge, William, 106
Big Brother Complex, 153–54
Bipolarity, 143–45
Bismarck, Otto Von, 106
Blair, Tony, 38, 48, 55–56, 58, 88
Bonn, Germany, 68
Bosnia, 4, 13, 24–25, 29–30, 98, 132,
150–52, 166–67
Brandt, Willy, 38
British Isles. *See* Great Britain, Ireland
Brussels, Belgium, 16, 97, 123, 128, 135,
137, 140, 151, 160
Budget deficit, 12, 43, 82, 95, 107–8,
111
Bulgaria, 4, 62, 83, 92, 149, 165–68
Bureaucracy, 70–71, 76, 134, 137–38
Business organization. *See* Employers'
association
Business unionism, 82

Catch-all parties, 56, 173

Catholic Church, 18, 39–40, 50, 87, 118, 120, 156–57, 162–64, 170
Catholicism, 6–8, 20, 39–40, 79, 113, 120; regional spread, 5, 13–14, 18–19, 25–26, 98, 158, 162–66
Catalonia, Spain, 16–17, 98
Chancellor. *See* Prime Minister
Chechenia, Russia, 46, 98
Chernobyl, Ukraine, 42
Chirac, Jacques, 34, 76–77, 93
Christian Democracy, 18, 32–33, 39–40, 79, 110–12, 120, 135–36; regional spread, 43–46, 59, 61, 75, 102, 160
Citizenship, 17, 35, 37
Civic nationality, 35, 37, 173
Civil law, 70, 173
Civil service, 70–71, 76, 156. *See also* Bureaucracy
Civil society, 35, 79–92, 102, 167–68, 173
Claes, Willy, 58
Class identification, 23, 27, 173
Clericalism, 18, 26, 45, 158, 162
Clientelism, 75, 158, 173
Clinton, Bill, 77, 88, 93
Closed circuit, 83, 86–87, 173
Coalition government, 43, 49, 58–62, 71–72, 112
Codetermination, 158. *See also* Employee participation
Cohabitation, 76
Cold War, 3, 87, 128, 143–45, 152
Collective bargaining, 81–85, 90–92, 102
Colonialism, 9, 11, 29–30, 141, 145–47, 160–62, 170–71
Command economy, 37–38
Common law, 70, 173
Commonwealth of Independent States (CIS), 98, 150
Communism, 9, 14–15, 19, 23–26, 31–40, 80, 89, 103, 120, 144; regional spread, 45–47, 60–62, 74, 91–92, 115–17, 158, 162–70
Consensus model, 71, 101, 173
Conservatism, 7, 23–24, 40, 43, 47, 54, 59–62, 110–12, 156, 162. *See also* Neo-conservatism

Constitution, 51, 68–70, 76, 136
Constructive vote of no confidence, 74
Corporatism, 39, 81–86, 92, 101–4, 112, 174
Corruption, 58, 75, 88, 158
Council of Europe, 121, 152
Crimea, Ukraine, 46
Croatia, 4, 13, 30, 62, 149, 152, 165–66
Cross-cutting social cleavages, 25, 98, 174
Cyprus, 4, 130, 138, 153, 171
Czechia, 4, 27, 55, 58, 62, 83, 92, 116–17, 151–54, 164; and Western Europe, 130, 149–51
Czechoslovakia, 3–4, 10–12, 15, 164

Dayton Agreement, 146, 167
De Gaulle, Charles, 11, 34, 76, 129, 132
De-alignment, 56, 174
Death penalty, 121, 152
Decolonization, 11, 145–47
Delors, Jacques, 129, 133, 135
Denmark, 2, 4, 27, 44, 131, 154, 158–59; colonialism, 146–47, 170; electoral system, 54–55; and EU 73, 124. *See also* Scandinavia
De-politicization, 74, 76, 85–86, 91, 162, 174
Deregulation, 43, 108–9, 174
Devolution, 44
Direct democracy, 72–73
Drugs, 73, 121, 132
Dual Power, 67, 130, 174

Economic policy, 43, 82–83, 100–1, 106–8, 114–17, 126–27
Education, 7, 16, 20, 35, 86–87, 107, 112, 118–19
Election campaign, 48, 52, 55–58, 80, 88
Election, 49, 51–62, 135
Electoral system, 51–54, 67, 74–75, 135
Employee participation, 102, 109, 158
Employers' association, 39, 57, 64, 72, 79–85, 101–4
Employment policy, 82–83, 101, 106–111, 116–17, 127
Enlightenment, 8, 61, 168

Environmentalism, 42–46, 59, 61, 87, 112

Erlander, Tage, 49

Estonia, 4, 15, 17, 72, 130, 149, 163

Ethnic cleansing 24, 30

Ethnic nationality, 14, 17, 37, 174

Ethnicity, 13–14, 37, 46, 97–99, 174

Euro, 1–2, 10, 12, 123–25

European Central Bank, 125–126

European Monetary Union (EMU), 64, 123–27, 129, 133

European Union (EU), 1–2, 10–12, 16–17, 70, 73, 86, 98–99, 123–38, 149; extension, 26, 137, 171; government, 130–38; international position, 13, 116, 126, 145–46, 149, 158–59; public policy, 43, 111, 123–28, 146

Executive power, 50–51, 63–64, 71–72

Family values, 32, 34, 87. *See also* Sexual morals

Farmers, 8, 22, 25–26, 39, 44, 47, 57, 86, 159

Fascism, 9,11, 32, 40–42, 81, 103, 162

Federalism, 16–17, 67–68, 97–99, 119, 130, 157, 161, 166

Feminism, 27, 41, 87, 111, 120. *See also* Women

Feudalism, 7, 93

Fifth Republic, 11, 76, 91, 157

Finland, 4, 44, 51, 73, 75, 129, 131, 145, 158–60. *See also* Scandinavia

Firearms, 121

First past the post system, 52, 135, 174

Flanders, Belgium, 49, 97, 119, 160–61

Floating voters, 56

France, 3–4, 131, 155–57; and EU, 128–32, 135–36; government, 11, 51–54, 61, 65, 68–72, 75–77; international position, 8–11, 139–41, 144–49, 151–55, 168; local and regional politics, 93–96; pressure groups and public policy, 83–91, 103–4, 114, 118, 120; social cleavages and ideologies, 19, 21, 26–30, 33–34, 39, 45–46

Frankfurt, Germany, 123–26

French Revolution, 8, 19, 50, 140, 155–56

Front national, 42, 77

Frozen party system, 43

Fugitives, 10, 13, 24, 28–30, 103, 140, 158, 164, 166, 168

Galicia, Spain, 98

Gaullism, 34

Geneva, Switzerland, 123, 161

Germany, 3–4, 10–12, 14, 131, 155–57; and EU, 128–29, 131–35; government, 53–56, 59–61, 64–65, 68–69; ideologies, 18, 20–22, 24, 27–30, 40–41, 44, 46; international position, 8–11, 15, 139–41, 148–49, 151, 153, 155; pressure groups and public policy, 83–84, 88–91, 102–3, 109–13, 119–20, 124; social cleavages and local and regional politics, 93–94, 97, 119; unification, 10, 12, 14, 22, 141, 145

Gerrymandering, 53, 174

Gibraltar, 4, 171

Glasnost, 169

Glorious Revolution, 8

Gonzalez, Felipe, 38, 163

Gorbachev, Mikhail, 10, 12

Grandes Ecoles, 70, 76, 114

Greece, 4, 7, 27, 30, 131, 142, 145, 154–55, 165, 168; and EU, 125, 129; and Turkey, 149, 152–53

Green Parties. *See* Environmentalism

Great Britain, 2, 4, 8, 131, 155–157; and EU, 129, 132, 135–36; government, 52, 54–56, 60, 63, 65, 67–73; international position, 8–11, 16–18, 139–41, 144–49, 154–55, 162, 170–71; local and regional politics, 93–96, 98; pressure groups and public policy, 84, 88–89, 104, 110–15, 118, 120, 124–27; social cleavages and ideologies, 19, 21–22, 29–30, 34–35, 44, 46

Havel, Vaclav, 164

Head of State, 7, 51, 58–59, 66, 68–69,
    162–63
Health care, 86, 106–7, 112, 115, 117
Helms, Jesse, 33
Hitler, Adolf, 9, 11, 40, 74
Holland, 4, 27, 30, 52, 68, 82, 94,
    118–21, 131, 147, 160–61; coali-
    tions, 44, 61; early statehood, 8,
    50; and EU, 124, 128, 133; reli-
    gious division, 18, 25; social pol-
    icy, 101, 109
Holocaust, 9, 11, 24, 40, 140–48
Homosexuality, 20, 87, 120
Housing policy, 87, 106–7, 110, 112,
    115, 117
Hungary, 4, 15, 17, 27, 94, 117, 130,
    154, 164–65; civil society, 84,
    91–92; under communism, 11, 91,
    116, 144; and Western Europe,
    130, 149–52

Iberian Peninsula. *See* Portugal, Spain
Iceland, 4, 95, 130, 170
Immigration, 10, 20, 28–30, 42, 103, 119
Impeachment, 75, 77
Industrial Revolution, 8, 155
Industry, 23, 26–27. *See also* Labor
    movement, Social class
Intergovernmental decision making,
    130–34, 174
International Labor Organization (ILO),
    117, 161
International Monetary fund (IMF), 117
Ireland, 4, 16, 18, 30, 73, 83, 96, 120,
    126, 131, 154–56
Iron Curtain, 6, 9–11, 143–44
Islam. *See* Muslims
Issue-network, 86
Istanbul, Turkey, 8, 140
Italy, 4, 7, 9, 81, 131, 156, 158; govern-
    ment, 54, 61, 65, 72, 75, 94, 98;
    international position, 29–30, 128,
    154–55, 171; pressure groups and
    public policy, 83–84, 114, 125;
    social cleavages and ideologies,
    20–21, 24, 33, 40, 45

Japan, 10, 151
Jews, 9, 11, 24, 40, 42, 140
Jospin, Lionel, 76
Judicial power, 50, 69–70, 74, 136

Keynesianism, 106, 108, 114
Kohl, Helmut, 40, 49, 56, 68, 74, 88, 93,
    109
Kosovo, Serbia, 13, 20, 24, 29–30, 73,
    132, 145–46, 166–67
Kuchma, Leonid, 170

Labor conditions, 81–85, 108–9, 114–15
Labor market, 101, 106, 111–12, 127
Labor movement, 8–10, 22–23, 31–32,
    50, 157. *See also* Communism,
    Social democracy, Working class
Labor relations, 81–85, 103, 108–9, 158
Labour Party, 44, 54, 156
Language, 4–6, 13–17, 44–46, 97–99,
    156–71
Latin America, 146–48, 162
Latvia, 4, 15, 17, 60, 72, 163
Le Pen, Jean-Marie, 42
Lega Nord, 20–21
Legislative power, 50–51, 63–68, 71–72
Legitimacy, 85, 174
Lenin, Vladimir, 9, 11, 129
Liberalism, 7–8, 18, 23, 32, 36, 44–47,
    59–62, 110–12, 160. *See also*
    Neo-conservatism
Liechtenstein, 4, 171
Lithuania, 4, 15, 72, 163
Lobbying, 80, 86
Local politics, 74, 72, 93–96, 109, 113
Locke, John, 35
Logrolling, 67, 101–102
London, Great Britain, 63, 120, 123–25
Low Countries. *See* Belgium, Holland
Luther, Martin, 8
Luxembourg, 4, 44, 90, 95, 128, 131,
    133, 160–61
Lviv, Ukraine, 139

Maastricht Treaty, 129–30, 133
Macedonia, 13, 17, 30, 62, 154, 165–66,
    168

Mafia, 21, 75, 116–17
Majority system, 52–55, 67, 72–75, 135, 174
Malta, 4, 130, 170–71
Marshall Aid, 10–11, 128, 143, 151
Martens, Wilfried, 49
Marx, Karl, 36
Marxism, 36–38
Mass media, 56, 72–73, 88–92, 121, 161
Middle class, 23, 25, 35, 39, 41, 56, 110
Middle East, 28, 42, 147–49. *See also* Arabs
Milan, Italy, 123
Milosevič, Slobodan, 72
Mitterand, François, 38, 77, 88, 108
Moldova, 4, 17, 167
Monaco, 4, 171
Monarchy, 33–34, 51, 58–59, 66, 68, 88, 157
Montenegro, 166
Montesquieu, Charles de, 50
Morocco, 29, 30
Multipolarity, 139, 149
Munich, Germany, 11
Muslims, 2, 20, 28–30, 42, 140, 148, 165–67, 170–71
Mussolini, Benito, 9, 11, 40

Napoleon, 8, 140, 153, 168
Nation-building, 3, 14–18, 42, 45, 155, 163, 166, 174
Nation-state, 14–17, 42, 50, 93, 127, 150–51, 159, 174
Nationalism, 28, 40, 42, 158. *See also* New nationalism
Nationalization, 114, 116
NATO, 13, 20, 24, 58, 144–46, 150–51, 164
Nazism, 9, 11, 15, 24, 40–41, 74, 81, 97, 102–3
Neo-conservatism, 43, 80
Netherlands. *See* Holland
Networking, 86–87, 92
New nationalism, 42–43, 160
New social movement, 10, 87, 175
Nobility, 8, 23, 68, 159
Nomenklatura privatization, 116, 175
Nordic Council, 158

Northern Ireland, 18, 44, 156
Norway, 4, 44, 73, 130, 154, 158–59, 170

Oil crisis, 10, 12, 42, 107, 129
Organization for Economic Cooperation and Development (OECD), 151
Organization for Security and Cooperation in Europe (OSCE), 151–52
Orthodox Faith, 5–7, 13, 18–20, 46, 87, 140–41, 166

Padania, Italy, 20–21, 54
Paris, France, 10, 12, 21, 29, 68, 123, 130, 146, 151, 157, 162
Parliament, 50–55, 63–68, 71–72, 74, 130, 134–35
Parliamentary system, 6, 8, 51, 71–74, 155–56, 163, 175
Party, 56–62
Party system, 43–47, 54, 58–62
Peaceful coexistence, 11, 144
Peasants, 8, 22. *See also* Farmers
Perestroika, 12, 169
Periphery, 21–22, 34. *See also* Regionalism
Pillarization, 25–26, 47, 118, 160, 175
Pluralism, 81, 85–87, 92, 175
Plurality system, 52–55, 175
Poland, 4, 20, 30, 62, 73–74, 77, 83–84, 91–94, 120, 140, 164; ideologies, 46, 62; political parties, 53–54; and Western Europe, 130, 149–52
Polarization, 45, 175
Polder Model, 101
Policy style, 101–4, 175
Political Action Committee (PAC), 80
Political spectrum, 31–47, 110–12, 119–21
Pope John Paul II, 164
Pope Leo XIII, 39
Pork barrel, 67
Portugal, 4, 27, 29, 45, 83, 114, 129, 131, 147, 149, 153, 162; fascism, 40, 81
Post-communism, 39, 45
Post-materialism, 47, 120
Prague, Czechia, 123, 151, 164

Presidential system, 11, 72–73, 75–77, 175
Pressure group, 79–88
Primary, 57
Prime Minister, 49–50, 58, 64, 74
Privatization, 73, 114, 116–17, 157, 175
Prodi, Romano, 125, 133, 136
Proportional representation, 25, 52–55, 72, 74, 135, 170, 175
Prostitution, 121
Protestantism, 5–8, 20, 25–26, 39–40, 87, 113, 120–21; regional spread, 18–19, 44, 98, 159–160, 163
Prussia, 8, 97, 164
Public administration, 71, 175
Public management, 71, 175

Racism, 24, 28–29, 41–43
Re-alignment, 56, 176
Referendum, 72–74, 158, 162
Reformation, 8
Regionalism, 20–22, 26, 44–45, 54, 67, 73, 156–58, 162
Regional politics, 74, 94–96. *See also* Federalism
Religion, 5–8, 10, 13–14, 18–20, 25–26, 28–30, 44–47, 98, 140, 156–71
Religious Right, 39–40
Renaissance, 8, 156, 168
Residual state, 107, 176
Rhenania-Westfalia, Germany, 98
Roma people, 165
Roman Empire, 7, 9, 146, 156, 168
Romania, 4, 27, 46, 77, 149, 167
Rome, Italy, 11, 21, 75, 128
Ruhr Area, Germany, 21–22, 98
Russia, 1–4, 9, 11–12, 14–15, 168–70; government, 50, 53, 74–77, 94, 96–98; international position, 8–12, 17, 139–54, 158, 163–68; pressure groups and public policy, 92, 104, 106, 115–17; social cleavages and ideologies, 24, 27, 37–38, 46–47. *See also* Communism
Russian Revolution, 9, 11, 37, 40, 106

St. Petersburg, Russia, 139
San Marino, 4, 171
Santer, Jacques, 133, 135
Sarajevo, Bosnia, 141, 166
Scandinavia, 4, 25, 44, 60, 68, 71, 82, 104, 110–11, 115, 119–20, 158–60, 170
Scandinavian Model, 159
Schengen Treaty, 129
School Issue, 20, 118. *See also* Education
Schröder, Gerhard, 38, 56, 61, 93, 124,
Scotland, Great Britain, 44, 73, 98, 156
Second ballot, 52 , 176
Secularization, 26, 28, 176
Semi-presidential system, 76–77, 176
Senate, 67, 71–72, 74, 76, 97
Separation of powers, 51, 63–70, 176
Serbia, 4, 13, 17, 20, 24, 30, 62, 72–73, 77, 150–52, 154, 165–66
Services, 26–28
Sexual harassment, 41, 108
Sexual morals, 20, 32, 41, 69, 73, 87–88, 119–21
Slovakia, 4, 17, 72, 154, 164
Slovenia, 4, 13, 60, 92, 94–95, 130, 149, 166
Social citizenship,106, 109
Social class, 7, 22–23, 44–47, 110–19, 156–57, 160. *See also* Farmers, Middle class, Working class
Social democracy, 7, 9, 19, 23, 25, 31–41, 56, 59, 80, 82, 106, 110–12, 120; regional spread, 43–47, 60–62, 158–60, 162–63
Social dumping, 127
Social policy, 7, 31–32, 37, 102–19, 127
Social security, 106–16, 127, 159
Solidarność, 46, 91–92
South Tirol, Italy, 98
Soviet Union. *See* Russia
Spain, 4, 29, 45, 61, 74, 89, 114, 120, 131, 146–47, 153–54, 162–63; civil war and fascism, 9, 11, 40; and EU, 129, 136; language division and federalism, 16–17, 26, 97–98, 119

Spill-over, 126, 129, 176
Stalin, Josef, 9, 11, 24, 143, 169, 157
State, 50–51, 79–81, 91, 105, 130, 176.
    See also Nation state
State paternalistic welfare state, 117, 176
Strasbourg, France, 128, 135–36, 140, 151
Strike, 36, 90–92, 117, 124, 127
Subsidiarity, 39, 79, 110, 176
Supranationality, 130, 132, 134, 176
Sweden, 2, 4, 19, 44, 49, 84, 96, 121,
    131, 145, 154, 158–60, 168; and
    EU, 73, 124, 129; social policy,
    113–14. *See also* Scandinavia
Swedish Model, 113–114
Switzerland, 4, 8, 14, 30, 50, 71–73, 121,
    130, 152, 161–62; language divi-
    sion and federalism, 16–18, 68,
    93, 97–98, 119

Taxation, 68, 93, 95–96, 108, 110–14
Thatcher, Margaret, 35, 48, 71, 104, 129
Third World, 10–11, 146–48. *See also*
    Africa, Asia, Colonialism, Latin
    America
Tito, Josip, 145, 166
Trade union, 39, 57, 64, 79–85, 87,
    90–92, 101–9, 159
Transnationality, 132
Trias Politica, 50, 69, 137, 176
Tripartism, 81–85, 90–92, 101–4, 137,
    158, 176
Turkey, 2–4, 28, 30, 119, 145, 149,
    153–154, 168, 171
Turkish Empire, 8–9, 11, 140–41, 165,
    167–68, 171

Ukraine, 4, 16–17, 46, 53, 68, 75, 77,
    104, 150, 154, 168–70
Unemployment, 12, 29, 42, 82–83, 101,
    106–9, 113–116, 127, 133, 160
Unipolarity, 139, 145–46, 149
United Kingdom. *See* Great Britain
United Nations (UN), 73, 145, 148, 161
United States (USA), 1–2, 5–8, 17–19,

50; government, 21, 33, 49–53,
    55, 57, 67, 69–71, 76, 80, 82;
    international position, 13, 24, 75,
    117, 126, 128, 139, 143–46,
    151–53; local and regional poli-
    tics, 93, 97–98; pressure groups
    and public policy, 80, 82, 86, 101,
    106, 118–21, 124, 126; social
    cleavages and ideologies, 20–23,
    26, 29–33, 36, 38, 48
University, 70, 118

Vatican City, 4, 171
Vienna, Austria, 110
Vietnam War, 87
Vote threshold, 53, 55, 74
Voting pattern, 43–48
Voting rights, 36–37, 41
Voucher capitalism, 116, 176

Wales, Great Britain, 73, 156
Wallony, Belgium, 17, 49, 97, 119,
    160–161
Warsaw Pact, 144–145
Weimar Republic, 9
Welfare, 107, 109
Welfare State, 10–11, 104–9, 116–17,
    159, 176
Western European Union (WEU), 150–51
Westminster model, 71, 176
Westphalia, Peace Treaty of, 8
Women, 27–28, 41, 58, 61, 101, 111–12,
    120–21, 148
Working class, 8, 22–27, 36–38, 47, 54,
    115. *See also* Labor movement
Works council, 102, 109
World War I, 9–11, 14–15, 106, 140–41,
    166
World War II, 9–11, 15, 40, 81, 106, 128,
    140, 142, 148, 158, 168–69

Yeltsin, Boris, 47, 75, 77, 92–93
Yugoslavia, 3–4, 10, 12–15, 29–30, 62,
    141–45, 165–67. *See also* Serbia

ABOUT THE AUTHOR

HANS SLOMP is Senior Lecturer in the Political Science Department at the University of Nymegen in Holland. He teaches European and American Politics and Labor Relations and has lectured at the New York State School of Industrial and Labor Relations, Cornell University, and at universities in Colombia and Peru. His other books include *Between Bargaining and Politics: An Introduction to European Labor Relations* (Praeger, 1998).

ISBN 0-275-96800-6

EAN

9 780275 968007

HARDCOVER BAR CODE